Beyond 1

Book 2

Communication with the Co-Creators Continues

Guy Steven Needler

OZARK
MOUNTAIN
PUBLISHING

For permission, serialization, condensation, adaptions, or for our catalog of other publications, write to Ozark Mountain Publishing, Inc., P.O. box 754, Huntsville, AR 72740, ATTN: Permissions Department.

Library of Congress Cataloging-in-Publication Data
Needler, Guy, 1961-
  Beyond the Source – Book 2; Communications with the Co-Creators Continues, by Guy Steven Needler
Dialogues through meditation with the last 6 of the twelve Co-Creators that operate outside of our own Source Entitiy.

1. Source Entities 2. Co-Creators 3. Origin 4. Metaphysics
I. Needler, Guy, 1961- II. Co-Creators III. Metaphysics IV. Title

Library of Congress Catalog Card Number: 2012938630

ISBN: 978-1-886940-44-4

Cover Art and Layout: www.noir33.com
Book set in: Times New Roman, Book Antiqua
Book Design: Tab Pillar

Published by:

OZARK
MOUNTAIN
PUBLISHING

PO Box 754
Huntsville, AR 72740

WWW.OZARKMT.COM
Printed in the United States of America

For my dear wife
Anne Elizabeth Milner
Now "Ascended"
(10th April 1957 – 24th December 2012)

Introduction
Continued Communications with the Origin's Twelve Source Entities

In *The History Of God – A Channelled Work*, I gave readers insights into how I started my higher level communications and managed to communicate with spiritual/energetic entities whilst gaining insights into the wonders all around us and the truth about our legends and myths. Through channelling, I also started my identification with The Origin and learned that The Origin created twelve Source Entities. The Origin and one of the Source Entities explained what The Origin is and the mechanics of the universe created by one of The Origin's creations, <u>our</u> Source Entity.

In the next book *Beyond the Source*, I continued my dialogue with our universe's Source Entity and commenced dialogue with the first six Source Entities—those that were closer energetically, so to speak, to my own energies. In *Beyond the Source* I gained insights into the wonders and workings of the multiverses created or not, as the case may be, by the first six Source Entities. I learned what entities inhabited their multiverses and how the multiverses and, indeed, the Source Entities themselves, were constructed.

If you've read these two books, then you will be delighted to know that this book, *Beyond the Source Book 2*, concludes those dialogues by focusing on Source Entities Seven through Twelve. In doing so, I was taken to the very edge of my capabilities!

To say that this was a difficult book to channel would be an understatement. There were times when I wondered whether I was capable of dealing with the information I was receiving and whether I would be able to put it into words that would be understandable without losing the essence of that information offered to me. There were other times when the amount of information I was receiving was so diverse that I had to stop and re-calibrate my own abilities to allow the state of "cosmic knowing" to take over so I could step up a level, take in the vista of a new and bigger picture and accept that I was expansive—capable of being stretched beyond what I felt was my elastic limit. Over and over this happened. In hindsight, the headaches, bags under the eyes and stress of needing to deliver the information resulting from this dialogue was more than worth it—

even though I questioned my sanity more than a dozen times whilst in the "thick of it." The world needs to know this information. My dear wife, Anne, has been fantastic in this respect, providing words of encouragement whilst editing text and ensuring I took some essential "down time." Additionally, encouragement from Dolores, Julia and the team at Ozark has been both timely and very well received; for this, I am truly grateful.

For those readers who have been following this journey of discovery, those dedicated to wanting to "know the truth," lifting their personal veil between themselves and the greater reality, I thank them from the bottom of my heart, for in doing so they are helping to raise the base frequencies of the Earth and its population.

Thank you and welcome back!

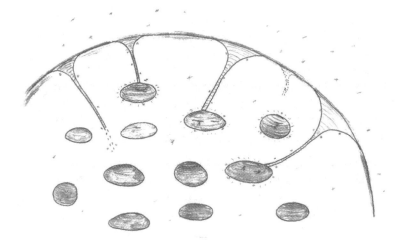

Figure 1: Conceptual Image of the Origin's First Contact with Its Source Entities

Chapter One
An Introduction to Source Entity Seven

Having just finished "Beyond the Source," I was glad of the proposition of a break. That was not to be. Having finished the manuscript for the communications with the first six Source Entities, I was instantly propelled into the generation of presentation material required to support my lecture at the "Awakening to Higher Consciousness Transformation Conference 2011" hosted by Ozark Mountain Publishing. Once I had finished the slides for the lecture, I started to feel the call of the Source Entity, the creator of our multiverse, to continue with the work of communicating with the remaining six Source Entities. Whatever happened to the rest I was advised to take, I will never know. One thing I did know was that I, along with others, was contributing to the inevitable ascension of the Earth and its inhabitants, and that this work could not be stopped for any reason.

Indeed, during the weeks after finishing "Beyond the Source," I had been receiving images of how the next Source Entity, Source Entity Seven, was constructed and how it environments had been created. A change is as good as a rest, obviously. I was just contemplating the images I had received and was starting to find myself tuning into Source Entity Seven when my own Source Entity offered some kind words of advice.

SE: As I stated when we signed off from our last dialogue, you are about to go further away from me than you have gone before. The difference in the frequencies are vast, but the work I have done in the background with you will enable you to build upon the protection required to support each step further away you make.

ME: What do you mean each step further away?

SE: Your memory is bad today.

ME: I have been reading up on the details contained in *The History of God*, not concentrating on the details of *Beyond the Source*.

SE: So I see. Listen, from now on, the frequential and dimensional distance that needs to be spanned by your consciousness will be stretched to its elastic limit every time you make contact with each new Source Entity. You will get further and further away from your incarnate self's base frequency. The period spent with each new Source Entity will be used to ease this level of stretch, allowing you the facility of stretching to the next Source by using your new "current" position as a stepping stone. I will, of course, be with you at all times, monitoring your progress and helping you adjust to the stretch as and when required, but there will be some side effects though.

ME: And what will these side effects be?

SE: You will feel like you are both tired and highly energized all at the same time. You will also feel physical responses to these very different frequencies. This will last for the whole time you are in communication with the next six Source Entities. I think you would use the terms "spaced out" and "arthritic."

ME: You mean the next eighteen or so months?

SE: Yes.

ME: Thank you for the warning.

SE: It's a pleasure. A word of serious advice here: you need to keep yourself as energetically neutral as possible. This will help with the assimilation of the new energies and frequencies. To do this, drink plenty of water, for it is a "physical" universal energy medium that has a common energy signature across frequencies and dimensions. Reduce the amount of alcohol and coffee that you drink to minimal levels normally and zero levels the day before and on the day of channelling. If you do drink alcohol, cleanse the system directly afterwards with equal amounts of water. You will also need to keep your body exercised and well rested.

Me: I don't think I am looking forward to feeling arthritic!

SE: Perhaps I used the wrong word. The feeling will be like you have joints that have a warm glow one day and cold glow the next.

ME: Sounds like rheumatism to me.

SE: But you will not lose the power in your limbs, and it will disappear directly after disconnection with Source Entity Twelve.

ME: No ramp down?

SE: No ramp down. It will be instantaneous.

ME: I can't wait!

SE: Then let us commence with the connection to Source Entity Seven.

Source Entity Seven–A Source Entity of Three Aspects

As I sat at the keyboard of my computer, I found myself being drawn to an image I had seen before. This image, I now know, is the visual representation of the Source Entity I was due to commence dialogue with—Source Entity Seven (SE7). I approached it slowly at first, trying to make the most of the image I was seeing in my mind's eye and the impressions I was getting. For all intents and purposes, it looked like two cells joined together with an overlapping middle section. As I got closer to it, I gained the impression that it had divided itself into essentially two areas/environments with the overlapping section in the middle creating a third "hybrid" environment, a mixture of the two larger areas. I wondered what we would talk about when SE7 made abrupt and direct contact.

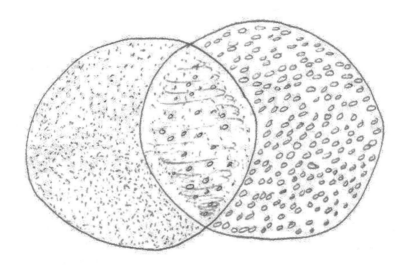

Figure 2: Source Entity Seven as 7a, 7b & 7c

SE7: G'day!

ME: What?

SE7: G'day! . . . Is this not the correct way to greet you?

ME: It's one way to greet someone but not one that I expected from a Source Entity.

SE7: No problem then if I access you to understand the best way to communicate?

This Source Entity was being very direct for what was essentially a first date! And it had an Australian accent as well! Quite bizarre!

ME: Be my guest.

As Source Entity Seven accessed my energies, I felt like my head was fizzing and was about to explode. Then it subsided and felt no different than normal.

SE7: Ah, that's better. I now know how to communicate in an appropriate manner with you.

I felt a tension in my head and an energy surge/shift. My eyes blurred a little. The accent was still there though. I decided that I had better live with it.

SE7: Sorry, just adjusting to an acceptable frequency for you. You will attune better as we continue with the dialogue.

I have to admit I was a little worried about the Australian accent but decided that the best thing to do was to ignore my preconceptions in its use. As I put this potential block in the clarity of our communication path to one side, I received an image and an understanding of its use by Source Entity Seven. Australia was the Earth's largest single country without a land-based border with its neighbors, and, it's the only country that shares the same border with the borders of the continent it's based on. This was the reason Source Entity Seven had chosen to speak to me with an Australian accent. It had recognized this unique condition and had studied the language and culture in order to communicate with me, thinking that most of Earth's incarnate inhabitants existed on this one large area. I also received the impression that it was a reasonable assumption for it to make as this was a common theme with those of its creations who associated themselves with a "planetary" body of sorts. I also noted that it considered Australia as a center of heightened awareness on this planet. With the reason for Source Entity Seven's method of communication now understood, I commenced the dialogue with renewed vigor and no underlying doubt.

SE7: Now that you understand the reasons for my choice of verbal communication, we can start if you like.

ME: Yes, please. I just found it a little strange at first and wanted to make sure I wasn't being delusional and was inventing the dialogue.

SE7: You are most definitely not inventing this dialogue. But I can tell you one thing: you are stretched very thin, and this lack of substance is the reason for your lower confidence level.

The Three Versions of Source Entity Seven

ME: I see. Well, I had better overcome that pretty quickly if I am not going to spoil this opportunity. Let's move on then. As I started to log into you, I received an image. It looked like you had arranged yourself into two areas that overlapped in the middle—rather like what two cells look like just before the point of divisional separation. Can you explain the reason for this? It looks like you have three environments: a left, a right and a combination of the left and right.

SE7: What you are seeing is actually two of me at a point in frozen separation.

ME: You mean there are two of you?

SE7: No, there are three. When I was planning how I would best contribute to The Origin's desire to evolve through devolution and separation, I decided to cut myself in half and create two independent but co-existent selves. At the point of separation, I saw the beauty in the possibility presented in constraining the separation to a partial condition. This partial condition—you might call it the "Siamese" section—that which was part of both of me that was separating at that point, developed an independent energetic signature of its own, creating a third version of me. This stopped me from continuing the separation as it provided a number of interesting opportunities.

ME: Am I reading this correctly then? You are now three independent but co-joined and coexistent entities, each with different thought processes and different activities?

SE7: Yes.

ME: Then why/how am I able to talk to you as a single entity? Am I just talking to one of you? Say, Source Entity Seven "A" (SE7A)

SE7: No, you are talking to a combined simulacrum of the three versions of me. This I/we have set up to initiate communication with you so that you didn't get confused with each of me talking at the same time, answering your questions simultaneously in three different ways.

ME: I thank you for your concern. Are you able to go back to your original singular condition, to that which you were before the point of separation?

SE7: No, the change was a permanent change. That is, unless all three of me decide, in fully committed unison, to enlist the help of The Origin to return us to singularity. This permanent change was my singular decision before separation.

ME: So you have no over-mind to control you all?

SE7: No

ME: You have no clock ticking in the background, which will re-set you back to singularity after a certain period of time?

SE7: No

ME: You have no re-set button to press if it all goes horribly wrong, or you want a change of strategy?

SE7: No

ME: Fascinating. When I have talked to the other Source Entities, those that had created areas of separation always had a bail-out facility somewhere.

SE7: Not me/us. The change was personally permanent.

ME: But you do have the ability to use The Origin to return you back to the singular should you all so wish.

SE7: Yes.

ME: So that is your collective bail-out.

SE7: Yes, I suppose it is. I/we hadn't thought of it in that way. We simply think of it as an opportunity for future experience, should we all collectively seek such a change. Such a change would only be sought by The Origin if all three of me desire it together. It cannot take place if only one or two parts of me want it, but one part does not.

ME: Can you merge two parts of you together.

SE7: No, for this would upset the equal balance we currently have.

ME: Can I talk to you (SE7A, SE7B & SE7C) separately as we progress this dialogue later.

SE7: If you wish.

This was a bit strange and was wonderful all at the same time. Here I was, communicating with what was Source Entity Seven—now in three separate but co-joined and coexistent parts but as a singular entity, this entity or shell being created specifically for communication with me. I felt VERY honored.

ME: Can I ask for clarification on why you felt it necessary to communicate with me in the singular rather than the collective.

SE7: Certainly, but first though, I see I need to give you a short lesson on singularity vs. collectivity vs. singularity through collectivity, for they are three different things, as is why I am able to communicate to you as a singular entity even though I am now three. We have, of course, created many others to assist in our evolution, as your Source Entity has. That is why you exist, but I will continue with defining singularity, collectivity, and singularity through collectivity.

Singularity

SE7: Singularity is when you have a unique and individualized entity that is independent of any other entity or group of similar entities. Although created and still part of its creator, it is given individuality as a sub-section of the entity which created it. A singular entity does not need to nor is [it] required to follow rules or conventions or styles of or for existence that may be created by those entities that may be similar to or exist in the same dimensional or frequential environment as the singular entity in question. This includes its creator. Although a singular entity may choose to adopt conformance to rules and conventions of those around it, it is ultimately not bound by them. A singular entity is responsible for its own actions, reactions, creativity, creations and subsequent evolution.

Collectivity

SE7: A collectivity is a group or groups of entities who, although have singularity, are bound together by the functionality of their collective existence. Singularly they are unable to function with the innate purpose that a truly singular entity is able to achieve. They achieve significantly more together "collectively" than they would do in one's or two's or even higher numbers. Their purpose is, therefore, achieved together as a collective, and as such, they work as singular, individualized units—each with a role to do that [which] is significant, not to themselves, but as a smaller part of the much, much bigger collective picture. They can be considered as single components on a computer's printed circuit board or the individual cells or atoms in a much larger biological entity. As a collective, all participating entities evolve together at the same time as the whole. No one entity's contribution is such that it can evolve at a faster pace than any other entity within the collective, nor would it desire to do so. An entity that is part of a collective considers only that which is good for or contributes towards the progressive evolution of the whole as a whole.

Singularity Through Collectivity

SE7: This occurs or is created when a group of entities are interconnected in a conscious and communicative capacity. They may even be interdependent in other more fundamental ways, ways that result in group connectivity, group thinking and group action. This then, results in a collective mind—each singular mind/entity a function of the whole. When a singularity through collectivity is created, it is due to the desire of a group of conscious entities, who are co-joined and/or coexistent to present themselves in the singular in totality. In doing this they create an "over-mind" allowing a single output/input to those external to their collective state, as a result of their collective reasoning. This provides the ability to communicate collectively or singularly.

ME: So the singularity through collectivity version is how you are currently communicating with me.

SE7: Correct. It was the best way to initiate the communication process, and it is the one we shall use unless you request otherwise. We note that you may wish to engage with us separately at some point in our dialogue.

ME: I would. Yes, please.

SE7: Then we will do so as and when the time is right to do so.

The Beginning, the Middle and the End

ME: Can you tell me why you intended to split yourself into two individual entities and then stopped when you saw the beauty in the possibility of the third?

SE7: I will have to start at the beginning of my first communication with The Origin to explain that. As with the other Source Entities, at the point of my becoming self-aware, I was contacted by The Origin to apprise me of the reason for my existence and what I needed to do to assist in the evolution of The Origin. Although I was not advised on what those Source Entities who were already self-aware and "contacted" had chosen to do in their contribution, I was previously and at that point, currently, in a position to know or witness what was being planned or "actioned" by them. The Origin deliberately negated to advise me on what they were doing lest it influence my own unique and individual choice, which The Origin valued above all else.

ME: Why did The Origin value your individual choice?

SE7: To maximize the diversity of evolutionary opportunities, which may not occur if I was influenced by direct and in-depth detail. There would be no use in me covering "existing" or "old" ground.

ME: Yes, I can imagine that would be a prerequisite dictate by The Origin, who would want to accelerate it evolution at the fastest and most efficient way possible.

SE7: That's right, it does, and that was the reason for my choosing to become two, which ended up being three. Apart from the Source Entity you call "Five" and the one that is not yet fully aware, I had noticed that the others divided themselves up internally whilst still maintaining an overall aspect that made them retain their wholeness. As a result of this observation, I decided to become two independent Source Entities with a link between the two. I discussed this and the "bail out" option as you described earlier with The Origin (for it is only The Origin that can return us to wholeness) who agreed with my strategy, and I continued. What happened next is as I have previously described. As I was in the process of separating out into the two versions of me, I noticed that a unique opportunity could be applied. If I maintained the equal overlapping area of the two versions of me and then froze the separation process in one position, this created a third middle option where we would all be separate but co-joined and co-existent. As I froze the separation at the point of equality, my consciousness divided into three and developed into three separate Source Entity personalities. But there was something else that I noticed as well. The periphery of the energies that separated us from each other was permeable, allowing energies that moved from, say, the left to the right or from Source Entity Seven "A" to move into Source Entity Seven "B" to actually cross the periphery or boundary energies. What's more, I noticed that there was a progressive opportunity in passing from one side of Source Entity Seven "A" to the point of interface between Source Entity Seven "A" (SE7A) and Source Entity Seven "B" (SE7B). This was duplicated in a progressive manner from Source Entity Seven "B" to the point of interface between Source Entity Seven "B" and Source Entity Seven "C" (SE7C).

ME: Was this dimensional, frequency, or evolutionary based?

SE7: All three. As with your Source Entity, I have twelve dimensions with each dimension inflated with twelve frequencies. Each of the twelve dimensions is a composite of the three base dimensions, thus allowing expansive form. However, these were duplicated in a whole sense when a certain evolutionary condition was met or could be achieved; this was multiplied by a factor of twelve. So I had in each Source Entity twelve evolutionary levels that were filled with twelve dimensions constructed with three composite dimensions per dimension which were inflated with twelve base frequency levels. That was not all though. The evolutionary opportunities increased as I scanned the progression from Source Entity Seven "A" through to Source Entity Seven "C." The high end of Source Entity Seven "C's" evolutionary levels were as high as an entity, which I/we had not yet created, could go to from an evolutionary perspective. This effectively gave me an evolutionary beginning, an evolutionary middle, and an evolutionary end.

Progression Between Source Entity Seven's Separate Parts

ME: So what are you saying is that an entity can travel, no, progress in an evolutionary way from one part of you to another, say from SE7A through SE7C.

SE7: Yes, in a manner of speaking.

ME: But that would mean that if all evolving entities had a progression path from SE7A through SE7C, then wouldn't SE7B and SE7C initially be devoid of evolving entities until such a time when enough entities were evolved enough to progress from say SE7A to SE7B and SE7B to SE7C?

SE7: If that was the way I/We had planned the progression of the entities we created, I would agree, but this is not the case.

ME: I had a suspicion that it wouldn't be as simple as that.

SE7: It's not, so I will explain. Each Source Entity Seven has an equal number of entities associated with it. They are small entities and number in their billions of quadrupillions. Each Source Entity has its own strategy for evolution and the way/s it constructs its environment for evolution. However, although each Source Entity Seven had this opportunity, the environments are similar in dimensional and frequential construction insomuch that they offer progression that is frequency-based whilst allowing dimensional passage at the will of the individual entity. The environments also have areas of energetic concentration that you would call "density" where they can work with the lower frequencies should they desire to do so. I will leave the explanation of each of the environments to those individual parts of me (SE7A, SE7B & SE7C) to explain to you separately, but suffice to say they also have the opportunity to exist in different dimensions concurrently or linearly.

When an entity that is based in SE7A has evolved enough, it has the opportunity to progress from, for instance, SE7A to SE7B and later to SE7C. The evolutionary opportunity for that entity is increased as it moves from one Source Entity Seven to another. If an entity that is based in SE7C desires, it may progress from SE7C to SE7B and later to SE7A. Again the evolutionary opportunity is progressive as it moves from one Source Entity Seven to next.

ME: So what about the progression for those entities that are based within SE7B? Which way do they go?

SE7: Entities that are based within SE7B can progress to either SE7C or SE7A first and then move on to that Source Entity Seven that they have not yet experienced. Simply put, they can progress from SE7B to SE7A to SE7C, or, SE7B to SE7C to SE7A.

ME: How do they do that? Do they have to traverse though that Source Entity Seven that they had previously experienced? Does that also still include evolutionary opportunities?

SE7: They can choose many ways to move from Source Entity Seven to Source Entity Seven, and this is not constrained to those entities who primarily originate in SE7B. Any of the entities in any of the Source Entity Sevens can chose to move to the Source Entity that is either on their closest Source Entity Seven to Source Entity Seven boundary or on the next Source Entity Seven to Source Entity Seven boundary, which is another Source Entity away.

An entity may choose to progress though the frequencies offered in a Specific Source Entity Seven's environment in order to transition to the border of the next Source Entity Seven or by-pass it. It may even choose to do this (transition) more than once with the second time potentially being the transitory transition to the Source Entity Seven not yet experienced where the entity may or may not choose to perfect the experiential content of certain experiences during this transitory period by doing one of these: 1) repeating the exercise; 2) just passing through the environment; or 3) conducting the whole evolutionary process again for purposes of perfection. An entity can choose to repeat the whole or part of the process as many times as it wishes. There are no rules in this function of existence nor are there restrictions.

ME: You mentioned that an entity can by-pass the need to transition through one Source Entity Seven to another. Does this mean that they can pass round the outside of the Source Entity that they would have normally transitioned through?

SE7: Yes, to a certain extent. You see, the interfacing boundary separating the environments whilst integrating the cohesion of the co-existence of the three Source Entity Sevens are twofold:

1) One contains the separate structure of the Source Entity specific environment and is dimensionally and frequentially independent of the environment;

2) The other contains the neutralized energies required to maintain the cohesion and co-existent existence of the three Source Entity Sevens in their integrated state. Because this boundary contains functions that are fully independent of the environments they contain, it creates an environment in its own right, albeit small.

ME: I have just gotten the impression that it is like the air in between a double glazed window with the inner window being the boundary for the environment that is one of the Source Entity Sevens and the outer window maintaining the cohesion. Is it this air gap that allows the entity to traverse between the Source Entity Sevens without the need to progress though them?

SE7: In part, yes. This is one of two ways. However, it is possibly the safest and fastest way to traverse between the three Source Entity Sevens. An entity can quite literally use this "air gap" to move to the nearest Source Entity Seven boundary interface and make the transition at this point of contact. It is a bit like the "null space" that you have in your Source Entity's environment to separate the universes from each other.

ME: What is the other way and why is the method above the safest?

SE7: The method I described in summary above is an environment in its own right and, therefore, offers a level of protection or energetic containment that is similar to that offered by a true Source Entity Seven environment but without the rules of evolution assigned to these environments. The second means an entity can use to transfer itself to the next Source Entity is to make the journey outside the boundary by using the inter-Source Entity void or space, i.e., by using the space that is, in essence, pure Origin energy.

ME: You mean they move from and to Source Entity environments by leaving the environment totally and entering into the absolute that is The Origin?

SE7: Yes.

ME: Why is that dangerous?

SE7: I didn't say it was dangerous. I said the first way was the safest and fastest.

ME: OK, so why would the first way be the fastest and safest way?

SE7: It's fast because its function is limited to what it is with no other complications or opportunities to be affected by the actions of those entities passing through it. It is safer because an entity can become overwhelmed to the point of distraction by being directly associated with the pure energies of The Origin if it is not prepared for them.

ME: What do you mean distracted?

SE7: Besotted to the point of being stuck in the bliss-like state of euphoria that is instantaneously experienced and results in a desire to stay in this state and not continue with the task at hand—that of moving to the next Source Entity Seven environment.

ME: How can that be? I am not besotted to the point of non-function when I go outside my Source Entity or, in fact, traverse the distances to you.

SE7: That is because you are being given a level of protection by your own Source Entity during your communications with the twelve Source Entities, and you are beloved of the Om.

I had heard this description of being "beloved of the Om" in the context of Hum and me before whilst compiling the text for The History of God book.

SE7: Being beloved of the Om means that you are part of the absolute fabric of the Source Entity, that which is the fabric of The Origin; hence, you have a certain level of built-in tolerance to these effects and accessibility to its energies, for they are part of you in a more holistic sense.

16

ME: Why would the OM be beloved then? My assumption is that all the entities created by my Source Entity were created out of its own energy, so wouldn't all of these entities be beloved?

SE7: No. In the instance of creating the entities used for its strategy for evolution, your Source Entity created a level of error during the process. This you know. What you have not been told is that those entities that were created first and were closest to your Source Entity, received a purity of energy that was not perpetuated during the remaining process of creativity. At the end of the process when your Source Entity claimed it was not paying the same level of attention as it had in the primary phase of creativity, it created the level of entity that you recognize as animals, plants, and even the , suns, and galaxies. The Om were simply the first to be created and, therefore, ended up being very close to pure Source Entity energy and, therefore, The Origin energy, as an entity could possibly be. Hence your ability to do what you are doing now. There are many other Om working with the Earth sphere, incarnate and not incarnate. Working in incarnately is a great sacrifice for an Om because of the risk of attracting lower frequencies without protection.

ME: I get the feeling that I can achieve a much higher level of connectivity with The Origin's creations whilst in the physical but that it needs working on.

SE7: You can, you will, and you will need to work at it.

I needed to move on so I changed the track of dialogue back to the space in-between the three parts of Source Entity Seven.

ME: Thank you for that extra information about the Om. I wasn't aware that the Om were that close to my Source Entity and, therefore, The Origin.

I made a mental note to discuss this further with my own Source Entity when the opportunity presented itself.

ME: Let's get back to the space within the boundaries between the three parts of you. Other than being the functional boundaries between your environments and providing a back door for entities to use as a faster method of moving from one Source Entity Seven to another, what other function does it provide?

SE7: It provides no other function that can be used by an entity, for its function is to be a boundary. It does have the properties of neutrality though. This is required to allow the interface between the different parts of me to exist simultaneously without interference.

Source Entity Seven's Entities and Flat Planets

ME: We previously talked about the entities that you created to populate the three environments of yourself. Can you describe them and their roles?

SE7: As you have been told previously, initially they were distributed equally across the three parts of me that were created. Their transition is a function of evolutionary progress that ultimately results in the number of entities resident in each part of me becoming un-equal. This level of "un-equality of residence" changes as the entities progress at differing speeds of evolution.

ME: What is their appearance?

SE7: Although they are energetic in nature in comparison to your own current physical condition, they have a habit of liking to cluster around areas of local density—what you might call "planets."

ME: Are these planets spherical as most of the planets are in my physical universe?

SE7: No, they are flat.

ME: Flat?

SE7: Yes, flat. This is because of the way the energy collects as dense matter. When the matter, energy matter, collects together and becomes dense enough to be used by the entities, it results in it being flat.

ME: Why is that?

SE7: Because when this energy becomes dense, it only becomes dense in what you would call "two dimensions."

ME: A flat planet. This is interesting. I thought that planets or areas of local density would be spherical. In fact, my Source Entity advised me that the sphere was the most common and natural shape for a planet to adopt.

SE7: In a fully physical universe dependent upon the first three dimensional components (tritaves) of the first full dimension, such as the one you exist within, this might be a common occurrence. The flat areas of local density act like islands in the fabric of the energetic environment of the particular Source Entity Seven they are associated with.

This would explain the affinity with those living on the Australian continent, I thought, for they see Australia as a large island, and the areas of local density are also considered to be islands rather than planets.

ME: Are they disk-like in shape?

SE7: No, for that would be an association with the dimensional requirements of a low dimensional tritave.

ME: So what is the shape of the areas of local density? (I was already receiving an image of a fragmented edge, rather like a coast line on earth.)

SE7: Fractal, for this is the usual shape adopted by a two-dimensional structure in a lower level dimension.

ME: How are your dimensions organized?

SE7: In a consistent way to The Origin. In fact, they are unchanged. I felt no need to change to a structure of my own design, especially when the separation of self into three separate but co-existent and interdependent Source Entities was decided upon. As a result of this, you will already have a good level of understanding of my/our environmental structure through your communications with The Origin.

ME: So you have 12 zones with 12 dimensions, each with 3 tritaves or dimensional components with 12 frequencies, 12x3x12x12 permutations of environmental conditions.

SE7: Yes.

ME: With each of them offering a separate and complete environment to exist within, should an entity choose to do so.

SE7: Yes, and they are also arranged in a way that supports evolutionary progression through the three parts of me.

ME: Would I be able to classify each permutation as a universe in its own right?

SE7: Yes, because a universe is an environment of known energy, frequency and dimension. Please note that matter is not a feature in all universes, for this is a function of lower dimension and frequency, linked together with intentional manifestation of the creator.

ME: You mean that a matter based universe has to be created intentionally? It does not exist as a function of its low frequency and dimension?

SE7: No. Matter-based universes, no matter how dense—and that can range from the super dense to the super sparse (thin, clear, fine)—do not and cannot exist without first being created. This is because the creative intention transmitted by the creating entity is the force by which energy of low frequency, existing in a low dimension, is manifest with or without "form." Only when it is manifest can it become matter "without form," which can then be translated to matter "with form." When it becomes matter "without form," it needs to be continually maintained to perpetuate its existence, lest it revert back to pure energy. When it becomes manifest as matter "with form," it needs to have individual localized maintenance on a continuous and continual basis. Hence, there is a hierarchy of entities within matter-based universes, dedicated to tending to the needs of the galaxies, systems and planets that are entities in their own right.

ME: Can I assume then, that evolution results in a progression from the lower frequencies/dimensions to the higher frequencies/dimensions as in my own multiverse?

SE7: You can, for this is a standard function of all of the frequencies and dimensions and energies associated with The Origin and its creations. This function, therefore, is passed down as an environmental prerequisite from the Source Entities to their/our creations—whether they be the environments themselves, the entities created to exist within them, or entities assigned with the creative capability to create universes within universes.

ME: So there is order to The Origin?

SE7: Very much so, and it is maintained throughout.

ME: OK, we have digressed a little here. What more can you tell me of the disk-like world/planets?

SE7: They are a matter type that has "form" but not what you would classify as matter "with form." This is simply because it does not have the level of density that you currently experience, and they are manifested in a different frequency and dimensional environment (universe). As a result, they are not consistent in their form factor, for they are constantly changing.

ME: What makes them change? Energetic influences or the entities assigned to their maintenance?

SE7: Both actually. You see, the way in which the entities work with each other and the planet results in a change in frequency of the energy of the matter. This results in a change in the cohesion properties of the planets "form" that results in essential maintenance to reduce the loss of form due to loss of cohesion. The entities maintaining the planet then have to change the functionality of the cohesive content of the energy of the matter to enable its form to be perpetuated. However, the work required to do this is not always achieved in a timely manner because of the amount of work they have to do to stabilize the changes that are happening. This results in minor changes in the planets' overall form factor but major changes to areas of what you would call the topography. Areas of high ground change to areas of low ground; denser areas become finer or totally disappear.

ME: Would that explain the earthquakes and volcanoes we get on earth?

SE7: Yes, for there is no other influence on your earth, which it is exposed to that affects it in a frequential and energetic way, as a direct result of the actions of the entities that exist or work "with-on" and "with-in" it. Your weather patterns are also affected by your frequencies. In fact, changes to the weather patterns are the first level of change that happens as a result in a change in frequency. They are your early warning system of an impending change to the planetary form, directly resulting from a change in frequency.

ME: Excuse me. Does this mean that the weird and extreme weather we are experiencing at the moment (April/May 2011) is a direct result of the changes in our frequency and not due to pollution-based global warming?

SE7: The pollution of and damage to your planet, resulting from your appetite for carbon-based energy does have an influence on your environment. However, the major changes you are experiencing are due to shifts in the earth's frequency, which is up and down like a . . . yo yo?

ME: Yo yo would be a good description. I guess this is a result of the critical mass required to assist in the ascension of our planet and its inhabitants actually increasing, but this good work is then being counteracted by local fighting between governments and people in other parts of the world.

SE7: It would be.

ME: Mmmm. We have such a hard time when things like earthquakes happen on the earth, and we suffer a terrible loss of life. Many vehicles for incarnate existence are destroyed in the process. How do entities that are working on or in the disk planets cope? How are they affected? Do they lose their creations or vehicle for existence in lower frequencies?

SE7: They are not in the need for a vehicle to allow them to exist or experience existence in the lower frequencies that pervade the planet. They also know what they are doing energetically and frequentially and, therefore, how their actions will affect the overall frequency of the matter that the planet is manifest from. Therefore, they have no disasters to run or recover from. They only have modification, relocation and recalibration of their work and how they interface with the planet.

Communication with the Separate Parts of Source Entity Seven

Beginning in my book "Beyond the Source," I began using the word "environment" (a more general and higher level description) in place of the word "universe"! This was a deliberate act to put the reader at ease with the possibly difficult concept of understanding a completely different multiversal structure than the one described by Source Entity One, the creator of our multiverse and the physical universe/environment humankind exists within—specifically, if the reader is using Source Entity One's multiverse as a datum to work from whilst reading about Source Entities Two through Twelve. Suffice to say that is the reason for the switch in nomenclature, and I apologize if it has caused any confusion.

A quick author's note here.

I am writing this text whilst I am sitting in a comfortable folding chair on the back patio of our little cottage in Crete. The energy here is so calm and clear compared even to our rural life in the UK that I wonder why I don't stay here all the time instead of coming from time to time. The aliens are here. Dare I say that now? They are our brothers in energetic existence. See "The History of God" for the story of my introduction to them. I see them all around me as I sit here. They have shown themselves to me in their true sprite-like forms as they hover around me. Before you ask, dear reader, they are not nature spirits for they have a completely different energy signature. They are interested in the energies I am working with whilst tuned into the collective that is Source Entity Seven. They say:

Aliens: We could use this [Source Entity] energy; it has a purity not experienced by us before. It would make our travel much quicker, and we would not need to modify the energies as we currently have to do when we need to jump frequencies.

The next day I noticed four of them following me whilst I was cycling up a rather long hill in the Cretan countryside. Initially, they followed me with one on each side and one front and back. They then moved around me to have all four in front of me and later darted in and out to be closer with me. They were interested in my mode of transport initially but had come to answer a question about their form that had just surfaced in my immediate memory.

Aliens: We are not of your dimensional realm and, therefore, cannot be considered as nature spirits assigned to maintain the earth. However, we do recognize that many humans sensitive to our frequencies, as you are, may well have seen us in the past and considered us as nature spirits because our form suits that expected of such entities in the imaginations of these individuals. You would call our form "Fairy"?

ME: That would be a good word to describe the form that you presented to me, yes. Your form is beautiful to behold, so I guess that humankind would prefer to relate you to something that works with nature, Earth's nature, rather than your being of extra-terrestrial (extra-dimensional?) origins.

Aliens: Yes, this is true. We must go now, for we have duties to attend to.

The comment by the Aliens about the energies associated with my communications with Source Entity Seven was such an interesting comment that I decided to put it to Source Entity Seven as a whole before I continued my communication with its individual parts.

ME: I have just had a conversation with some entities that are on my planet/area of local density, the Earth, about the purity of the energies that are a result of the communication system (conduit?) set up to allow my temporary link with you whilst conducting this dialogue. Did you catch what they said?

SE7: Yes, while we have our communication link I am with you all of the time. I assign a part of myself to recognize when you want to continue communications so that I can continue where we left off. This part of me follows your every move to ensure I can respond to your request for communication in the instant you request it. I agree it is a most interesting comment from your "Aliens," but I can see why they are interested in the energy being used.

ME: So why are they?

SE7: They see that the energy used to create the conduit you have to communicate with me is a mixture of my base energy and your own base energy. We created this together with a little help from your own Source Entity. Because it traverses the frequencies and dimensional states from one Source Entity to another Source Entity via the intermediate energies of The Origin, it spans three environments. This is rare as energies and their frequencies go because they tend to be a product of their universal environment and do not span dimensions or base frequencies. Based upon this, your Aliens see the opportunity to use this as a carrier wave or a fast track/road that can be used to bridge the dimensions without the need to manufacture a process or energetic vehicle that negates the need for evolutionary conditions being met by an entity before travel between the dimensions can be achieved without such constructs. They would only be able to travel between your Source Entity and

24

me in its unrefined state, so they would still need to "work" the energy to use it for the translations they are interested in.

ME: Thank you for that answer. I would now like to communicate with that part of you that became what I call Source Entity Seven "A."

SE7: No problem. Please note that the link and the feel of the communication will be the same as it is now. You should experience no difference in energetic signature either.

ME: Thank you.

Source Entity Seven A

I had now signed off from the collective that was Source Entity Seven and waited with eager anticipation to commence dialogue with the "first" part of Source Entity Seven. I did not have to wait long.

SE7A: I trust you are at ease?

ME: I certainly am.

SE7A: Then let us commence communication.

ME: I have received two different images whilst connected to your collective of three versions. The first was of an entity that was moving over the surface of one of the flat planets/areas of local density. Its appearance was, well, I can only describe it as a very flat ameoba. In fact, the more I study the image in my mind's eye, the more it looks like a sentient version of the planet it is traversing. Its shape looks almost identical—right down to the topography of its surface. Why is that?

SE7A: The entities that work with the "planets" assume their (the planets') basic energy signature when they first become associated with the planet for the work they will be doing with it. The entity itself can assume any form factor required to suit this relationship, for when an entity desires to work with a particular planet, it enters into a relationship with the planet for the duration of the work to be done. In this particular instance, the entity in the image you saw was almost the same size as the planet.

ME: How does that work? Surely an entity that is almost the size of the planet it is associated with would crush or destroy any other entities or life that are part of that planet's normal condition.

SE7A: Not in this case, for the planets in this particular environment can only have a population of one.

ME: One?

SE7A: One.

ME: Forgive my confusion. I am making the assumption that all planets have a large number of smaller entities living on, within or with them.

SE7A: Not all planets in your own universe have entities associated with them, so why would one of my environments be any different?

ME: Very true. So what is the work that this particular entity is doing with this planet?

SE7A: It is experiencing existence as a planet. That is why it is almost as big as the planet it is associated with. Later, when it has assumed the exact same size and shape and has totally covered the full surface of the planet, it will stabilize its energy signature in totality to that of the planet and will exist and behave like the planet itself. In fact, for all intents and purposes, it will be the planet, right down to accepting another entity to work with it.

ME: And that entity would work with the other entity exactly as if it were a solitary planet with no inhabitants or energetic partners?

SE7A: That's right, the objective being that the new entity seeking a relationship with the planet does not nor will ever know that it is working with another entity and not the real planet.

ME: But could that not be the same for the entity I saw in my perception? Could another entity have already beaten the one I observed to it, so to speak, and achieved the same relationship?

SE7A: Absolutely. This is the beauty of this type of work.

ME: But I have just seen a scenario where it would be possible to have many multiples of entities all doing the same thing, all-encompassing the planet with which they want to establish a relationship with a none of them knowing that they are really covering or creating a relationship with another entity and not a real planet.

SE7A: Yes, it can and does happen.

ME: It does? So what is the maximum number of times this has happened with a single planet concurrently?

SE7A: Four thousand three hundred and twenty two times.

ME: What!? How long did that last?

SE7A: Approximately two hundred billion, trillion of your solar years before the first (last to create a relationship) entity broke its relationship with the planet/entity it was associated with.

ME: Did this create a cascade of entities breaking their relationships with their "planets"?

SE7A: No. The eventual reduction of entities breaking relationships took treble the amount of time it did to create it.

ME: Why was that?

SE7A: Because other entities joined the build-up after others had broken their relationships, and some of them wanted to experience existence as a planet throughout a number of environmental/planetary changes.

ME: What would those changes be, with reference to a relationship with a single entity? I would have expected changes to only be possible with the association of large numbers of entities working with the planet.

SE7A: One would be evolution as a result of interaction with a single entity. Don't forget that the size of the entity compensates for the lack of a lot of much smaller entities. Some of the changes experienced by the planet might be these:

- An increase in frequency either planet-wide or localized;
- A decrease in frequency either planet-wide or localized;
- Energetic changes to the structure of the planet resulting in the following changes in form;
  - Localized areas of different energetic function;

- o Incompatibility with other entities' energy signatures, resulting in a planet's refusal to enter into a relationship;
- o Localized fragmentation of the overall form of the planet, resulting in its fragmentation;
- o Migration to higher frequencies and dimensions or even to one of the other Source Entity's environments.

ME: So based upon this, the number of entities that associate with a planet is not relative to the evolutionary progression of the planet and what it can achieve during a relationship and the entity/ies it has a relationship with?

SE7A: No, it's the quality of the relationship that counts.

ME: Thank you. I also received another image/set of images. The sky was full of entities that had the appearance of dandelion seeds being blown with the wind. However, these had purpose, for they were in a strict formation.

SE7A: Those entities are a collective of gravity pilots. They move around the planets that they are working with looking for gravitational anomalies—areas where the gravity is not as it should be for a specific part of the planet in comparison with its density within its environment.

ME: So do these entities change the gravity in the area where there are anomalies? Do they repair the gravity in the area of the anomaly, creating a stable area?

SE7A: No, not in the slightest. The reason for them seeking out the gravitational anomalies is to gain energy. They need the energy in the anomalies to allow them to exist, procreate, and maintain their distance from the surface of the planet.

ME: But how can that be working with the planet?

SE7A: It isn't, it is just perpetuation of their existence.

ME: Mmmm. So what are they doing? How are they working with the planet?

SE7A: They provide a transport medium for those entities that want to move from planet to planet but are incapable of doing it themselves.

ME: Wait a minute. I thought all of your entities were energetic, and as a result, they would be able to move from planet to planet energetically.

SE7A: Not all entities in my environment are capable of moving from one planet to another of their own volition.

ME: Why not?

SE7A: Because they are associated with the planet where they exist. They are tied to that planet's energy signature. Remember what SE7 (SE7A, SE7B and SE7C collectively) told you about the planets being like islands and that the entities that exist on them relate to your continent/country of Australia?

ME: Yes.

SE7A: Well, one of the parallels is that most Australians, I see from your memories, stay in Australia. This is the same for most of the entities whose existence is linked with their planet—they stay with it. The parallel is similar. Australians can generally only move to other islands or continents by boat or by airplane. They can't transport themselves by using their own volition or intention. They can only move by using a vehicle of some kind, and in the instance of the entities working with the flat planets, the vehicle is the gravity pilots rather than a boat or an airplane.

ME: How do the gravity pilots transport the flat planet inhabitants? By lifting them up? Or do they have another method?

SE7A: They use the gravity waves that they create to change their position in relation to the planet to locally warp the space around the entity that desires to move its location to both re-assign its energetic signature to that of the new location, the planet the entity desires to move to, and to instantaneously transport it. In doing this, the gravity pilot also transports itself to the new location.

ME: And it doesn't return to its planet of origin?

SE7A: No, it remains with the planet it has moved to. Moreover, it is linked to the entity it transported and will transport that entity to the next planet it desires to experience.

ME: I am getting the impression that these gravity pilots exist throughout your environment, move from planet to planet at will, and continue to do so until that point in time when they are associated with one of the entities based on the surface. Once they are associated, they stay together for as long as they feel the need to maintain the association.

I have just received another image of a whole and vast number of these "gravity pilots" moving from planet to planet.

SE7A: Yes, they move around in what you would call a herd . . . no, flight . . . yes, flight . . . that is a better name. These flights are populated by gravity pilots that are not associated with a land-based entity. As they gain individual associations, they break away from the flight and assume a partnership role with the land-based entity, and as stated above, this continues until the land-based entity feels a need to remain for an indefinite period on the planet it currently sees itself. If it desires to stay for eternity, so to speak, it relinquishes its association with the gravity pilot to allow it to gain a new partner so that it can continue its own evolution. I know that I have not spoken about the experience, learning, and evolution of these entities, so I will elaborate on this now.

There is a symbiotic relationship between an individual land-based entity and its gravity pilot. The gravity pilot itself is not able to generate its own experiences and so needs another entity to do this for it. So the gravity pilot offers its service of transportation to the land-based entity in exchange for access to the experiences, learning, and subsequent evolutionary content generated by the land-based entity itself. In essence, they share the experience, learning and subsequent evolutionary content that is generated as a result of their working together.

ME: That really is working together. Why are the land-based entities not able to move from one planet to another on their own?

Figure 3: A Gravity Pilot

SE7A: Because the whole point of this environment is based around the need to work together and share the rewards. In this particular example, two entirely different beings are able to work together for the benefit of each other.

ME: Sounds very harmonious to me.

SE7A: It is, and it works very well, too.

ME: I have just remembered a question I meant to ask on the energetic content of the land-based entities and what work the gravity pilots do with the planets.

SE7A: The land-based entities are constructed out of the energies that are used to create the planet it resides on; they are tied to the planet as a result. In essence, they are individualized units of the planet itself and as such the attraction to the planet of their first creation is so strong that there is no way they can separate themselves from the planet without the co-operative help of another entity, one that is not tied down to the energy signature of the planet.

ME: Are you suggesting that the land-based entities are actually the planet itself, localized, individualized units/parts of the planet?

31

SE7A: Yes, that is exactly what I am saying. They are fragments of the planet itself that are able to move around the surface of the planet and, if so desired, migrate to the other planets that are part of my environment.

ME: I have just had a thought.

SE7A: No, you mean the real you, the higher self you, the energetic self you, has had a thought and passed it down the frequencies to that part of you that is participating in this dialogue.

ME: Ok. Ok. Yes, that would be a correct description of the process of me thinking.

SE7A: You're drinking alcohol.

ME: What? Err…

SE7A: You are drinking alcohol.

I had succumbed to the materialistic desire of half a pint of beer. I felt I needed one after the work I had done over the day.

ME: Yes, err, yes, I have, am, was. It's only a half pint. It's not a lot, honestly.

SE7A: Any alcohol that is introduced into the human body is detrimental, especially when partaking in the activity that you are currently working on. The effect of alcohol is profound. It has an effect on the pineal gland in the human brain, which is associated with the spiritual eye. This means that your ability to receive the imagery that I give you will be warped and distorted and not as accurate as a result.

ME: I am profoundly sorry. I simply did not realize.

SE7A: You were advised of this by your own Source Entity?

ME: Not in the way you have described it. To be perfectly honest, I thought that because our connection was stable, I would, mmmm, get away with it.

SE7A: Well, you won't. Let us continue. You need to drink an equal amount of water first.

Considering myself thoroughly reprimanded, I went straight to the kitchen and drank a little over a half pint of water. I hate it when this happens. If I am not able to keep things to myself over the vast distances of The Origin, that distance that is between SE7A and me, then how am I going to keep myself to myself here on Earth? I sighed and continued the dialogue.

SE7A: That's better. You are able to cope with the energies again now.

I have to say it was true. I suddenly felt the buzz of the alcohol disappear as fast as it had come.

SE7A: The buzz was a frequency-based response. This resulted from a lower frequency interacting with a high frequency that is not native to you or your Source Entity. I used the water to stabilize the chemical process that had started. This helped to correct your frequency change which, in turn, negated the buzz.

ME: Oh, I see. Thank you. So where were we before my reprimand?

I felt like a school boy caught stealing a sweet from the sweet shop. I was all embarrassed.

SE7A: Do not dwell on the past. Learn the lesson and move on.

ME: Good advice. Sorry. Where were we? Ah yes, talking about the land-based entities being individualized parts of the planet they are associated with.

SE7A: Correct. These individualized units or parts are essentially mobile planetary units. You see, the planet has to experience and evolve in its own right. Everything with a level of awareness has this requirement. It is a prerequisite for existence.

ME: So why are they mobile?

SE7A. To give the larger entity, the planet, the opportunity to experience different things, including existence and experience on other planetary bodies.

ME: Are you suggesting that the land-based entities, these mobile units of planet are able to pass on their experience, learning and evolution back to that part of them that is the whole planet?

SE7A: That is exactly what I am saying. What's more, it is entirely possible for a group or, indeed, the whole of the planets indigenous land-based but mobile units to migrate to a different planet in order to allow them to experience more and pass that back to their greater whole, their home planets.

ME: Hold on. Are you saying that the planet, by using the individualized mobile land-based units of itself, can move en-mass to another planet?

SE7A: Yes.

ME: And, I suppose, they use the gravity pilots to do this?

SE7A: Yes. You see. The gravity pilots are linked but are not wholly indigenous to their first planet of domicile. They are created elsewhere within my environment.

ME: Sorry, I got the impression that they were born or something on the planets that they were associated with.

SE7A: No. They are part of the fabric of the environment. They are, if you like, the environment's transport system.

ME: I am getting confused now. I thought you said that they were working with the planets and that they look for (I quickly checked my previous notes) and used the gravitational anomalies to provide them with energy to procreate.

SE7A: Correct, but they use this energy to multiply in areas away from the planet they are working with. The work they do with the planets and its individualized land-based units is basically one of transportation. Remember that although they pervade the environment, they do not have a natural home or ability to experience, learn or evolve—hence, the association with a planet and its land-based entities or individualized units. They evolve through association; their work is the transportation of the land-based entities to other planets, where both the land-based entity, the planet the land-based entity originates from, and the gravity pilot gain experience, learning and evolution.

ME: And they sometimes do this en-mass.

SE7A: They sometimes move in smaller numbers or groups. More often, they move to another planet as a singular planetary unit-gravity pilot combination. It is quite possible for a planet to have none of its indigenous land-based units actually resident on its surface if the units themselves are spread or distributed throughout the environment.

ME: I have just had another thought. In the dialogue above, I made this statement: "Are you saying that the planet, by using the individualized mobile land-based units of itself, can move en–mass to another planet?" And you said. "Yes."

SE7A: Yes, I did.

ME: Then, sorry, but I am thinking of the right words to say here. Is it possible for a planet to completely separate itself out into smaller units and experience existence in a totally fragmented way?

SE7A: Yes, that is one option that the planet can take. It is one that many entities take to experience, learn and evolve in an accelerated manner. In the example that you have just stated though, the planet must create enough of its land-based units in one go, so to speak, to destabilize its inherent planetary structure. This is necessary because it allows the planet to separate its consciousness into smaller but nevertheless co-existent, coadunate existence. The coadunate existence is a necessary requirement for reversing the separation process, for without it, the planet cannot collect its separate parts and recreate the whole planet. The planet MUST at some point recreate itself.

ME: Why must it recreate its whole self?

SE7A: This is the only way that the planet can assimilate wholistically all of the experiences that its previously existing individual units and those units that were created when the whole was dissolved have accumulated and share them with the re-integrated units. When the planet becomes one again it needs to act and behave as one. In doing so, everything that is or was the planet in both its separated and collective "whole" states needs to be reprogramd, if you like, into a condition that represents a whole planet and not a collective of smaller coadunate parts.

ME: So there is a difference between a "whole" and a "coadunation"?

SE7A: Yes. Most collectives, although described as a "whole," are actually a collective of "coadunate" entities—they are co-joined, individualized units that have control over their decisions and evolution whilst sharing their experiences with other members of their coadunate collective. A "whole" is a collective of individualized units that do not have control over their decisions and

35

evolution. In fact, they do not evolve in an individual basis. Instead, they evolve as a "whole."

ME: So the planetary parts are a hybrid. They are given individualized intelligence and evolutionary components when separated from the "whole," communicating through coadunation but lose this individuality and coadunation when they are re-integrated as a single whole planet.

SE7A: Correct, well stated and understood.

ME: So how many planets are totally dissolved into a coadunate of individualized planetary land-based units?

SE7A: Not many. I see that you are going to press me for a number.

ME: You read my mind.

SE7A: Always. The figure would approximate three hundred thousand million planets that have or are currently experiencing existence in this format.

ME: One thing I haven't asked yet is what the land-based entities look like.

SE7A: That is not a simple question to answer, for they are not all the same.

ME: You mean they are as diverse as the flora and fauna on Earth?

SE7A: Not in the slightest. They are created in a form that allows the planet the optimal opportunity to experience itself from a surface-based perspective.

I will give you an example, but I will have to explain this in physical terms to you, for you would not understand it otherwise.

ME: OK, fire away.

SE7A: They have the characteristics of what I can only describe as rock, a mineral.

ME: How do they function? I got the impression that they move around the surface. Is this right?

In some of my other dialogues, I have encountered entities that are "PART" of the rock/mineral content of a planet but are not "OF" it. They are "consciousness" associated with the rock and move around

36

the planet by moving their consciousness from one rock structure to another on the sub-atomic level. They literally pervade the planet.

SE7A: These individualized units of planet and planetary consciousness initially grow out of the surface of the planet, if that is the correct way to portray it, and achieve a form factor that is totally resultant of the minerals that form their body. As an example, if they were composed of the mineral you call quartz, they would initially assume the form factor of quartz. If it was pure carbon, it would be the form factor of pure carbon. The planets are not made of such basic elements, and so this should be used in illustration only because I have no other way to describe it in your language. Nevertheless, I will try.

The land-based entities have the ability to change molecular structure of the mineral to create an alloy of minerals and metals. They move around the surface by rolling themselves.

ME: I just received an image of them moving rather like the track on a caterpillar tractor or a military tank.

SE7A: That is one way they achieve movement. The motivational force they use is the attractivity that exists between the minerals and metals that they use in their "alloy" and the minerals that are part of the surface or sub-surface of the planet. They literally move by using the forces of molecular attractivity. To achieve this movement on a constant basis, they are continuously modifying their alloy. Continuous modification of their alloy of minerals means that there is a continuous level of motion through attractivity. Once the attractivity has created motion, the area of alloy is changed to a neutral alloy so as not to stop the movement through attractivity with that area of land that has been passed.

SE7A: When they want to create something, they create the tools required to create that which is desired by creating an alloy of themselves relative to the task at hand. This also includes incorporating an alloy of the materials that are in the area of the planet they are currently near. When they want to create something bigger than that which they can achieve on their own, they merge together, creating an alloy of many land-based entities. They also use and incorporate an alloy of the planet's minerals that are found in the area that they are working with or within. When they create a structure or shelter for other entities, they create the form out of this

37

alloy of themselves and the planetary minerals and metals and then change the alloy so that they can move away from the form of their creation. During the leaving process, they program the molecular structure of the alloy of the structure left by leaving part of their collective intention and allowing the structure to perform the tasks it was designed to do. The entities then dissolve their collective alloy and become separate individual units again.

ME: And all this is happening whilst the other entities/planets cover each other to experience existence as another planet?

SE7A: Yes, that and other things with other land-based entities as well. We must end this dialogue here as you need to progress on to your dialogue with Source Entity Seven "B."

ME: Before we finish, I note that there are no galaxies or suns.

SE7A: No, that's right. The permutation of space that you are observing has no need for entities to be present in the form of galaxies and suns (stars). That is because the energies required to support the entities (including the gravity pilots) that are either the planets or the entities that reside on the surface of the planets are available throughout the environment and are not a function of fission or fusion that your physical universe experiences. Also, the largest size entities in my environment are, in fact, the flat planets themselves. They are evenly dispersed around the volume of the environment rather than in clusters of star systems and galaxies. If they were to group themselves into similar shapes that may be construed as a star system or a galaxy, they would not create a new larger entity, one that has the role of such an entity. Instead, they would merely be in a group of planets that form a shape of some sort.

ME: Why did you not create galaxies or stars?

SE7A: First, the galaxies and stars that you are referring to are a product of the lower frequencies in your dimension. Within the dimensions in my environment there are no frequencies low enough to result in the manifestation of physical phenomena. Also, because the environment is energetically "in order," so to speak, there is no need for a larger entity to be in existence to "sweep up" and collect all of the stray energies and materials created by such energies.

ME: I keep getting a picture in my mind of a white back drop to your environment.

SE7A: Yes, that is another reason for not needing the entities you refer to as stars. As you know, stars create heat and light in your physical universe, plus other energies necessary for the continued existence of the human body and other carbon-based entities. As my entities are essentially energetic in nature, they are exempt from the need for such basic elemental fuels. The appearance, in your mind's eye, of my environment is, therefore, a representation of what you would expect to see from your own perspective, should your physical eyes be capable of de-coding the frequencies that inflate this environment.

ME: So essentially, you have a universe that is full of planets and entities, and that's it.

SE7A: As a very high level summary, you would be correct, but, of course, there is much more to my environment than this short dialogue can expose. One such addition that I will give you before I let you commence communication with Source Entity Seven "B" is that at certain periods in their existence all of the flat planets link up together and make what you would call a hollow sphere.

ME: Like a big 3D jigsaw puzzle (I was thinking of the Wikipedia logo).

SE7A: Yes, sort of.

ME: Why do they do that?

SE7A: To share their learning and to identify which entities will be moving on to the next environment.

ME: How often has this happened?

SE7A: Only six times since their creation. It is a very special occasion when it happens, and we are not due such an a event for some time yet, as the entities currently in my environment are a little slow evolution wise.

ME: Any reason for that?

SE7A: It just happens that way sometimes. Consider your own planet. It went backwards, did it not?

ME: Yes, it did.

SE7A: Well, it's not a unique occurrence. It happens throughout the environments created by The Origin's Source Entities. Now you need to prepare yourself, for Source Entity Seven "B" is waiting for you.

Source Entity Seven B

SE7B: Hello!

ME: Sorry?

SE7B: Hello.

ME: Is that Source Entity Seven "A"?

SE7B: No its Seven "B."

ME: I am sorry. You caught me out a bit there. I didn't expect such a fast change over, and your voice has the same tone as SE7A. Also, I was advised to prepare first.

SE7B: You did prepare.

ME: Sorry, but I don't recall it.

SE7B: You, that is, your energetic self, prepared itself to receive my energies. You calibrated your frequencies to that which makes communication easier.

ME: Well, that bit of me that is communicating with you is under the delusion that it is cut off from the rest of me whilst incarnate. Ah, now I understand. My greater self doing the work in the background might explain why certain things happen automatically and so easily. It is preparing me for the work by working in the background to maintain and control the energies that maintain and control the link.

SE7B: OK, I don't see it that way. All I see is a single entity, one that is not of my creation, communicating with me.

ME: Interesting. Thank you for that clarification. I must take that into consideration when I communicate with the remaining Source Entities.

So, you are the intermediate Source Entity Seven, the one that was created out of the area that overlapped between the initial aspects of Source Entity Seven when it decided to separate itself out into two.

SE7B: Correct. You see, what happened was that when this separation was taking place, that which was Source Entity Seven separated its sentience to become Source Entity Seven A & B. This process took place at the same time as the demarcation of the areas of Source Entity Seven that was to become Seven "A" &" B." As this happened, there was a third temporary entity created, me, which caused that which was still Source Entity Seven (holistically) to hold the process in stasis and reconsider its options based upon what had happened.

ME: Were you self-aware at that point?

SE7B: Not as a separate entity, but I was as part of that which was holistically Source Entity Seven.

ME: So when did you become self-aware?

SE7B: My self-awareness only became a function of my individuality after my separation from the holistic aspect of that which was/is Source Entity Seven.

ME: And that aspect is still available as a communication medium because I first made contact with it/you as this collective aspect?

SE7B: It is. It still functions as the whole and must always function as the whole.

ME: Why is that?

SE7B: Simply because there may be a point in our evolutionary development where we wish to become fully one again. As a result, we need to keep part of the holistic aspect of Source Entity Seven in reserve, so to speak, as the initiating entity for such a decision to take form and start the process of re-integration. Or, to initiate communication with entities such as yourself.

ME: You expect to re-integrate at some time then?

SE7B: Not sometime soon, but it could well happen—specifically if the opportunities for evolution are expended in our current configuration, which they are very much not. But let me get back to our discussion on me. You asked about when I became self-aware?

ME: Yes I did. The Source Entities I have contacted to date have all suggested that they became self-aware over a long period, and that when they realized that they were self-aware, that was the point in

41

which The Origin contacted them and advised them of their reason for "being" in existence. Clearly, this would have already happened with the full aspect of Source Entity Seven, which means that you must have gained both individuality and the collective memory/experiences of Source Entity Seven as part of the separation process, including knowledge of the separation process, the reasons for it, and the decision to stop the separation at the point of your creation.

SE7B: You're good, aren't you?

ME: Errrr!? Well it is logical, isn't it?

SE7B: Not to everyone. I was told you were good for such a small being.

ME: Thank you for the compliments. I am just doing my job.

SE7B: Let's continue.

ME: It must have been/is strange being both an individualized part of Source Entity Seven and actually being the whole Source Entity Seven concurrently.

SE7B: No, the separation was instantaneous and that part of us/Source Entity Seven that is/remains as the whole, as a higher function of us rather like your being a temporarily separate part of your energetic self. You are still one, but you are separate—you are separately together, separately one, and so am I. We are similar in this particular aspect.

ME: The separation program must have contained all the details of the separate aspects of Source Entity Seven, which you would have inherited.

SE7B: We all did. However, my creation was, as previously stated, a bit of a surprise. As a result, the full aspect of Source Entity Seven stopped the process at that point to both review what had happened and perpetuate my existence.

ME: Perpetuate your existence?

SE7B: Yes, because if the process was not stopped, the initial plan of a separation into two would have continued, and I would have become non-existent. In this instance, we three are one as we are still joined, the joining being me.

ME: On earth it is always difficult for the supposedly unwanted or unplanned child. That child always feels that they are not loved by their parents. Do you have this thought in the back of your mind?

SE7B: Not in the slightest. I was always in existence anyway.

ME: How do you mean?

SE7B: I am essentially Source Entity Seven; as a result, I existed before the separation, and I will exist after re-integration whenever that takes place.

ME: And you feel that way because you have inherited all of the memories and functions of Source Entity Seven?

SE7B: Yes, but know this. From my perspective, there is no difference between being integrated and being separate, at least not now.

ME: Why not now?

SE7B: Because I am now separate but together. The act of being separate is happening now, not as a possibility or a "what if" scenario. It has happened, is happening, will happen, could have and did happen. There is no issue with that with me as the event is an event in event space. Source Entity Seven stopped the separation process where it is now because it saw the beauty in what happened. In its mind it was a perfect outcome, one that supports the evolutionary requirement.

ME: And that evolutionary requirement that has been supported is?

SE7B: To experience, learn and evolve.

ME: Of course. OK, I am convinced. Let's talk about what you have created within the period of event space you have been in existence.

SE7B: I would like that.

ME: Your environment is equal in size to Source Entity Seven "A" and Seven "C" from my visual data.

SE7B: Yes, it is but I have incorporated a set of dimensions within dimensions. Source Entity Seven "A" created an environment that was populated with what you recognized as flat planets. That was only one environmental area, one universe if you want to call it that.

ME: But when I spoke to Source Entity Seven, it said that it copied the structure of The Origin in the 12x3x12 format, missing, of course, the 12 zones, which Source Entities cannot, I assume create.

SE7B: It did. However, Source Entity Seven "A" only used one of those dimensional permutations and, as a result, it constructed a single universal environment. I, on the other hand, decided to use the full suite of possible permutations and "add-in" all of these permutations within the permutations of space that were available. Everything is still as it was explained to you by Source Entity Seven from the perspective of the main structure of "US" as separate aspects of Source Entity Seven. It is just that I have split it down further for my environment.

ME: That makes 12x3x12x12x3x12 different permutations of space (186,624 permutations or different/simultaneous universes).

SE7B: Yes, but that is not all. The progression from one permutation to another is not linear or indeed logical, for it changes in relation to that which has been experienced by the entity experiencing it. In essence, the universe they move onto next is relevant to that which they need to experience next but in a way that is not so much progressive but transgressive. As a result, they can and do experience as many permutations of space as is necessary for their evolution. The order in which they experience them can either lead them to quickly traverse my environment, allowing them to move on to Source Entity Seven "A" or "C's" environment after the shortest possible exposure to the smallest number of permutations of space, or they can experience all of them, or all of them and some of them more than once or twice, making them take a longer time.

ME: You mean your environment is like an ever changing MAZE, where re-tracing your steps, if you get lost, does not help you get out of the maze or indeed to the center of the maze.

SE7B: Correct. Fun, isn't it?

ME: I am glad I am not one of your entities!

SE7B: Why, they enjoy the challenge!

ME: This environment sounds a little like the entities in Source Entity Six's environment where there are universe-sized entities that can exist either singularly or as part of the structure of another universal entity, each having the ability to exist within and without each other simultaneously and in multiples of numbers.

SE7B: That would be useful only as a thought process to enable you to expand your understanding of what can be. The basics of my environment are such that each permutation of space is capable of holding and does hold all of the permutations of space at what you would understand as being the micro level. So to keep it easy, each permutation of space holds within it 430 permutations of space, each a universe in its own right, with dimensions, tritaves and frequency bands. Whereas the entities in Source Entity Six's environments are entities in their own right, these are purely energetic environments.

ME: But all energy can become a self-aware entity given long enough, can it not?

SE7B: It can, provided it is allowed to. In this instance the energy in each permutation of space is programmed to do a certain job. Sentience, at whatever level "energy" is allowed to attain, is not necessary in this instance.

ME: Thank you for that explanation. One of the things that has been going through my mind whilst we have been discussing the structure of your environment is the mechanism used to identify which universe an entity is allowed to move onto next.

SE7B: The universes themselves decide what entity can move onto which universe and how long they should stay there.

ME: What? I thought you said they weren't sentient.

SE7B: They aren't. But they are programmed, so to speak, to do certain functions that allow my/our entities to experience what they need to experience before they move onto the environments that are Source Entity Seven A and C.

ME: Hold on here. How can a universe decide on which entity it accepts, especially when there are so many entities involved?

SE7B: As an entity progresses through the universes, it gains what you might call a signature or a code relevant to what has been experienced and where.

ME: I think I see what you are alluding to. I have just received an image of a multifaceted shape passing through a gateway of equal

45

but opposite facets, sort of the square peg in a square hole imagery except this has lots and lots of different sides, angles and curves to it.

SE7B: Yes, I see what you are describing is a key; this would be a reasonable method of description even though it is limited.

ME: If it is limited, can you give me a better illustration?

SE7B: Certainly. You see, when an entity progresses through my environment, each universe they interact with gives them a certain signature or coding. This coding opens the door to various universes that are the best next environment for a particular entity to experience, including the optimal progression permutation.

ME: I thought you said that your environment was a maze.

SE7B: No, you said that, but the analogy still remains.

ME: How?

SE7B: Because the entities themselves do not know what those permutations are.

ME: Oh.

SE7B: Also, the permutation that may next be experienced by the entity that is close to finishing its time in one universe may well change as a result of what it has experienced.

ME: So the code/signature of an entity can change from the potential of accessing one set of universes at the start of experiencing a new universe to a different set of universes at the end of that particular universal experience/set of experiences. Hence, the changing maze imagery I received.

SE7B: Yes.

ME: Can you give me any more information on this code or signature the entities generate through their experiences in the various universes.

SE7B: Let me see. The image in your head that I have just sent is illustrative only as it is a difficult subject for you to understand.

I received two images:

1.   The first image was one of a cylindrical key that had a specific and complicated form factor that was the positive

"male" version of a negative "female" version, the lock being the "female" version. It had many layers or levels. It could be inserted into the first level and then had to be rotated to allow the first and second level to pass through. The same was true for a third, fourth and fifth, etc., level. These form factors changed sometimes, so the sixth level may be one shape before it was inserted into the lock, if say it was only the fourth level that was inserted, but if the fifth was inserted, the conditions of experience and evolution may have changed this and affected the form factor of the six and subsequent levels by either making a change to the form factor or not, as the case may be.

2. The second image was that of a person riding down a water chute with doors and deflectors at various stages down the chute. These doors/deflectors would be presented to the person as they progressed down the chute. Imagery would be presented to the person, and they would select a door as a result of the imagery experienced. This, in turn, would result in a deflector closing off a part of the chute and allowing the person to only progress in the direction relating to the imagery and door. Various permutations would be in front of the person riding the water chute that they were not aware of. In my mind's eye I could see a system that looked rather "root like" with the exception of the roots sometimes linking up again and even going back on themselves to an earlier although potentially different point. On the back of this person was a map. The map indicated where and when the person had been and, therefore, what the permutations of the next universal environment that could be experienced were available to the person concerned. The water chute knows this information, and this is taken into account when the person makes certain decisions in choosing doors, based upon the imagery presented to them. It was essentially like a personalized and portable Akashic record with everything about the individual recorded by it, including the next possible permutations of the code. It was very complicated.

SE7B: Good summary. Note though that although the entity itself is not aware of the new possible permutations available to it, its personal record has this and travels with the entity at all times. The universes are illustrated by the functions of the "lock" and the "water chute." The entities are illustrated by the "key" and the "person riding" the water chute.

ME: Before I ask the inevitable question of what your entities look like if I were able to see them with my physical eyes, that is, I would like to know the work that they do to enable them to traverse the maze that is your environment.

SE7B: They evolve.

ME: Clearly. Evolution is a prerequisite for sustained existence in my book.

SE7B: It is one of the reasons why The Origin allowed us to create smaller versions of ourselves. Evolution is an inevitable result of the experiential content of existence.

ME: There are more reasons?

SE7B: Yes, of course. Although evolution is the prime facia reason for an entity's existence, it is not the only reason for its creation.

ME: Ah! So what would the reason for an entity's creation be?

SE7B: Entertainment.

ME: What?

SE7B: Entertainment. Maybe I have this word wrong. Maybe I should have used distraction or even company or help.

ME: From my standpoint, all of those words might describe the reason to create an entity. A creator would no longer be alone in its task, it would have help in working on and completing its task, and/or it would be distracted from its own task/workload, as well as entertained by the efforts of its creations in trying to do those tasks.

SE7B: Diversity would also be a word I would use.

ME: Why?

SE7B: Because the more entities an entity creates to help it deliver its commitment to the evolution of The Origin, the greater the number of permutations that can be employed to experience, learn and evolve whilst essentially experiencing the same thing, but from different angles. This is the main advantage of diversity and is the result of creating a high number of entities.

ME: Fine. Can we move on to the work they do?

SE7B: Certainly. There are three types of entity, and they each have different work to do.

ME: The number three seems to be a recurring theme with Source Entity Seven.

SE7B: Only in so much as we have three environments. I will continue with the work of each entity type.

ME: Can I stop you a moment? When you said there were three entity types, I momentarily picked up the number four, but that quickly changed back to three, actually no, it was three and a half. Why was that?

SE7B: There was a fourth, but that entity line was terminated. The image of three and a half was primarily because that's exactly what it was doing—the role of an entity that was based upon three and a half, i.e., it was an in-between entity that was doing half the role of one series of entities and half the role of another.

ME: Would this not have been advantageous from an evolutionary perspective.

SE7B: No, it was surplus to requirements.

ME: Why?

SE7B: Because once the entities have achieved all that they can achieve whilst doing the work that they are working on, they move on to do the work of one of the other two types of entity. Eventually they gain experience in all three work types.

ME: So what you are suggesting is that the fourth entity type would only experience the diversity of experience that was eventually and inevitability experienced by the other three entities.

SE7B: Correct.

ME: I also feel another difference in the fourth entity.

SE7B: Yes, there was one. It was a hybrid of all three, and that was not the point.

ME: Why not?

SE7B: Because the whole objective was to have three individual entity types that were specialized in some way relative to the work that they do. Once they had experienced all they needed to experience as a result of the work they were essentially designed for, they had to swap roles with another entity, one that had completed all of its work so they could experience what you would call frustration.

ME: What? Experience frustration?

SE7B: Yes, as I have just stated, they are designed for a particular type of work. Once they have, err, graduated from the work that they were designed for, they are then tasked to work on subjects within the new work that they are not designed to work on. This results in the exposure to frustration as they obviously remember the ability to perform tasks in a seamless fashion.

However, frustration and necessity are the birth place of creativity, and it is the need to perform the tasks for the work that they are not designed for that results in the creation of constructs or tools to allow them to perform as required in their new "working" environment.

ME: So it's the need to create that helps the entity evolve?

SE7B: Creativity is the other main reason for existence. To be a creator is to be a God whilst being part of God. What's more, it is the most direct route that an entity can take to becoming closer to its creator. Creation is next on the list of the ten most important things an entity must do whilst individualized from its creator. The first, of course, is evolution.

ME: So if evolution and creation were the top two items in a list of ten an entity needs to do whilst being individualized, what are the other eight?

SE7B: I didn't see that one coming, much! However, it is a universal list, so to speak, and one that must be shared with your readers.

So here is a list of the Top Ten things an entity MUST do whilst individualized:

1.   Evolve

2.   Create

3.   Learn

4.   Experience

5.   Develop

6.   Interact (with others)

7.   Innovate

8.   Discover

9.   Intellectualize

10.   Become aware of self

The tenth in line is the **first** thing an entity needs to do once created. The last, evolution, being the result of all the other things being actioned. The rest are in a sort of "loose" order and are not entirely dependent upon each other for an entity's progression from self-awareness to evolution.

Entertainment is achieved by my observing how my entities progress.

ME: So what I need to know now is what your entities look like, including what they have created.

SE7B: I, and I say I, have created two types of entities.

ME: I had a flash of the number three then. Why would I have received that? Oh, hang on, you mentioned that we have three entities in the last dialogue *(there was a one week gap in the generation of the text above compared to that text which was currently being channelled)*, with a fourth being discarded as it was a hybrid.

SE7B: Yes, that is correct. I did say "I" created two entities. The third and the discarded fourth are the result of the combined creativity of SE7.

This was starting to get complicated all of a sudden.

ME: Ah, so let's keep this simple then. From my standpoint, you are part of/an aspect of Source Entity Seven, and as such you must have been, in part, involved in the creation of the third and fourth entities. Is this a reasonable way to understand it?

SE7B: I would say so. If it helps you understand, then yes, by all means, use that method of recognition. Although in truth and actuality, "I" created two of them and "I" as part of the whole entity that is Source Entity Seven took part in the creation of the other two entities. However "I" took the decision to remove the fourth hybrid version from individual existence.

ME: Thank you for the clarification. What happened to those entities that were the hybrids? Surely they must have been sentient at that point in their creation.

SE7B: They had, indeed, gained a level of self-awareness at that point in event space when I decided to terminate their existence.

ME: But would that not be classified as genocide?

SE7B: No, not in the slightest.

ME: Why not?

SE7B: Because they were not lost. In essence they never existed before they were created, as you never existed before you were created.

ME: You mean existed as an individual unit of the Source Entity (my Source Entity, SE1 – God). The energies that I am always existed as part of the Source Entity and, of course, The Origin.

SE7B: Correct. But they were not simply re-absorbed into my energies. They were modified to allow them to be one of the three remaining types of entities. To re-absorb them would have been a waste of my creativity (not of energy). It was a relatively simple process to modify the energies of the already existing entities into those of another type

ME: How did you choose which entity they were modified into?

SE7B: By looking at their attributes to establish what the percentage, if you like, of their hybrid make-up was and whether they had more attributes of one type than another. If they had, say 50% of the attributes of type 1, 30% attributes of type 2 and 20% attributes of type 3, then that entity would be modified to be 100% type 1. On the other hand, if there was an equal spread of type 1, type 2 and type 3 attributes within a specific entity, then that entity was either asked to decide what type it would prefer to be, or if it was undecided, it was placed in what you would call a "pool," a holding area where the total number of entities that were undecided or showed no particular preference would be equally divided into the three entity types and modified accordingly. That way I achieved the best re-distribution possible of individualized Source Entity Seven/Source Entity Seven "B" energy.

ME: I thought it would be easy to change the energy that was the entity's back into your core energy?

SE7B: It is, but as I said earlier, it would have been a waste of my creativity. Not only that, removing life from individualized existence, specifically if it has achieved the sentient state of life, is to remove the opportunity to allow an individual the right to evolve, and my opportunity to benefit from that evolution. What's more, there is an unwritten rule between the Source Entities that states that a sentient entity must make dissolution back into its source its own choice and not the choice of the creating Source Entity.

ME: I thought that an entity sought communion or re-integration with its Source Entity through the route of evolution only. Surely re-integration or dissolution bypasses that function.

SE7B: No. You see, there is a major difference in the end product that I will explain further. Re-integration as a result of evolutionary progression results in an entity becoming one with its Source Entity, one with its God. It is integral whilst maintaining individualized thought processes and as a result it augments the functionality of the mind of the Source Entity it is fully integrated into. It gives it extra processing power if you like.

However, when an entity, through its own volition decides to end its individuality, it both re-integrates and fully dissolves its energies back into the energies of the Source Entity, giving up its right to individualized existence forever. The bulk energies of the Source Entity are, therefore, increased by the product of the total Source Entity energies, plus those of the individualized entities energies, and that evolutionary content that the entity had already accrued, no matter how small it is/was.

ME: Can this ever be reversed?

SE7B: Of course. The entity itself is not aware of this functionality as it can only be activated by the creating Source Entity.

ME: So how and when does that work?

SE7B: The signature, structure and accrued functionality of the individualized energies of that entity wishing to lose its individuality and become fully one with its Source Entity are recorded, together with the distributed locations of its energetic components, i.e., those areas within the Source Entity where they are put to best use. In essence, the re-integrated entity can be spread across the full totality that is the Source Entity they were created by. Each energetic component is able to be put to use in some part of the Source Entity it is re-integrating into because the locations, functions and signatures are known by the Source Entity. In the event that it needs or desires to create an individualized part of itself to perform a certain task, it can take those parts of the integrated entity either in whole or in part and individualize it. It can even re-activate those memories and evolutionary content should it be necessary or advantageous to do so.

ME: Are you suggesting that a new individualized entity can be created either as a whole and perfect re-build of that entity that gave up its individuality? Or it can create a completely new entity that is constructed of the chosen composite parts of several entities who chose to give up their individuality by using separate parts, each composite part specifically chosen because of the speciality of the work the new entity is being assigned to?

SE7B: Correct.

ME: And this also includes the composite memories and evolutionary content?

SE7B: Yes, it does.

ME: So what happens to this entity once created?

SE7B: It performs the task it was created for.

ME: And after that?

SE7B: It is given the opportunity to either re-integrate into the creating Source Entity or to commence the standard evolutionary journey by identifying which environment it would like to start this within.

ME: Why would you go to all the hassle of re-individualization, either a whole or composite entity, when, as a Source Entity, you could just create a new entity?

SE7B: There are two reasons for that. First, there is a specific window during the existence of a Source Entity where it is at its best, creativity-wise. This window is specific to the creation of individualized autonomous entities. This is a cyclic function of Source Entity existence, and as such the need to re-individualize an entity may be outside the optimal part of this cycle. Second, once an individualized entity is created it is specialized into autonomous individualized evolutionary energy, and this specialization remains even in dissolution, so it becomes much easier to re-assemble specialized components of evolutionary energy into whatever a Source Entity wants, such as the total re-construction of a previous entity or the creation of a new entity made up of the composite parts of other dissolved entities rather than to create one from scratch.

ME: That is interesting. I wasn't aware that Source Entities have cycles to work within.

SE7B: Everything has cycles to work within. It is part of the flow of energy around The Origin, and as such we need to work with that flow. Even The Origin does.

I made a mental note to discuss this with The Origin in the next book, which I now know will make the "Beyond the Source" books a trilogy. It will have the subtitle "The Origin Speaks" and will focus fully on dialogue with The Origin.

ME: Ok, I will discuss this with The Origin in later dialogues. I would like to discuss the physiology of the three entity types you have—if indeed, they have physiology.

SE7B: No problem. As I stated before, each of these entities has a role to play, and its specialized form is relative to the work it does. As such it enjoys the benefit of being a "round peg in a round hole" in the first instance. However, as it progresses, it then moves to an environment where it is not the round peg in the round hole and, therefore, experiences difficulty in performing its new role and even experiences frustration. To progress this dialogue, I will now explain the form of the entity, the work it performs and the advantage of that form.

The first entity is energetic in nature. It has the ability to change its magnetic properties at what you would call the sub-atomic level, allowing it to corral the native energies within the environment and create areas of high nuclear activity. You might call them suns or stars. These areas of nuclear activity are used as energy stores for the other two entities to use and work with, allowing them to create. The only issue here is that they need to be maintained from within the area of activity. In essence, the entity uses its magnetic properties to create a cage effectively stopping the energies being corralled from moving away from each other. What's more, these energies need to be compressed over a period of time to maintain the nuclear process. This requires the magnetic field, the cage, to be reduced in size when required. Don't get me wrong, the magnetic field is not the only medium being used to control this process. There are many more, and the first entity has the ability to use many more. It is just that you would only be able to understand/relate to the use of magnetism. The other mediums would and could only be described by what your science fiction writers call force-fields, but that is a very non-descript and general piece of terminology.

ME: Is the corralling of energy to create areas of nuclear activity all that they do? How could they learn and evolve by just doing this type of work?

SE7B: My entities are not as complicated as those created by your Source Entity, so in this instance, learning how to corral the energies, creating the nuclear condition and maintaining that condition relative to the changes in energetic content both inside and outside the cage they have created whilst meeting the demands of those entities that are using the energies for creative purposes is a full-time task—especially as each entity has over a million areas of nuclear activity to maintain. The objective of this form of entity is to create, maintain and serve.

The second form is primarily energetic in nature but has the ability to change its density. It has no magnetic or other energetic functionality that is or can be associated with the ability to contain a nuclear condition. However, it can use its ability to change its density to make the tools necessary to use such energies. This entity can assume any form factor required to achieve its goal—being the use of nuclear energies to form materials for the use of the third entity type. The objective of this form of entity is to overcome obstacles, create, and serve.

The third entity type is semi physical in nature and would appear to be like a net or cloud that travels through the environment, gathering up the materials created by the second entity type for the purpose of forming the pure material content required to make the objects described in the dialogue you had with Source Entity Seven A's environment—such as the flat planets, their component parts and the creation of the component parts for the other physical entities that exist in this environment, such as the gravity pilots. The objective of this entity is to create the physical from the energetic.

ME: Between them, I would guess that they work as a team and create the content for your environment and the entities for Source Entity Seven A's environment. They are true creators

SE7B: Yes, but they are creators that rely on each other and are limited in what they do. As you can see, each of these works apart from the first entity in a downstream manner—one creating the product for the other to work with. This is why they must each experience each other's work environment and work load.

The additional piece of learning here is, as previously explained, each of them has to experience and perform the other's tasks by using its own ingenuity and specialized skills in order to overcome the difficulties it faces in trying to perform the tasks of the others that are relative to the type of entity and its specialism. This is the learning, appreciation and evolutionary stage.

Figure 4: Source Entity 7b's Three Entities

ME: Re-reading our dialogue, I don't see that you have described the form factor of your entities.

SE7B: It would be difficult for you to visualize that which is purely energetic and formless, which, of course, is what the first two are. The third type has a sort of loose form—hence, the net or cloud-like description that has been described to you in the most logical way possible.

ME: Touché. When these flat planets or the materials for these flat planets are created, how are they transported to Source Entity Seven A's environment?

SE7B: Via the interface at the outside of the three environments. The same one that allows entities to move from Source Entity Seven A's environment to my environment or my entities to [move to] Source Entity Seven C's environment.

ME: OK, that's clear. Thank you.

SE7B: It is now time for you to communicate with Source Entity Seven "C." It is waiting for you and has been observing the communication methods you used to establish a continued dialogue with Source Entity Seven "A" and me. Further and final communication with Source Entity Seven "collectively" will follow directly afterward in order to finalize these dialogues and help with the redirection of the link to the Source Entity you will refer to as "Eight." I bid you farewell as a singular entity and will communicate with you in totality as Source Entity Seven later.

Source Entity Seven C

And with that last sentence the link between the second or "B" aspect of Source Entity Seven was dissolved. Even before this link was dissolved, I felt another link taking place, that of Source Entity Seven "C."

It should be noted here though that the overall link to Source Entity Seven in "totality" was never lost. Indeed, it was consistently present as a "carrier wave" (See glossary) for the smaller more directional communication links with the separate "A" and "B" aspects of Source Entity Seven. As a result of this, it is still in place and will be used for the dialogue that I am about to have with Source Entity Seven "C."

As I thought about the up-coming dialogue with Source Entity Seven "C," the link automatically established itself. I intuitively knew that this is a function of my energetic self and not something that I have established with that part of me that is associated with the physical. I wonder how I did that? Then, in my mind's eye, I suddenly saw the environment that Source Entity Seven "C" created and was stunned to see that it was like a ball of water hanging in space. I remembered a previous dialogue with Source Entity Two (see Beyond the Source), whose third environment was fluidic in nature. But the fluidic nature that Source Entity Two described to me was based upon an ever changing state of rotational attractivity and not what obviously looked like a liquid to me.

I was intrigued to find an environment that was clearly "physical" in appearance in an area of The Origin where most, if not all, of the environments created by the Source Entities I had communicated with at that point in time were energetic. I eagerly sought Source Entity Seven "C" to establish if this image and my interpretation were reasonable. I do have to say though that the prospect of an environment that was liquid in consistency was not likely, for in my understanding, a liquid is a function of the physical universe in which I or part of me currently existed. Was I pre-empting the information I was receiving? I decided to not overlay this information with my own thought processes and commenced the dialogue with Source Entity "C."

ME: I feel that you have made contact with me. Can we speak?

SE7C: G'day.

Again, said in an Australian accent, the accent used by Source Entity Seven "in totality." I had gotten used to a neutral accent with Source Entity Seven "B" (not commented on in the text), and as a result, it took me by surprise.

ME: You caught me unawares then. I had become used to "B's" neutral accent.

SE7C: I can adopt a neutral accent if you wish. I was following that communication method used by our "totality." I trust what you are receiving now is to your acceptance.

ME: Sorry, I didn't need you to change your accent to suit my requirements. What you had was fine. It just caught me out, but I do thank you for thinking of me and my limitations.

SE7C: You are not as limited as you think. In fact, there is quite a crowd forming around the galaxy your earth sphere is manifested in. The beings in the crowd are watching with intense interest the human who is in contact with The Origin and the Source Entities. To travel around a universe where one is existing is one thing. To travel around the multiverse of a Source Entity is another, but to be able to break through the barrier of a Source Entity and its environment, dip into the environments of other Source Entities and communicate directly with The Origin is quite another. You are creating quite a stir. You are a sensation.

ME: You are embarrassing me.

SE7C: Why would I want to do that? I have no need or desire to. Ah! I see your heritage. Now I see why and how you can do what you are doing. You are OM.

I had been told this before (that I was OM) but had decided to put it to one side. I did not want to promote illusions of grandeur. Instead, I felt very silly that it had come up again, especially as it was suggested that I was drawing a crowd. And not only that, an intergalactic one to boot!

Quite out of the blue, and with no knowledge of this dialogue, my wife had received the same information in one of her meditations. Scary!

I decided to forge onward with my agenda of questions rather than dwell on such an ego-inflating subject but was headed off at the pass by Source Entity Seven "C." It had something else to say about me.

SE7C: I will explain to you something about yourself that your own Source Entity has not shared with you yet. You clearly have the ability to move outside of the structure of your Source Entity's multiverse. When you first started to use the rather mechanical means you invented to help you move up the frequencies, you truncated the 430 frequency bands (12 dimensions x 3 dimensional components x 12 frequency bands = 432. Taking into account that the first three dimensional components (tritaves) are effectively "one" in the lowest dimension, this makes it 430 frequency bands because the rest of the tritaves are considered individual within the full dimension in which they exist. Also, note that as a frequency band is associated with a particular dimensional component, in actuality it becomes a permutation of space, a universe in its own right) that are associated with your multiverse, to 100—hence, your rather round figure of 100 levels. Your Source Entity did not deny the figure. Because you had traversed the 430 levels in 100 steps and not 430, you missed out certain levels. When you achieved this, you attracted the attention of your Source Entity and The Origin, who commenced dialogue with you in order to encourage you and let your ability grow. They saw your evolutionary opportunities and were/are keen to see you progress.

ME: If that is true then, the levels that mankind's universe exists within also span the lower two frequency bands/levels of the lowest tritave in the second full dimension. That is, humanity can/will occupy the twelve frequency bands/levels in the first full dimension, plus the first two frequency bands of the first tritave in the next full dimension. That equals fourteen and makes sense.

SE7C: Correct. Mankind is ascending and will soon be able to occupy, in part, those two levels, the ones you call levels thirteen and fourteen, which, to current physical mankind's perspective would be classed as energetic. This is why you established that the physical universe is made up of 14 levels. It is because part of the universe that mankind occupies is moving up the frequencies. At some point in mankind's evolution, the lower frequencies will be closed to mankind because mankind will have ascended beyond the need for interaction with the physical.

ME: Ah, now it makes sense. I was struggling with that one. To me, it just did not add up. I was getting worried that I was getting conflicting information. I was starting the think that I had gotten something totally wrong or was missing something, which I obviously was.

SE7C: Everything is revealed at the right time. One other thing that you need to be aware of is the way you operate. You effectively cut across the frequencies, tritaves and dimensions in any way you feel fit. You are not limited to the linear progression or dimensional/tritave/frequential movement that many entities are. You are fully free. This is why you can communicate with the other Source Entities. This is another reason why you grabbed the attention of your Source Entity and The Origin. It is also the main reason why you are being allowed to communicate with me and the other Source Entities.

Know this: Most entities are currently restricted to the confines of their Source Entity and can only communicate with their Source

Entity and The Origin as a direct line of communication. Being able to circumnavigate this restriction is an honor. Use it wisely. Use it well.

ME: I will. Thank you. You also seem to know now that I am OM. I have been told this before by my own Source Entity, Byron, Hum and an intuitive friend, but to be honest, I have not given it too much thought. However, I did have a flash of information whilst considering what I had typed as my "personal thoughts" (in italics above). The information (and I am really sensitive about typing this, let alone including it in this book) suggests that the OM is an abbreviation of two words in English, Original Material or Original Manifestation. I also received the information/impression that this Original Material/Manifestation is "Origin" energy remaining from the creation of the twelve Origins, the experiment that failed. Is this suggesting that I or my energy is from The Origin and NOT from my Source Entity? How can this be? People will be thinking that I am getting delusional.

SE7C: No, you are not delusional nor should you be concerned. You should be honored to know such information. You may recall that in your communications with "B," you were advised that the fourth set of entities in its environment were either re-assigned to be one of the other three or were assimilated into "B" for use at or in a future event. You may also remember that in the event that an entity chose assimilation where the energy that was the fourth entity type was broken up and used for other purposes—including full and partial integration into that which it was as the previous entity or used to create another entirely new composite entity, it retained the signature of energy that was given individuality, purpose and the ability to experience, learn and evolve.

ME: Yes, I do remember that.

SE7C: Well, when The Origin reintegrated those energies that it had used to create the twelve Origins, the signature of that energy was not lost. It was merely integrated back into use for the creation of the Source Entities. The Source Entities, us, were actually created using some of this energy with "Origin" characteristics. However, when it was amalgamated into the Source Entities, it did not mix very well. It maintained its own boundaries and was difficult to share evenly and equally among all the Source Entities when we were created. It

62

was like mixing oil with water, so to speak. When your Source Entity created the energies it was to use to populate its environment, giving it the signature of the ability to experience, learn and evolve, the energies that were of Original Manifestation energy were the first to be let loose. You (incarnate you) are part of one of those energies.

ME: Why was I not told this by my Source Entity or The Origin?

SE7C: Quite simply, you were not supposed to know then.

ME: So why are you telling me now?

SE7C: Because of the need to accelerate your knowledge. You have/are progressing faster than planned in your current state and need to know why you are supposedly breaking the rules. You have no rules. You and the OM are Original Material, and you are part of The Original Manifestation.

ME: Should not my Source Entity have told me this, or at least The Origin. Why you?

SE7C: It was not important what "Source" was used for your gaining this information; it was all about the timing. You are a child of The Origin with a foster parent of the Source Entity. Your Source Entity set you free in its initial casting out of energy to create the beings that populated its environment. Similar versions of the OM are in other Source entities, but for some reason your Source Entity had the lion's share of the energies. This is possibly because it was the first, by a few nanoseconds, to be created when The Origin created the twelve Source Entities. It is no mistake you call your Source Entity, Source Entity One.

ME: So there are, err, globules of OM everywhere—within and without the Source Entities?

SE7C: Within the Source Entities, yes. But as I said, your Source Entity seems to have the lion's share of this energy. Without the Source Entities? No, this is not a regular occurrence—hence, why you are causing a bit of a stir. In fact, you are one of five OM to be "re-born" from your Source Entity who have the ability to move outside their fostering Source Entity. The other four—*my mind went back to the memory of the four individuals I saw in a waking meditation some thirty odd years ago, telling me that all that I knew and was working on was correct, but it was not the right time for me to progress it further*—that are associated with you have not incarnated with you in the physical plane nor will they, for they are supporting you and your work, which I am told goes beyond that which you are currently experiencing.

ME: Can I, should I ask you what that is now?

SE7C: No, it would be a distraction. You will get plenty of time for that in the extended and exclusive dialogue you are due to have with The Origin in the text you already know will be called "The Origin Speaks."

ME: Sorry, I am getting a bit flustered at this information. I have one more question. Shouldn't I be able to do more than I am? I mean, shouldn't I have more faculties/powers? I feel that if I am of the OM, of The Origin's Original Material/Manifestation, should I not be performing miracles? Shouldn't I be a great Yogi materializing this, that and the other? Levitating, teleporting, saving individuals and countries from starvation and strife? Teaching the truth on a grand scale?

SE7C: No, first I am advised that YOU chose the level of functionality you currently have whilst this small part of you is projected into the physical. I also note that you understand that the lower down the frequencies you go, the less functionality you have. This is very much in "play" here. Second, being OM only really gives you a signature that originates from The Origin's creativity and not directly from your Source Entity's creativity. Your abilities whilst in the energetic are similar to both Source Entity and Origin but majoring on The Origin with, of course, the exception being that you can traverse beyond your Source Entity and the other Source Entities, which is an Origin-based function. Is that not miracle enough for you, especially when such a small part of you is in the physical? You are doing what you signed up to do. On a worldwide scale, your books and your lectures/talks, both in groups and one on one, are starting to help increase mankind's understanding of your Source Entity's multiverse and that which is beyond, The Origin and the other Source Entities. You are also helping to increase the frequencies of the earth. Ah! I see that you have residual memory of your ability; this can be a big distraction and could inhibit you if you dwell on it too long. My advice is that you be content with what you are doing and move on with your purpose.

ME: OK, enough of me, or what I currently don't recognize as me. Let's move on, as you say. When I first contacted you, I received an image of your environment as being like a sphere of liquid, rather like water. Is that right? I find it hard to believe that you have an environment made up of, err, water.

SE7C: It isn't water but the make-up of the energy might give it similar properties to water or any other liquid you have on earth.

ME: What do you mean similar properties to water?

SE7C: Looking at the way entities in your universe move/transport themselves in this most dense of environments, it would have a similar effect on the entities that exist in my environment. For example, it offers a significant level of resistance to their personal freedom of movement.

ME: I keep getting this picture of an aquarium or huge, universe-sized goldfish bowl.

SE7C: That is because your information data bank is only able to give you a universe sized goldfish bowl as an example of how the combination of frequencies is constructed in my environment.

I received more conceptual information from Source Entity Seven "C."

ME: I feel that you have just given me a rather radical concept to consider here in describing your environment. *(I must stop using the word, "environment.")* This is a real conundrum to me. The frequencies, dimensions and dimensional components are all interwoven with no clear demarcation like there is in my Source Entity's multiverse.

SE7C: Correct. They are all merged together, nothing being separate but everything being together. It makes things compact. That is why you perceived the liquid-like condition of my environment.

ME: Isn't this a bit like the "composite dimensions" that Source Entity Six described to me in *Beyond the Source*?

SE7C: No, only in name, and that name is only used to help you understand, which clearly at this point in our dialogue, you don't.

ME: Hold on. Give me chance. I have just received some clarity in the image that I am receiving. The ball or goldfish bowl is not really liquid in appearance; it is more like steel, round shiny and hard. That's it; it looks like a ball bearing! It was the shiny outer surface that took me by surprise. A drop of liquid has some reflective properties in my physical universe, and so does a ball bearing.

I was starting to realize that the sphere was a common shape. It had appeared in some way in all the different Source Entities' multiverses I had encountered; it even looked like it was a common shape within The Origin. I decided to mentally file this away and ask The Origin about this possible "constant" later.

SE7C: The perceived appearance of my environment is merely metaphorical. That which you are seeing/perceiving is a direct result of the intertwining. Is this the correct word?

ME: It will do.

SE7C: The intertwining of the dimensions, dimensional components and the frequencies provides you with no logical datum point to use. In essence, they are all one. Let me explain further.
This environment is a bit like a mobius loop within a mobius loop within a mobius loop. I can see you frowning.

ME: You bet I'm frowning. I can see a headache coming on.

SE7C: Let me give you an example. The area that would be occupied logically in your Source Entity's environment is as follows:

A full dimension is constructed of three dimensional components or tritaves. Each tritave, except the first three tritaves, which are used to create the base full dimension only, are inflated with twelve base frequency sets. This structure is duplicated in what you would recognize as an upward manner.

ME: Yes, I know this quite well, and we just discussed it. Thank you.

SE7C: Bear with me. Well, in my environment, one of the tritaves can be substituted with a base frequency or, indeed, a full dimension. Also, a full dimension can be substituted with a base frequency or a tritave. Similarly a base frequency can be substituted with a full dimension or a tritave or both. With all of this happening concurrently, one can see an intricate weave of dimensional component, base frequency and full dimension. Try to imagine it as the biggest knot you have ever seen!

I tried. It was difficult. And, yes, dear reader, my head hurt.

SE7C: It is best not to try too hard. I see that you are looking from the outside of me/my environment.

ME: Yes, it still looks like a steel ball. But wait, I get the impression that there are, just as you insinuated by the word "Knot"—lots and lots of little loops with each loop being a connection to each of the dimensions, tritaves and frequency bands. It is as if they are all joined together even though they can and do pervade each other's logical "space." As you say, each of the components of frequency dimension or dimensional component (tritave) can replace each other. And again, as you say, this is not restricted in a one for one replacement as, for instance, two or even three full dimensions can sit in the location/position or whatever of say, a single frequency band. Or even a single tritave can be positioned in its logical position, plus that of a full dimension or a frequency band. Just then, I saw the connections between the environmental components twisting and weaving as the locations changed. It is a bit like an ever changing knot. It even looks like a bucket of snakes, except that the snakes are all linked together. It is quite bizarre.

SE7C: It is not bizarre to me because it has purpose.

ME: OK, that's a good thing to start with. What is the purpose of this ever changing, fully substitutional knot of a ball bearing-looking environment?

SE7C: Its purpose is simply to create confusion in terms of an entity's orientation within the environment.

ME: What do you mean confusion? I would have thought that confusion was a fairly small purpose for an environment with such a complicated structure.

SE7C: Not in the slightest, for this is a most taxing environment to exist within. The method of evolution is in the functionality of the environment and how the entity works with it. I can see you frowning again, so I will explain further.

The environment changes in a way that is not logical to its representation. Because the individual tritaves can either be next to a frequency band, be a frequency band, or be a full dimension rather than a component of a full dimension, their characteristics are not consistent with the characteristics of a tritave—for example, in its correct and logical structural position. This means that movement from one permutation of space to another is not recognizable as ascension or descension.

ME: So you are suggesting that ascension is not possible in this environment and that this is a function of its structure?

SE7C: That is a very good point. Actually, there is only one level of ascension available to the entity as a result of working with this environment. And as you quite rightly suggested, this is a function of its structure. Please note though that the amount of work undertaken by my entities to work and traverse this environment does not go unrewarded, for the equivalent ascension profile is equal to two of those evolutionary levels attained by existing within Source Entity A & B's environments. In actuality, it is equivalent to the evolution gained by working in and graduating from "A" and "B's" combined environments.

ME: Thank you. I have been receiving images and feelings of dual existence whilst in this mixed up evolutionary arena. Can you explain what I am receiving, for it is something that I am having difficulty translating into recognizable imagery.

SE7C: OK, I can see your difficulty. When an entity that is working in what you would call the frequency band associated with a particular dimensional component and is, in turn, associated with a full dimension, it is able to move on to the next frequency band through its work in experiencing that which it desires to experience. It doesn't just move on to the next logical frequency band.

ME: No, don't explain further; let me see if I can understand what is happening. I think I understand now. It moves into the space that is associated with the dimensional component/full dimension etc. That is, "in the place of" that next frequency band. This means that it occupies and exists within the space between the permutation of space that would be the next logical step if the next step was to be into a frequency band. Not only that, I get the feeling that it ends up in two places at once as a result. Further, the entity, with the space being what it is, what I would classify as a permutation of non-space, does not really occupy it because for the entity, it does not really exist. It leaves a part of itself in the frequency band that it previously occupied whilst the other part, that part that is looking for the next permutation to exist and work within, looks for the frequency band that would logically be next in line. It has to traverse all of the different permutations of non-space to find it, and that may and does include working with those energies that are associated with the non-space before it can progress because progression can only really happen in the frequency bands. The entities can end up being in two environments concurrently on a permanent basis if not careful, space and non-space, because the entity has the possibility of becoming lost. It has to hone its personal multi-dimensional, multi-frequency, multi-dimensional component (tritave) navigation system to the most accurate it can ever be in order to be successful. By learning from its experiences and applying that learning, the entity eventually finds the frequency band that is next in whatever guise it assumes. Once it has done that, the entity can "reel" in that part of itself that remained in the previous frequency band, that part of it that remained in the frequency band that the entity had "grown out of" being used as a sort of life line, a datum to help it recognize where it had been and where to try next in its quest for the next frequency band.

And . . .

WOW, I just received an image of this environment that illustrated the movement of the entities around this environment like a huge three dimensional super highway multifaceted junction with roads going everywhere, up, down, left and right, with entities jumping from one road to another, each missing each other by fractions of an inch. It is "packed" with entities desperate to find the next frequency band, whether it be replacing a dimensional component a full dimension or existing as it is, a frequency band. No wonder it had the appearance of a steel ball. The energies required to hold it together must be immense!

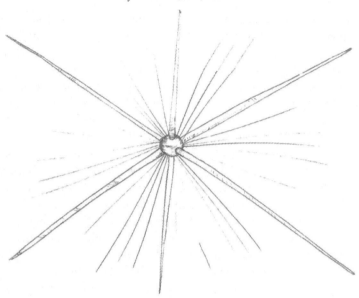

Figure 5: 3D Super Highway Junction

SE7C: How very well done. You are getting the hang of this, aren't you? I, of course, hold it together with ease, for the environment is me, and I am the environment. But you knew this. The whole objective of my environment, me, is to teach the entities that either primarily exist within it or that migrate to it from one of the other environments created by Source Entities Seven "A" and "B" how to operate in a multi-dimensional, multi-tritave, multi-frequency environment by not being hung up on the structure of it—to teach the entity the methods and ways of multiversal existence created by a multi-dimensional, multi-tritave, multi-frequency environment and allow them to traverse from one part to another without the need for linear progression whilst having linear progression, if you understand what I mean. Evolution is all about experience and the learning from such experience; as such, it is linear in its progression. The ability for an entity to be truly multiversal in its functionality is a prima facie requirement for existence and its progression towards the return to its creator. An entity cannot truly be a creator if it is not able to function in the same way as ITS creator. This is a fundamental law—one that exists for all entities created by all of the Source Entities who, in turn, were created by The Origin.

ME: So this environment you have created, that you are, seems to be more important than that of the other two Source Entities Seven "A" and "B."

SE7C: No one Source Entity is more important that the other for we all contribute to the evolution of The Origin. I have simply created a multiversal navigation conundrum, a classroom if you like, for the collective entity population of Source Entity Seven "in totality." This allows them to experience all of the things necessary to operate in the ways a creator should do.

ME: Hold on. I have just picked up something else. All of this work, this teaching your entities to be master multiversal navigators is aligned to the image I picked up when I talked to Source Entity Five. Where all of the entities created by all of the Source Entities become equals with their creating Source Entities, and, the Source Entities all become equals with The Origin. More importantly, they all evolve together up to a level not yet experienced by The Origin, one it needs to move beyond the part of itself that it is currently aware of. The Origin created the Source Entities to help it achieve this "quantum" evolutionary leap.

SE7C: Again, very well done.

I felt Source Entity Seven "C" smile. It was the smile of knowing that I was starting to "get it." There was something very important going on here. I had "tripped up" on something. Something of such importance that it was not only important that mankind understood what was happening through the books created by my limited dialogues with The Origin and the Source Entities, but the word was being spread throughout the Source Entities and their creations by other entities like me. I felt very small in the sudden realization of my very limited understanding of this "huge" big picture and mentally logged the need to discuss this in more detail with The Origin directly.

ME: Hold on, this is even more important than I imagined. All of the entities that are part of you, that is, the whole of you, Source Entity Seven in totality, are being trained through experiential means to populate The Origin when the point in its existence arrives where we all ascend together, and we are all entities in equal standing.

SE7C: Go on.

ME: When all of the entities that have been created by the twelve Source Entities evolve to the point of equality with their creators and the Source Entities evolve to the point of equality with The Origin, everything ascends to the next level. At this point The Origin moves outside of its sphere of understanding of self by a percentage point, so to speak. This movement effectively multiplies the area of awareness of self to a level where the full awareness of self is a smaller part of an area that is both known and unknown. It quadruples the area of awareness to an area of awareness/non-awareness, to an area of knowledge of existence but not of experiential knowledge. It is like we know that we live on a planet in a galaxy in a universe that is part of a multiverse, but we only know a fraction of a percentage of the solar system our planet exists within. In actuality, we don't really know the planet we exist on as physical beings. We know bits of it, but certainly not all of it. But as our understanding of self and our environment grows, together with our technical and spiritual abilities, we detect more of our environment—that which was beyond our previous level of detection. We add it to the map. Well, we try to map it, but unless we experience that which is in those areas of space that is newly mapped, we are not fully aware of its properties. It is there but not there.

SE7C: What you are trying to say is that The Origin will become aware of that which is a greater part of itself but will need help in expanding its awareness of its expanded self.

ME: Yes. Ok, you seem to have put in two lines what I have taken thirteen or even seventeen lines of text to do.

SE7C: Naturally. I can explain further if you like.

ME: Please do. This is getting most interesting.

SE7C: To put it in simple terms my particular environment is designed to train those entities that either begin in my environment or progress to my environment in the art of navigation. I will explain further. The entities that exist in all aspects of Source Entity Seven, including "A" and "B," Source Entity Seven in "totality," and me are endeavoring to create a team of entities that contain all of the important aspects of existence necessary to allow them to grow into creators. This will allow them to create their own environments and hence populate that part of The Origin that becomes available for experiential use when the expansion/ascension occurs.

The entities that "graduate" from this environment will be master navigators. They will be able to traverse and exist within and without the energies, frequencies, dimensions, tritaves and zones that make up the known and unknown area of the newly ascended Origin and populate it with newly ascended Source Entities.

ME: Wait. Hold on a moment. What do you mean, newly ascended Source Entities? At the last count I made twelve. Do you expect there to be more?

SE7C: As you have seen in your visualizations, all entities will eventually become equals. As they become equal to their creators, they attain the same status as their creator and so will become Source Entities in their own right. In essence, the created will become the creator and will adopt the same status and reason for being in existence. They will be different from The Original Source Entities though insomuch as they will be able to find and adapt themselves to a location within The Origin that they feel is in keeping with their plans for experiential creativity and evolution. Each of them will be able to work outside the need to be "static" within The Origin's area.

As you are aware, when The Origin created the twelve Source Entities, we were/are all stationary within The Origin's area of awareness. We do not move. There is no need for us to move, for we occupy that area which The Origin was aware of when it created us. It will expand its area of awareness to a greater level when we all ascend. You used the word "quadruple," I believe, but this is not a correct word to use to describe The Origin's increase in size. The area of The Origin's awareness of self will increase when it becomes an area of knowledgeable awareness/non-awareness. Everything will expand and multiply: the zones, the dimensions, the tritaves, the frequencies and the energies. The word "quadruple" should be, therefore, explained as being a multiple of a multiple of a multiple of a multiple of the zones, the dimensions, the tritaves, the frequencies and the energies. It will be unbelievably larger than that which we are currently experiencing. And yet, it will still not be a percentage point of the total area of that which is The Origin.

ME: I am getting an image of a huge sphere, one that has levels within levels within levels. As one's perspective moves further away from the center, the level of intricacy multiplies on a multiple of an exponential scale each time one moves away from the center by a fraction of a percentage point.

SE7C: Yes, now you are getting it. Now do you understand?

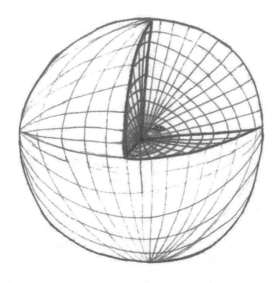

Figure 6: Conceptual Image of the Levels and Layers of The Origin

ME: I think so. If I can just explain in summary. The anticipated expansion in The Origin resulting from the collective ascension of entity, Source Entity and Origin will be so big that it will be able to satisfy the same area occupied by a single Source Entity now, for all of the current Source Entities and all of the entities created by the twelve Source Entities that will be elevated to Source Entity status in every way shape and form.

SE7C: Correct.

ME: That's AWESOME!

SE7C: Isn't it just? But it's more than that. The area will be so big that the newly ascended Source Entities will not be side to side, so to speak. They can be hidden away from each other in some part of the newly expanded area of awareness/non-awareness of self that The Origin will experience—hence, the need to be master navigators of that which is The Origin. These navigators will be called upon by the newly ascended Source Entities/themselves to guide them through the maze that will be the area of awareness/non-awareness of self that The Origin will be post-ascension. They will need to be able to traverse all conundrums that will be placed before them. That is why my environment is designed the way it is. To allow the entities to experience their environment as a conundrum and learn how to navigate it, to learn how to move outside the maze so to speak, to see the maze as if seeing it from above and drop down to that area required to be experienced. The introduction of these new Source Entities will greatly accelerate The Origin's ability to increase its awareness of self and to evolve. It will be the start of a wondrous time.

ME: What will happen to The Original twelve Source Entities?

SE7C: We will assist The Origin in its own explorations of self. We will start again but in a different way.

Again, I made a mental note of this discussion as one that I will progress with The Origin in "The Origin Speaks."

ME: I have just noticed that I haven't asked you what your entities look like yet.

SE7C: What they look like is of no consequence, for in my environment they need no physical or energetic form. All those entities that come from "A" and "B's" environments are converted to the formlessness required to work in this environment; hence, I cannot give you a form, for they neither need one nor use one, physically or energetically.

It is time for you to move on and conclude your dialogue with Source Entity Seven "in totality" before moving on to Source Entity Eight. Go now.

ME: I thank you for your "time" and wisdom.

SE7C: It was, as you call it, a pleasure.

And with that the third Aspect of Source Entity Seven, Source Entity Seven "C" was gone. Almost immediately, I felt the combined energy signature of Source Entity Seven "in totality" as it approached me to conclude our dialogue.

In Closing with Source Entity Seven "In Totality"

ME: It is an interesting feeling when you all become one again. I mean, you all have separate energetic signatures, which I might add are quite distinct from each other even though they somehow have a feeling of commonality. It's almost like, to use radio (RF) engineering as an example, you have the same carrier wave but have different frequencies to signify your independence, your singularity. But when you are addressing me as a collective, as Source Entity Seven in "in totality," it is like the carrier wave is the same, but the frequency of your signature when you are "in totality" is the average of the total frequency of the three aspects of you. Does this sound reasonable?

SE7: Of course. You see, when I split into two and then recognized the opportunity for a third aspect, the frequencies above and below my base frequency were occupied by the newly individual aspects of myself, the third aspect remained in The Original frequency, which simplistically put is the average of the three separate frequencies. That is, if you added them up together and divided them by three you would return to The Original base frequency.

ME: I expect that is because the frequencies above and below the base frequency, those occupied by Source Entities 7A and 7C, are equidistant from The Original base signature.

SE7: Correct. And that is why it feels like it's the same.

ME: I am honored to receive the information from SE7C about what could/will happen when we all ascend and become Source Entities in our own right.

SE7: You should be. You are the first of your kind to receive such information. It is important that you pass it on for all to recognize and understand, for it will make a difference in the way incarnate mankind interacts with each other, specifically those who are on the path of enlightenment and ascension.

ME: How do you know of our ascension? I mean, you are so far removed from my Source Entity and its work, and you have your own work to focus on.

SE7: You are aware that we are all linked, linked to allow the evolutionary content we collect to be passed on to The Origin?

ME: Yes.

SE7: Well, the Source Entities also benefit from the evolutionary content of each other, and as a result, we all receive each other's experience, learning and evolution so that we can all evolve at the same time. Even the Source Entity that is not yet aware (I will call this Source Entity "Twelve" later in this book.) benefits, as we benefit from its slow road to awareness. As a result of this link I/we know how each other's creations are "doing," so to speak. That is how and why I and each of the other Source Entities can and do offer you advice.

ME: And all of this information is being shared on an instantaneous basis I suppose.

SE7: You suppose right.

What I/we have shared with you these past few weeks is but a minor summary of what we perform and create on an on-going basis. In your current state, you will never be able to comprehend more than the very basics of what your Source Entity achieves, let alone what the other Source Entities are working on. Do not take this as an indication of failure to overcome your limitations but more of a statement of "what is" based upon the limitations you have given yourself currently.

To be able to do what you are doing with these self-administered limitations—and you don't know how limited you have made yourself in the vehicle you have chosen—is creating quite a stir. You are showing what can be done given very little training and with none of the tremendous focus and single-minded determination that spans a lifetime (which is what most need) to get anywhere near the levels you have achieved. Keep it up; teach others, for this is an important time for both you and the humanity that is in the lowest of dimensions and frequencies of your Source Entity.

Go now, for you have dwelled long enough with me/us. It is time for you to move on to Source Entity Eight.

And as with the other dialogues with Source Entities One through Six, the link with Source Entity Seven "in totality" was broken. But as with the links with the other Source Entities, I knew that although they were severed from a continued dialogue perspective, I was now in a position where I could re-initiate contact with any of the Source

Entities at will. It was like not knowing someone's phone number and, therefore, not knowing that they were there or even existed, but when the phone number was available, they could be contacted at any time and at a moment's notice.

I looked around the vast unfathomable space that was The Origin and found this to be true. Having established an initial link with seven of the Source Entities I could now "phone them up," so to speak, at any time. I felt privileged to have this ability. It was a wondrous gift. I vowed to myself that I would use it wisely and for the education of the human race. This, I noted, is why I am on this planet here and now—to help with incarnate mankind's education. Again, it was another privilege, one that must not be squandered, which I must accept patiently. I felt very humble all of a sudden.

Chapter Two
Source Entity Eight

I have to admit that at this point in the dialogue—including those with the other Source Entities—that I was a little surprised that Source Entity Seven (that is, the three aspects of Source Entity Seven) took up twice as much text as the previous Six Source Entities had to date. On reflection I decided that this was a function of the three aspects essentially having the equivalent of three Source Entity environments with each being a Source Entity in its own right, which, so it seemed was in its own version of The Origin's environment. That is, they, the three, were in the confines and, therefore, the environment that was Source Entity Seven. In some respects and to all intents, they were independent of each other while clearly still part of the "totality" that was Source Entity Seven. I was considering this whilst I felt the attunement taking place that would allow me to commence communication with Source Entity Eight,

which I noted had already projected an image of its extremities to me. It was as if I was in space and was approaching a spherical shape that was covered in large cone shaped spikes. However, just before I had the chance to consider this image further, my own Source Entity had something to say.

Figure 1: Conceptual Image of Source Entity Eights External Structure (the associated continuum, are represented by the cone shape)

SE: I just I wanted to congratulate you on your progress so far. You are progressing with this work faster than expected and improving in all sorts of ways. Your desire to contact and communicate with as many people as possible about God (me) and the greater reality (the other Source Entities and The Origin) is a wonderful sight to behold as is your desire to be seen as an approachable man on the ground, explaining the greater reality in ways that are understandable to the common man, as well as the spiritually adept. This is and will be your greatest strength. To answer one of your own questions—the time is not far away when you will be a full-time teacher of the truth, for the doors are opening in the correct sequence. Enjoy the synchronicity and effortlessness of my multiverse and its function (workings); marvel at its splendor, its simplicity, its grandeur; go with its natural flow of energies and inherent evolutionary opportunities; be at one and at peace with it. See how it interlinks with the works of the other Source Entities and understand your place, your destiny, your inheritance within The Origin's plans, for we are all part of The Origin's great plan.

ME: Wow! That was a bit of a grand speech, wasn't it? What caused that?

SE: The need for you to recognize the importance that you are doing your "life's work," for it is not about living what you would call a "normal life." It is about being of service within a most important function of the *omniverse*.

This was a new word, one that even a humble incarnate as myself recognized as being above, well above, the concept of a multiverse.

ME: Now you have my interest. What is an *omniverse*?

SE: Simply put, The Origin.

ME: Hold on here. Why did I pick up the word "continuum" then?

SE: Because The Origin contains all functions with the continuums being a fraction of them. This is something you will discuss at length with Source Entity Eight, for it is entirely composed of continuum. The plural of continuum is continuum—hence, the imagery it just presented to you.

ME: This sounds like a good time to link up with Source Entity Eight.

I made yet another mental note to talk to The Origin on the functions of an omniverse.

SE: There is no time (event space) like the present.

SE8: This sounds like it is the correct event space to check in then.

ME: That, err, was quick. I expected to perform some preliminary work on my communication link with you first.

SE8: Why? We have already been in communication.

ME: WHAT? Run that one by me again, will you? I think you might have misunderstood.

SE8: On the contrary, it is you who is the one who misunderstood, for we have spoken before and on many subjects.

ME: I can see that it is time for my head to hurt. But wait; just let me think about this for a moment. My Source Entity said you are made up entirely from continuum. Does this mean that we communicated whilst the I part of me that is the energetic was in another continuum?

SE8: Yes, for I am spread throughout the known omniverse (Origin).

In my mind's eye I saw that this was true. Source Entity Eight pervaded the space of the known Origin, that part of it that was within its area of self-awareness. There was one other thing though. (Only one? That will be the day!) How can that last statement relate to the image I saw in my mind's eye, the image of a sphere covered in cone shaped spikes? I decided that there was only one thing to do—ask Source Entity Eight what the image and the statement about Source Entity Eight pervading The Origin as a continuum within a continuum meant. Moreover, how did this relate me having previously communicated with Source Entity Eight? I was dying to know. I do like these conundrums.

How and When I Previously Communicated with Source Entity Eight

ME: OK, both the myriad readers/truth seekers out there and I want to know how and when I have been talking with you before. Let's start with the when. Sorry. It sounds a bit blunt, but I have quite a selfish interest here. Once I have gotten this little titbit out of the way, we can continue with the usual routine. Is that OK with you?

SE8: Of course. Communicating with you again is going to be fun.

I was starting to get the impression that there was something going on here and that I really wasn't the new boy in town that I thought I was—at least, not if I included that part of me, the greater part that was still mainly energetic. I decided to use this thought as a springboard for what I hoped would be a logical and quick answer.

SE8: Quite simply, we have communicated many times whilst you were fully energetic. We planned the communication process we are about to start right down to the finite points of the minute details. This was a very important piece of planning work, for we needed to understand what you were going to be able to both understand and relay back to those who would seek to know more about the greater reality of existence beyond the environment that is your Source Entity. This is because the concepts surrounding my environment that we are going to discuss are difficult at best for incarnate humankind to understand, even in the most basic sense.

ME: So, bearing in mind that you "Source Entities" are sharing each other's information and evolutionary growth on an instantaneous and continual basis, can you tell me whether or not I have whilst in the energetic form made a similar level of pre-planning and preparation for the dialogues to date and that I am due to have?

SE8: Yes, you have. Of course, the level of planning has been varied and dependent upon the level of information you were expecting to work with, including the energies of the Source Entities you have and will communicate with. In this instance you may have noticed a pattern in the level of dialogue and complexity in the concepts increasing in complexity the further away from your own Source Entity you go.

ME: Well, I have noticed that the depth of information that I would have liked to extract has been not so much limited as more generalised. I have also noticed that the energies surrounding the Source Entities I have enjoyed dialogue with has been significantly different each time. Although it was significant, it was not insurmountable. I could work with it and even tune into it and get used to working with those energies. I even noticed that the more I continued dialogue with a new Source Entity, the more I could understand the information and receive more conceptual data. I reckon that the Source Entities I have communicated with to date have been in a certain order to allow me to ramp up each time, allowing me to move onwards and upwards in terms of my communicative (energetic link) abilities. Thus, I was able to use each

Source Entity communicated with as a stepping stone for the next one. I guess that my going from my own Source Entity to Source Entity Four would have been an impossible task?

SE8: Correct. You may remember a previous dialogue (see *Beyond the Source* Book 1) where your progression outwards from your own Source Entity was described as being out on a lanyard, with the lanyard being "let out" the further you go to meet that metaphorical distance needed to travel to meet the next Source Entity in your list.

ME: Actually, I do.

SE8: Well, that was in place to make sure that you did not or could not move out too far or start communication with the wrong Source Entity. It was designed to keep you in the correct sequence. In fact, what you don't know is that metaphorically speaking, the Source Entities have placed themselves in a sort of line or in order set distances away from your start point with your Source Entity to ensure that this strategy worked. WE ARE ALL WORKING WITH YOU TO SUPPORT YOU IN YOUR MOST IMPORTANT TASK.

ME: Wow! . . Sorry, but that's all I can muster. The suggestion that you are all, err, moving around to suit my communication strategy is just a bit too much for me to handle right now. Specifically, as I am just a small energetic being.

SE8: Don't malign yourself. You have no idea what you are really like when fully energetic.

ME: Clearly not. It's just a bit of a surprise to note the amount of pre-planning even though I am not cognisant of the full details that must have happened to allow all of this to occur.

Right I now need to refocus and continue the task at hand rather than feeling small in the bigger picture of what is happening in the greater reality.

SE8: Good, I am raring to go.

Source Entity Eight — A Continuum of Continuums

ME: Just to repeat some of our previous dialogue, one of the images I picked up was of you as a sphere covered in cone- shaped spikes. If you are supposed to be interspaced/pervade The Origin and be a continuum of continuum, how can that image relate to this very high level description of you?

At this point in the dialogue, dear reader, I knew that this was going to get difficult, so I decided that it would be a good idea to quote Source Entity Four's and Source Entity Five's comments on continuum for reference purposes.

SE4: "As you rise through the frequencies, you move away from that which you experience at the previous frequency and start to experience that which is present in the new frequency. That is, using your own frequencies as an example, because things like the desk you sit at (of a slightly lower frequency than yourself and therefore solid) will no longer be part of your new frequentic level. You will, however, experience other things that are consistent with your experience or expectation of what a solid object such as your desk is. This is because frequencies overlap to a certain extent, and you are still within a single dimensional continuum. Now if you consider a change from one dimension to another, then you have to consider a bigger picture—that of the dimension and the frequencies. When you move from dimension to dimension you also move from the frequency set that is aligned to the dimension being moved from to the frequency set that is aligned to the dimension being moved to."

SE5: "....there is only one environment that can be called a continuum, one that involves dimension, frequency, energy and the recognition of the passage of events and time, which is where you are right now. A parallel dimension of equal content could be classified as a continuum but only if it has the full complement of the four components specified above. None do in YOUR universe. You need to be in a "multiversal" environment to have this effect take place."

Below is the Wikipedia description.

"Materials, such as solids, liquids and gases are composed of molecules separated by empty space. On a macroscopic scale, materials have cracks and discontinuities. However, certain physical phenomena can be modeled assuming the materials exist as a continuum, meaning the matter in the body is continuously distributed and fills the entire region of space it occupies. A continuum is a body that can be continually sub-divided into infinitesimal elements with properties being those of the bulk material."

(ref: http://en.wikipedia.org/wiki/Continuum_mechanics).

Confused? Me too! But the comment about the "body" being continuously distributed, filling the entire region of space it occupies is very close to Source Entity Eight pervading the known area of self-awareness of The Origin. The mathematics to support this is VERY impressive! I wonder if it is anywhere near correct.

SE8: Ah, yes. No, it's woefully inadequate and goes nowhere near explaining any part of a continuum within me or The Origin. In fact, there is no humanly derived mathematics that can be used to model me.

Well, that answers that question on definition and our mathematical prowess to explain what a continuum is.

SE8: So without, so within.

ME: What is that supposed to mean?

SE8: That is the best way to understand a continuum; everything that is within is without as well. You see, the image of the cones on my supposed exterior form are the same in reverse inside the sphere.

ME: Now you are losing me.

SE8: The cone is both a geometric shape and a mathematical constant. It is also one of the shapes used to convey higher information. As a mathematical constant, it can be used in myriad ways.

ME: You mean it is like the number associated with Pi (3.14159265, etc.).

SE8: Yes, with the exception that it is a multi-dimensional, multi-frequential constant and, therefore, is a mathematical cornerstone to the mathematical explanation of my construction, so to speak.

ME: So the image I received of you as a sphere-covered in cones, which may or may not be inside out within you is a symbolic representation of the way you are constructed.

SE8: Bingo! . . . Is that the right word?

ME: It will do. We use it as an expletive for the recognition of understanding of something. Eureka! would have been a more appropriate way of expressing your concurrence of my miniscule level of understanding though.

SE8: Then my use was correct, a diminutive word for the miniscule level of understanding of the concept.

ME: I very much don't think that I even understand it on even a miniscule level yet. Can you go into a bit more detail for me?

SE8: With pleasure. But first let me tell you this. All 3D geometrical shapes are geometric explanation of a mathematical constant. I limit myself here to the use of 3D as there are 4D, 5D, 6D, 7D, etc., up to 12D geometrical shapes that are also constants, including that which humankind is not currently aware of. Some of your mathematicians are starting to understand this, but they need to include the wider multiversal environment and the energies associated with The Origin before they will start to make any sense of the maths surrounding it. It is the use of such mathematical constants that are the major language of the planets, stars and the galaxies and of whatever presentation, form and function within most of the environments created by the Source Entities that can be classified in some way as the physical representations of energetic constructs, a physical universe if you like. However, a physical universe, such as the one your vehicle (physical body) currently resides in, cannot be classified as a continuum as it does not contain all of the elements required to be classified as one. As Source Entity Five stated in its dialogue with you on the subject, you need to have the "multiversal" content to classify an environment as a continuum.

The sphere in your image represents all that currently is The Origin with the cones representing the mathematical constants, or pit props if you like, that hold me in my current position within that which is currently The Origin. Each of these has a loci which is in contact with each other at a mathematical point of, err, let's say, absolute zero. I can see you frowning, so let me explain what absolute zero is.

ME: You bet. I thought that zero was zero with a plus and minus component above and below for positive and negative values of figures.

SE8: It is not a concept that mankind has to consider yet in its limited recognition of self, environment and creator. Absolute zero is a zero that is manifest from a group of converging mathematical constants that are individually derived but collectively dependent whilst still being independently calculable. The absolute zero is that point or mathematical location where a locus of the individual loci of a group of constants occurs simultaneously, the physical representation of such a condition not being possible due to the fact that "physicality" is a single universal phenomenon and not multiversal. However, there are instances where a simulacrum of physicality can occur in non-physical universes due to similarity in resonant frequency. But you already know this from previous dialogues.

ME: You talk about "that which is currently The Origin." What do you mean by that?

SE8: I haven't finished yet.

ME: I know, but I feel that the readers would like to understand.

SE8: Simply put, it is what you have recently been told by Source Entity Seven "in totality." That at some point The Origin will evolve and expand its area of awareness of self further. The expansiveness of The Origin will be multiplied to the point of infinity in your mind, but it will still be a mere fraction of what is possible for The Origin to be. Currently, The Origin is a fraction of one percent aware of itself. The expansion in the area of self-awareness will bring the area of awareness un-mapped experientially to a little under one percent of its totality.

ME: Ah, OK. I was just making sure that there was not anything else happening to The Origin. I was just making sure that I didn't miss anything.

SE8: Ha, ha, ha, ha, ha! How naive you are. The Origin is always changing, and for you to say that you don't want to miss anything? Well, I will tell you this. When you have finished all of your current lifetimes' work on the subject of helping mankind understand the truth, and you have some considerable distance to go, you will still know nothing in comparison to what IS.

ME: OK. OK. It was a foolish thing to say. I am blushing now. I think it's time for me to let you carry on in your explanation of the relevance of the imagery I received about your structure.

SE8: Thank you. Please note that I was not trying to put you down. Far from it. It's just that it was a good joke to me. Your comment reflected mankind's self-centered "know it all" arrogance. Even The Origin doesn't know everything; hence, its need to create the Source Entities to help it in its own quest to experience, learn and evolve. I am sorry; I just found it very funny for a moment.

ME: That's alright.

I was starting to chuckle to myself; tears were forming in the corner of my eyes as I, too, saw the joke!

SE8: It's good to laugh. We Source Entities do it all the time. We have so much fun in doing what we do that we can't help but laugh.

I wondered how a Source Entity would laugh. No, don't ask that question!

ME: How does a Source Entity laugh?

I failed on that piece of temptation.

SE8: How we laugh is unexplainable to you. But I will tell you this: when a Source Entity laughs the whole of its environment receives unfathomable love. Everything and everyone within its environment/s feels a wonderful sense of "well-being" for a split second.

ME: I think I have felt this once or twice in my life.

SE8: All of mankind has.

ME: Thank you.

SE8: It's a pleasure.

I mentally logged in to one of those moments that I believed were associated with me having a snippet of full self-awareness and realized that this may have been one of those moments when our Source Entity laughed. It felt wonderful.

SE8: Now then, let's continue to talk about how the imagery you received explains my form and function. I will repeat what I previously said.

"The sphere in your image represents all that currently is The Origin with the cones representing the mathematical constants, or pit props if you like, that hold me in the position that I am in within that which is currently The Origin. Each of these has loci which are in contact with each other at a mathematical point of absolute zero." Got it so far?

ME: Yes.

SE8: Good. The cones are on the outside because they represent the number of continuum that I am constructed of. In essence, they are on the inside, figuratively speaking. Therefore, each of the tips of the cones is in contact with each other at the center point of the sphere that represents my epicenter of existence within the area of The Origin that is its current area of self-awareness. If you were to expand your consciousness, you would notice that each of the continuum are placed close enough to one other to allow the exterior surfaces to touch each other, creating an interface between the continuum where an entity could pass from one continuum to another. The gaps in the middle, i.e., where the continuum do not touch, are those areas where the maintenance of the structure of the continuum can be addressed. These gaps are absolutely necessary and vital to the overall balance of energies as there must be an equal area of non-continuum to continuum to allow the structure to be maintained. Do not, however, be confused by the word non-continuum for the area of non-continuum is a continuum in its own right. Am I making myself clearly understood here?

ME: I think so. But I don't understand why you need an equal amount of single non-continuum to multiple continuum.

SE8: Simply put, there has to be a balance. The sum of the whole has to equal the one, and the one has to equal the sum of the whole. That, my friend, is the basis of continuum mechanics. Everything that exists within, exists without, whilst still being within. That is the only way that a continuum can maintain its structure and independence. That and with a little help from my continuum mechanical maintenance entities.

ME: That sounds like the opportunity for a lead in to my next question. Who and what are these continuum mechanical maintenance entities?

The Maintenance of Continuum Within the Continuum

SE8: They are entities whose sole purpose in existence within my environment is to maintain the stability of the continuum and the continuum within my continuum. Their most important work is to maintain the location of the locus, for this is the lynch pin that holds the continuum together.

ME: I would have expected that a locus, especially if it is the locus of a series of loci, would be stable. By the tone of your dialogue above, you are suggesting that this is not the case, and that it needs to be maintained in some way.

SE8: Your expectation would be correct where the locus in an area of stability. But The Origin, and as a result, I, in my dissemination throughout The Origin, are not stable. We will never be stable.

ME: Why is that? I would have thought that The Origin, being the vast expanse that it is would have an inherent level of stability, especially as it is the basis for everything that is.

SE8: You are talking about dimensional stability, I feel.

ME: Yeeees!

SE8: Well, I am talking about evolutionary stability. You see, evolutionary stability has an effect on dimensional stability, specifically where The Origin is concerned.

ME: Right! Err, how?

SE8: You will remember that in previous dialogues you have been told about the ascension of The Origin and that its evolution creates this ascension. That its ascension will allow it to expand its area of self-awareness even though it will not be cognizant of the details of those new areas of self-awareness.

ME: Yes, I do.

SE8: Well, the area of expansion of self-awareness is not even. What I mean by this is that it is not expansion in the spherical sense of the word. It is more uneven, lumpy. It is as result of this lumpiness that the locus of the loci changes location within me, and, therefore, The Origin. Now then, we are not at that point of expansion resulting from ascension yet. However, The Origin is expanding. It's always expanding, and the expansion is in its level of experiential detail of its current area of self-awareness. It is this expansion that creates evolutionary pressure, which results in minor changes in the external perimeter of the area of self-awareness of The Origin and, therefore, the position of the locus.

ME: So The Origin has dimensional area?

SE8: In a sense, yes. You see, its area is unfathomable even to us, as none of us has really been able to calculate what size, if you like, The Origin will be when it reaches recognition of one hundred percent of its area of self-awareness. But please note here that the dimensional area is a function of evolution, not a so-called measureable metric that you would use in the universe that the Earth is within.

ME: As I understand it then, these entities whose job it is to maintain the position of the locus must be able to understand or measure in some way the changes to the outer edges of you as a continuum within The Origin, and make adjustments as appropriate.

SE8: Spot on. Do not think that it is just the locus that they have to work with. The locus is the product of the absolute zero points of the loci.

ME: And they have to manipulate the levels of absolute zero to compensate for the changes in The Origin's area of self-awareness, which affects you as a continuum within the totality of that part of The Origin which is known in detail . . .

SE8: . . . And that it is becoming self-aware of.

ME: We finish in tandem.

SE8: We do.

ME: Based upon that then, the levels of absolute zero are not, in fact, absolute zero.

SE8: No, for absolute zero is not a fixed mathematical point. It is dependent upon the area, position (within me) and dimensional, dimensional component, frequential and energetic components associated with the continuum it is absolute zero of and, therefore, a loci for. What you are looking for is a fixed point of zero. A fixed point of zero is an altogether different thing.

Just when I thought I was on a roller, I score a bogey!

ME: Go on, tell me. What is a fixed point of zero?

SE8: Quite simply the expression of that position or locus that is always collectively achieved by the mathematical representation of all of the possible positions achievable by the locus or collective positions of absolute zero of all of the continuum at any point in the evolution of The Origin. I will give it a word you can understand, a datum. A datum that is always created even though stable rather than being a start or a point of origin.

ME: I can imagine a few mathematicians having a field day over discussing that statement. They won't believe a word of it.

SE8: I would like to see them disprove it. It is what holds everything together. Scientists rarely, if ever, see the fundamental basis for WHAT IS, for they are always working with the PRODUCTS of what is.

ME: OK, I would like to go back to the entities who maintain the different continuum. How and what do they do to maintain the overall continuum environment and the point of absolute zero?

SE8: As explained above. The point of absolute zero for each of the continuum is based upon the evolutionary periphery that the base of the "cone" that represents the continuum and its contact with the outer periphery of the continuum, that is me, and the outer edge of The Origin's area of self-awareness, and its subsequent point of contact with the other continuum cones, so to speak. Simplistically put, the entities are constantly calculating, if you like, the levels of evolutionary pressures in the area of the continuum they are responsible for and noting how it affects their position of absolute zero. This is done concurrently and simultaneously throughout the continuum and its component continuum. This continual calculation results in the constant and consistent movement of the point of absolute zero in conjunction with the movements of the other points of absolute zero that represent the locus of the loci.

Figure 2: Conceptual Image of Source Entity Eight's Internal Structure (the points of the internal cones are the loci of the associated continuum, which are represented by the cone shape)

ME: I just received an image of the points moving in and out and round and round with all of the points staying in contact with each other all of the time.

SE8: The image you have received would be a correct representation apart from one thing.

ME: What's that?

SE8: Sometimes there is a disconnect, and one of the continuum loci's loses contact with the locus.

ME: What?! When does that happen? More importantly, how can it happen, especially if the fixed point of zero is, err, fixed?

SE8: Very good question. The fixed point of zero is what it is, fixed. So when the odd occasion occurs where the loci, the point of absolute zero of a continuum, either moves away from the locus as a result of incorrect calculative action on the part of the maintaining entities or as the result of a sudden and rapid change in evolution, the loci of the continuum remains in contact by a continuum thread so to speak. Call it a bungee rope if you like, for it allows the loci of the continuum to remain in place whilst the bulk of the continuum is adjusted to be in the correct position from a geometric perspective.

The reason this happens is because evolution is not an exact science. It happens in fits and starts. Devolution can also be experienced as can evolutionary compression, evolutionary expansion, evolutionary expression and evolutionary stretch, which by the way is not the same as evolutionary expansion.

ME: I had heard of loss of evolution, devolution, but not the others. Can you explain them for me?

How the Different Forms of Evolution Affect Source Entity Eight's Continuum

SE8: I will split them out and illustrate how they affect the order within my continuum.

Rapid Evolution: This is where the evolution itself happens at an accelerated rate due to the continued recognition by an entity or group of entities (this can include a whole universe) of what experience processes are creating the evolutionary opportunity and actively planning to use them to increase their evolutionary progression.

This has the ability to affect the geometry of the continuum in a way that is equal to an expansion outwards from the center, effectively increasing the distance from the locus to the so-called base of the cone. The diameter of the base of the cone of the continuum increases accordingly to account for the supposed increase of the theoretical spherical radius of self-awareness. The loci's (point of absolute zero) connectivity to the locus is not affected with this type of evolution and is controllable.

Slow Evolution: This occurs where the evolution itself happens at a slower than expected/normal rate. In slow evolution, the recognition of evolutionary opportunities is either not made or is spasmodic with the entity or entities not learning the processes and actions that created the possible evolution.

This has the ability to affect the geometry of the continuum, the so-called base of the cone, in a minimal way because it is slower than normal growth. In this instance, and this is the same with static evolution and devolution, evolutionary stretch can be experienced if the other continuum are experiencing accelerated evolutionary growth simultaneously. This is not the same as "Logarithmic Evolution" (see below).

Static Evolution: This exists where the evolutionary progress is in stasis. It is neither progressing in a positive or negative way. In this instance, positive evolution that is being experienced in one part of the continuum is being balanced by negative evolution in another part of the continuum. In both instances, the processes surrounding the positive and negative evolutionary effects to the overall continuum are not being learnt and progressed.

The effect from a geometric expression is equal to an undulation on the outer edges of the continuum, creating a sort of rippling effect.

In the event of rapid evolution being experienced in all other continuum, an elastic limit can be reached where the outer edge of the holding continuum must move with the evolutionary tension created by the other continuum. In this instance, the static evolutionary condition is changed to reflect an increase in the level of evolution in some part to "catch up" with the evolving continuum and their effect on the outer surface of the holding continuum, me.

Reversed Evolution (Devolution): This is where evolution is effectively going backwards. In this instance, there is no learning from the action of the entity or entities, and the same ground is being covered over and over again with no sign of reversal. The entities operate in ignorance of their condition and need significant external help to aid recovery.

In this instance, the continuum shrinks towards the loci, the effective geometry of the continuum loses its "area" as the diameter of the so-called base of the cone is reduced relative to the distance from the loci and its previous positional condition. Visually, the outer edge of the continuum that the devolving continuum exists within appears to disappear towards the loci of the continuum, following the base, creating what looks like a hole in the surface of the holding continuum, me.

As with static evolution, in the event of rapid evolution being experienced in all other continuum, an elastic limit can be reached where the outer edge of the holding continuum, me, must move with the evolutionary tension created by the other continuum. In this instance, the devolving evolutionary condition is changed to reflect an increase in the level of evolution to the static evolutionary condition, migrating on to very small amounts of positive progression by default, irrespective of the actions of the entities occupying the continuum.

Evolutionary Compression: This is where a group of nearby (close) continuum or all continuum within my continuum are in a devolutionary regression, affecting the positive evolutionary progression of an evolving continuum. They effectively slow down or reverse the evolutionary progression being made by that continuum that is experiencing positive evolutionary content. However, as there is an opposing "pressure" effect of the positive evolution in the continuum that resists the devolution. The continuum is not reduced in evolutionary size geometrically speaking but is instead compressed, putting evolutionary strain on the exterior of the continuums' structure and the height of the frequencies possible within the continuum.

In this way actual continuum devolution experienced as a function of the effect of other neighboring continuum devolving is not experienced but does stop significant progression. This, by the way, also affects me as the holding continuum as I evolve as a result of the work of the entities working within the continuum.

Evolutionary Expansion: This is compartmentalized evolution within a continuum. Here a certain percentage of the area of the continuum experiences evolutionary progression and another does not, providing pockets of evolutionary progression and static evolutionary progression. In some rare instances, this can even contain small pockets of devolution.

In this instance, the exterior geometry of the continuum shows areas of deformation in a convex or concave manner, where it is affected by the type of evolution being locally experienced. Full continuum-based evolutionary progression cannot be experienced until the compartmentalization effect is harmonized and eliminated.

Evolutionary Expression: This occurs as the result of the content of evolutionary reflectivity expressed by a continuum where the neighboring continuum is experiencing accelerated evolution of any type. The expression in this instance is the perceived evolutionary growth of the neighboring continuum experienced as a result of the work of the entities populating the neighboring continuum and not as a result of the work of its own entities.

Source Entity Eight

In essence, this means that the continuum is reflecting an equal amount of evolutionary progression, albeit with no substance, in an insubstantial and non-experiential way to that being experienced by its neighbor. From a geometric representation of the continuum, the visual appearance would seem to be identical to its progressing neighbor without having the actual evolution to back up the visual appearance. Its loci remaining in the correct position within the locus is the only way to quantify the true evolutionary state of the continuum without actually entering the continuum and experientially experiencing the evolution first hand.

Evolutionary Stretch: This is the opposite of evolutionary compression. It is where a group of nearby (close) continuum or all continuum within my continuum are in an evolutionary progression, affecting the static evolutionary progression of a continuum. They effectively speed up or reverse the evolutionary progression being made by that continuum that is experiencing static or even devolutionary content. An opposing "negative pressure" or vacuum effect of the static evolution in the continuum that resists the evolution is experienced by the continuum. The continuum is not increased in evolutionary size geometrically speaking but is, instead, stretched, putting evolutionary strain on the exterior of the continuums' structure.

In this way actual continuum evolution experienced as a function of the effect of other neighboring continuum, devolution or evolutionary stasis is not experienced. This also affects me as the holding continuum.

Geometric/Exponential Evolution: This type of evolution can happen in a progressive and regressive state, depending upon the work that is undertaken by the incumbent entities. It is the rate of evolutionary progression or regression (devolution) resulting from, in the case of evolutionary progress, the absolute 100% effectiveness of the previous evolutionary content affecting the opportunity for evolutionary progress that is experienced in the next phase by a factored ratio equal to the difference between the two levels of evolution, pre-evolution and post-evolution. If successful, this ratio is passed on to the next phase and the next phase until errors affect the geometric content of the progression, and the progression, "if expressed as a curve," tails off so to speak. In the event of geometric/exponential devolution, the ratio works in reverse and the continuum experiencing such devolution quickly and rapidly loses its evolutionary standing.

A continuum experiencing geometric evolution will create both "evolutionary stretch" within itself (if too fast) and in neighboring continuum and "evolutionary expression" in continuum which are neighbors of the neighboring continuum.

A continuum experiencing geometric devolution will create both "evolutionary compression" within itself (if too fast) and in neighboring continuum and "evolutionary expression" expressed as a negative reflection in the continuum which are neighbors of the neighboring continuum, together with all of the effects of the structure of the continuum expected in evolutionary "compression" and "expression."

Logarithmic Evolution: Is similarly expressed in mathematical terms, insomuch as it is the inverse of geometric/exponential evolution/devolution. Whereas with geometric evolution, the continuum experiences extremely rapid evolutionary progression or regression expressed as a ratio between the initiating and the resultant evolution, creating the springboard for geometric evolution/devolution in the next evolutionary phase. With logarithmic evolution, the progression or regression (evolution/devolution) is very slow. In this instance, the growth or decay can be mathematically expressed as a known base of logarithmic function.

This type of evolution/devolution has little or no effect on its neighboring continuum. It can be, however, affected by neighboring continuum experiencing geometric evolutionary content in which case it experiences "evolutionary stretch" in the case of the neighboring continuum experiencing geometric evolution, and "evolutionary compression" in the case of the neighboring continuum experiencing geometric devolution.

ME: Wow. I had no idea there were that many different versions of evolution.

SE8: Well, there are more, but you would not be able to comprehend them. In any case these are the most important.

As I contemplated what I had just been told by Source Entity Eight, especially about how its energies created a continuum within the area that is now classified as the currently known area of The Origin's self-awareness, my mind turned toward the information I had received about how big the newly recognized area of self-awareness was expected to be within The Origin. I remembered the comment given to me that The Original twelve Source Entities will leave The Original area and will move into the greater, newly recognized area of self-awareness of The Origin to help it define ways to experience it and evolve further. I then realized that I was being given more information—information that was pertinent to Source Entity Eight's new role.

Source Entity Eight was to be the basis for the structure resulting from the ascension of The Origin to its next level of awareness. In the process, it would experience a level of evolutionary stretch never before experienced by a Source Entity. It was to become the framework for the navigation of the newly self-aware Origin. It would be populated with Source Entity Seven "C's" Navigators, and Source Entity Eight will be the framework of the Maze that will be the new and old areas of The Origin's areas of self-awareness and experiential knowledge and evolution. The Navigators will know every method of navigation necessary to allow effective movement throughout the new expanse of The Origin. The Jigsaw puzzle was starting to fall into place, micro-piece by micro-piece.

A few days after writing the dialogue with Source Entity Eight above, I was sitting in an airplane bound for Shanghai, China, anticipating whatever levels of turbulence we might encounter. More importantly, what energetic shields I would throw in front of the plane to smooth the air density out to a nice medium density, a density that would result in no turbulence. This was a tried and tested process for dealing with turbulence that I had developed from a method I used in my late teenage years to clear clouds by giving them energy. I was considering this and my dislike of turbulence (hence my invention of the energetic shields) when I suddenly saw how ridiculous this line of thought was.

Here I am, a man able to traverse with my mind all of the Source Entities' multiverse, and beyond, as well as the multiverses of eleven other Source Entities, including their creator, The Origin, and its environment. And ironically enough, that part of me that is projected into the physical is not only reduced to traveling the minute distances around this planet in "uneven" comparison to galactic and multiversal terms by the slow mechanical means offered by flying, but is (I am) also worried about turbulence. I might even cause it for God's sake!

How pathetic, I thought, that the association with the physical had caught me out yet again. That the association with the physical and its sensations were so compelling that even a spirit, such as I, was taken off guard and conned by its apparent all-consuming sensation-based experience being reality rather than focusing on the subject of The Origin and its creations, the twelve Source Entities, being the real reality.

The real me being an energetic being with a very small part of me projected into the bag of meat we lovingly call the human body. The human body I was using being just that: a body, a vehicle, a temporary biological construct, a temporary convenience enabling me to experience existence at the very bottom of the dimensions and frequencies, just like this airplane I was sitting in. It was a mechanical construct of transportational convenience. I sat back in my chair and detached myself from the un-reality of the physical (considering the greater reality of The Origin and its Source Entities) and re-established my link with Source Entity Eight.

In doing so, I also felt the detachment necessary for breaking through the facade of the physical, allowing contact with entities in the higher frequencies and beyond. I saw my human body as the piece of meat it was and smiled to myself. In doing so, tears started to stream from my eyes. These were the tears that presented to me the sign that I had come to recognize as "evidence of absolute truth" in my experiences and information received in my dialogues with the Source Entity, its peers, and The Origin. They were tears of absolute joy born from the recognition of the truth. It was a Wonderful feeling!

ME: I had no idea that there were so many types of evolution. Although it's incredible to think that the cumulative effect of the entities existing within not only a universe but a continuum can have the types of effect we have just discussed on their universal environment and the continuum it is contained within. Not forgetting the effect on the surrounding continuum and of course, you.

SE8: Of course. You see, each of the entities in my continuum are powerful creators in their own right, and as such, they are able to accelerate and decelerate the evolutionary content of their environment accordingly. This allows them to moderate (control) how and when they evolve, including what activities and experiences lead to the evolution they want to experience.

ME: Hold on a bit. I am getting the impression here that your entities are doing things in reverse to what I and other entities I have encountered.

SE8: Such as?

ME: Well, in the dialogues I have experienced to date, entities experience different things in order to learn and evolve. The evolutionary content is a product of the subsequent experiences and learning undertaken.

SE8: Go on.

ME: Well, reading between the lines, your entities appear to change the evolutionary content, or should I say, "signature," in this case, of the continuum and the universes contained within the continuum. The objective is to experience the existence opportunities that are only available at certain levels of evolution. This creates a resultant level of "real" evolution as a product of the types of experience required and the evolutionary signature demanded of the continuum necessary to create such experience and subsequent learning and real evolution. Would this be correct?

SE8: It might be.

ME: What do you mean "it might be"?

SE8: There has to be agreement with those entities who control and maintain the continuum first, including those entities who control and maintain the neighboring continuum, for as you know from the previous communications we have had, the evolutionary content experienced or contrived for the benefit of real evolution, affects those continuum surrounding the continuum in question.

ME: So what you are saying to me is that any changes to the evolutionary status of a continuum that are made to enable different experiential learning conditions to be available for experience are agreed upon by basically all the entities concerned before the change is made.

SE8: Not only that. They have to agree with the need or desire for the change requested. You see, the entities in a particular continuum may be happily working their way through a number of evolutionary experiences at that point in time of the request. The real evolutionary content of which might be of real evolutionary benefit to them, and they may not have completed the work and want to see through. Moreover, the change requested may also affect their continuum in a way that is either limited in evolutionary content for them or even puts them in a position of real evolutionary stasis/devolution.

ME: Hold on a moment. All this is very well, but what this means to me is that there is not only one evolution, the evolution, real evolution, that is accrued by a continuum and its entities, but there is a sub-evolution that is used to force experiences that would not be available to a continuum or its entities if it stuck to its normal real accrued evolutionary schedule. Not only that, but the opportunity to use the sub-evolutionary opportunities actually has the potential to affect the real evolutionary progression of a continuum and its entities in a negative way.

SE8: Correct. But the beauty of it is that in accepting the possibility of evolutionary stasis for the benefit of another continuum, a continuum and its occupants can accrue more evolutionary points, so to speak, than it would do normally. In essence, it creates a sort of leapfrog effect.

ME: Now you are confusing me. Are you suggesting that modification of what I will now classify as "sub-evolution," that is, sub-evolution in your environment that affects real evolution in a negative way, results in positive evolution simply because it is related to "self-sacrifice," and I say "self-sacrifice" in the "collective entity within a multiverse within a continuum" way?

SE8: In a nutshell, yes. You see, the most powerful evolutionary tool an entity can use is one of self-sacrifice for the benefit of others. This includes the individual and the collective versions, not to forget universal, multiversal and continuum-based evolutionary sacrifice. Any self-sacrifice for the benefit of others results in evolutionary gain above and beyond that gained in normal experiential existence.

ME: Why is that?

SE8: Because it requires no knowledge of the outcome of the sacrificial act by those making the decision. It is "the" only decision any entity can make without precognition of the resulting effect of the decision. This includes decisions made by any entity or collective of entities in whatever format, be it singular, universal, multiversal or continuum-based.

ME: So you are telling me that there are some decisions that are blind decisions, even at the energetic level?

SE8: Of course. Evolution wouldn't be the fun it is if there wasn't.

ME: And every entity that has created or has been created knows this?

SE8: Yes. And that includes all entities created by all Source Entities, for it is an Origin decreed onmiversal rule.

ME: That's amazing.

SE8: What is?

ME: That there is a rule that affects everything and everyone no matter which Source Entity created them, the entity, the universe, the multiverse or continuum. It is the same for everything and everyone.

SE8: Well, there are many other rules of a similar nature, but now is not the time to discuss them.

ME: OK, I can live with that. It was getting complicated anyway. Especially the bit about what I call sub-evolution affecting real evolution in a quantum leap sort of way when decisions are made based upon self-sacrifice with no knowledge of the outcome for the entity, universe, multiverse or continuum.

Maintenance Control Entities

SE8: Good. Let's talk about your next subject.

ME: Which is?

SE8: What the entities do who maintain my continuum. Apart, that is, from coping with the evolutionary conditions discussed, and how and why they maintain the loci's positional relationship with the locus of the continuum that is me.

ME: Sounds like a plan to me. I guess the best way to kick this off then is to ask you a rather fundamental question first. What form do your continuum maintenance entities have? What work do they do other than the maintenance of the position of the loci, and are they the same for all continuum?

SE8: So this is one of your famous nested questions.

ME: Famous, I hardly think that my questions or, indeed, the structure of them is famous.

SE8: You may not, but I can guarantee they are from where I am standing, so to speak. They are so famous they are being counted.

ME: Counted??!! Good grief, I must remember to ask questions in a linear fashion in the future then, to avoid further infamy.

SE8: Don't force it, we, the Source Entities that is, greatly enjoy your nested questions. Let's carry on with the first part of your question: what form do my continuum entities take?

First of all, let me elaborate a little on the starting point of a maintenance entity's existence shortly after creation.

All of the entities that were created for evolutionary existence are given a choice.

1.   They can either be an entity whose role it is to work and evolve, passing on their evolutionary content to their continuum controller and hence myself.

2.   They can be one of two different types of continuum maintenance entity.

        a.   The first type work within the continuum maintaining the geometric relationship between the continuum, the loci to the locus and the evolutionary balance.

        b.   The second type work in-between the continuum, maintaining the relationships between the continuum and the effects each continuum's evolutionary condition has on each neighboring continuum whilst also being a continuum controller. This is a singular job and is extremely important.

At the start of their initial existence, each newly created entity is tested for functional compatibility and is assigned the correct position for their aptitude accordingly.

ME: I thought you said that they had a choice?

SE8: They do to a certain extent, but that extent is only relative to the type of aptitude they have. There are sub-roles you know, and these are filled by entities who have a desire to be involved with the maintenance of the continuum, but who do not desire to be part of the decision process that is required to be adhered to when considering issues of evolutionary concern. These entities may even desire to stay in the service of continuum maintenance for an agreed period only before entering into the continuum as an evolving entity.

ME: Hold on, are you suggesting that entities that are of service to the maintenance of the continuum do not evolve?

SE8: Of course, they evolve. Every entity evolves. It is just that they do not evolve as a result of their own volition, their own work; instead, they evolve as a result of being of service, which is a slower process when compared to working on one's own evolution within the confines of the continuum. Evolutionary progression is always faster if one is at what you call "the coal face." (See glossary for definition.)

ME: I would have thought that being of service is a faster evolutionary route than as being an evolving entity.

SE8: In any Source Entities' environments, the only way that an entity can evolve fast is through being party to their own development by the interaction with other entities and the environment they exist within. If an entity is "being of service" whilst being involved in the process of being in control of their own evolution, and the object of their being of service results in them making a conscious decision to give up items of their own evolutionary opportunities so that they can be of service to the evolutionary opportunities of other entities, then they can enjoy greater levels of evolution than those accrued by simply being of service—that is done without the underlying knowledge of evolutionary law. That law states that an entity who gives up its own evolutionary opportunities for the benefit of others and does this without the possibility of any selfish decision to gain evolutionary progression under the disguise of self-evolutionary gain through initial magnanimous action of self-sacrifice for eventual self-gain, then they will gain progression faster than they would have in a normal existence where they are only concerned with their own evolution. The problem here is that my entities know the omniversal law of evolution and, therefore, have to put themselves into areas of existence and experience where they could, in fact, terminate their existence if they are being of benefit to others. For them, the only way they can be of true service is if they make true self-sacrifice, the ultimate sacrifice of self-termination, where their own termination is achieved in the full knowledge of their own ultimate demise but in the full knowledge that they have achieved an improvement in the evolutionary condition of those entities that the sacrifice is made for.

ME: So what happens to them when they make this ultimate self-sacrifice, one that they make in the knowledge that they will be terminated because, and help me out here, they know the omniversal law of evolution of being of service and the resultant opportunities in evolutionary progression? So why would they choose this particular route if it is to all intents and purposes the end of the line in their own individualized existence?

SE8: Pride.

ME: Pride?

SE8: Pride.

ME: Go on. You are losing me.

SE8: My entities experience an immense feeling of pride when they decide to make this level of service, especially when it is to directly benefit another entity—and specifically, if they have been in existence for a long time. You see, these opportunities don't come up very often. In fact, they are quite rare, so when an entity has this sort of opportunity presented to them, they take it.

ME: Sorry. I still don't see why self-termination is OK if it's for the benefit of others. It is a foreign concept to me.

SE8: Would it be so foreign to you if you knew that I and ultimately The Origin benefitted greatly from the evolutionary content of such an act?

ME: No, I suppose not, for that is ultimately why we are in existence.

SE8: Then now you know why they do it. Please note here that they are not totally lost, for once they make this level of sacrifice, they are re-instated and removed from the need to work within the confines of the continuum and can evolve at an accelerated pace purely as a result of being of service to the maintenance of the continuum. In essence, they are elevated in their positional and evolutionary rank, so to speak. Although they made the ultimate sacrifice in the name of being of ultimate service, they have done so without the knowledge of their ultimate survival. These entities are of a rare quality and are best placed in supervisory positions within those teams of entities who choose to maintain the continuum from an external perspective rather than an evolutionary position within the confines of the continuum.

Continuum Maintenance Entity Form Factors

ME: OK, so can you tell me a little about the form factor, if any, these entities take for their maintenance roles?

SE8: This may be difficult for you to understand, so I will need to elaborate a little, specifically as neither you nor anyone else in the Earth sphere has any knowledge or experience of true continuum mechanics.

ME: OK, we can but try.

This is the point in these dialogues where I was expecting a conversation where my head would hurt again. Ah well, here we go!

SE8: As you are aware from previous dialogues on the subject of continuum construction, the construct is created from the components of full dimension, dimensional componentry, frequency and energy that exist outside the frequencies?

ME: Yes, I am with you so far.

SE8: Well, the entities themselves have to be created from a combination of higher factors of those continuum component parts to enable them to manipulate them. In essence, they exist as a composite construct of their own, one not attracted to being part of those components that make up the continuum itself. They are, if you like, slippery. They need to be like the oil in the water. They can be part of the water, but they can never be a component part of the water so to speak. What's more, they also need to be sticky so that they can attract the component parts of the continuum and manipulate them, creating the boundaries that are necessary for the compartmentalization of the continuum, which needs to have a construct that has a structure to it, one that allows the distortion of the geometry of the continuum that results from local and indigenous evolutionary conditions.

Figure 3: Conceptual Image of the Make-Up of SE8's Entities (an alloy)

ME: I have an image in my mind that shows them as an alloy, so to speak, an alloy of all of the energies that are either present in the natural make-up of the continuum or synthesizable by manipulating the interaction between the natural energies. That includes those energies that are synthesized from a culmination of synthesized energies and further synthesis of the synthesis.

SE8: That would be a good analogy. They have to be capable of working with any possible combination of energies and their relative materials. However, there is another component that needs to be taken into account as well.

ME: What's that?

SE8: The all important component of evolution. Evolution has a significant impact on the energies within and without the continuum. You are aware of how evolution affects the continuum from our previous dialogue, and I can imagine you are able to understand how evolution affects the energies of a continuum and its incumbent entities.

ME: Well, yes, I can.

SE8: Then you will understand that the energies of the maintenance entity are also affected in a way that is consistent but not entirely in synchronization with the evolutionary changes. At least not at first, for they need to learn how to manipulate their own energies by forcing a localized evolutionary condition around themselves that effectively puts them outside of the evolutionary envelope of the continuum.

ME: So you are suggesting that they are not only slippery in terms of their energetic content and how it relates to the energies of the continuum but also in terms of their evolutionary content and how that affects or is affected by the evolutionary content within and without the continuum.

SE8: Correct. They are totally autonomous in every respect.

ME: So how do they manipulate the energies, and, I would guess, the evolutionary content of the continuum they are associated with?

SE8: Simply by becoming one with the whole of the location they are dealing with. They become the area of the location by infiltrating the energies and replacing them with their own of the same type. That type must have frequency, dimension, dimensional componentry, energy and evolutionary content, not to mention positional content relative to the loci.

ME: That sounds like they work a bit like a cancer cell in the human body which emulates the characteristics of a certain organ but is not linked to it or able to function like it and has a function all its own.

SE8: I can see the analogy, but I would suggest it is not a true description of how a maintenance entity works.

ME: How would you describe it then, as I thought that it was a reasonable description?

SE8: It would be better described in terms of a master key that was able to unlock all the doors in all the hotels in your world. And not only that, the key would be able to change the characteristics of the lock that it was inserted into so that only itself and one other could use it at any time in the future. What I must say though is that this analogy suggests a form factor of some kind, and as this is one of the parts of your nested question, I will answer it now.

As you may have guessed by now, a physical or energetic form factor is neither necessary nor required in many of the environments that the Source Entities you have communicated with to date. Your own form factor is a very transient state, as you well know. The length of the transience is a factor of the ability to control the decay at the cellular level by use of the incumbent entities' intentions or will. This, however, is not strictly the case in my continuum-based environment.

Form without Form!

ME: Go on. You have my attention now.

SE8: Ha, ha, ha, no, no, it's not the sort of form factor that you would ever recognize as a form factor dedicated to the environment that an entity would exist and experience within.

ME: I didn't see that one coming. No really, I am joking. It is quite obvious that the level of form factor of one of the maintenance entities would be something that was not only so completely different from anything else expected, that it could not be from my current incarnate perspective anything other than energetic. Even though it has a form of some type, that type is un-recognizable as a form to me.

SE8: Stop apologizing for your joke. We appreciate humor here, it is an essential part of existence of any being.

ME: That's OK. Shall we continue?

SE8: Yes. Mmmm, let me see how I can explain their form factor, for it is not something that you have been exposed to yet.

You see, the form that my entities take is based upon the twelfth dimensional geometric form. This is a form that is able to manipulate the very structural fabric of a portion of the continuum an entity works with—that is, both the internal and external structures associated with a particular continuum.

ME: So how do they do it? How do they manage to manipulate the fabric of a continuum? This seems to be a major role that they play.

SE 8: They do it by becoming that which they intend to change. That which they intend to change could be anything from an external barrier between the environment between the continuum and the continuum itself. It could be or a localized area that is showing promise from an evolutionary perspective, one that would benefit from being manipulated in some way to augment the evolutionary experience through manipulating the evolutionary content of the area being considered for manipulation. I appreciate that this seems a bit convoluted, but that is exactly what it is, convoluted and iterative.

I can see that you are a bit lost so I will explain further in terms that you can understand.

If you can imagine creating a plan of a house or even a much larger building, and that the house or large building is built faithfully to the plan, so you have a building which is built to plan. Now imagine that the building needs an overhaul. The plan remains the same, but the architecture of the inside is changed to suit new requirements. The new plan is overlaid over the old plan to see the difference between the two and to see what has to be done to make the changes required to support the architectural requirements of the new plan. The old architecture is then stripped out, and the new architecture is installed. It is the process of overlaying the new architecture over the old that is used by my maintenance entities. They become the old architecture in every possible way, effectively replacing the energies that were the old architecture allowing those energies to be put to one side. Consider it as a scaffold replacing a scaffold. The entity then makes the changes necessary to support the specific changes required of the continuum, including those interfacing entities or components of the continuum undergoing change within itself, thus effectively changing the geometry of the scaffold or in this case the continuum's structure. Once it has done this and the new structure is working well, taking into account that adjustments may be

111

necessary, the working structure of the continuum is introduced, and the entity moves on to the next job.

ME: So what you are saying is that the maintenance entity creates a sort of bridge between that structure that the continuum currently has and that which it needs to be in order to augment the evolutionary opportunities that can be experienced as a result of the proposed changes to the continuum. Once these proposed changes have been under a trial-run, so to speak, they are introduced as a permanent feature, albeit for the period of time required for the entity to create a longer term replacement, one that allows the entity to move on to its next role.

SE8: That's it in a nutshell. You see, there is no point in creating something that will fail, especially if it is to have a medium to long term function.

ME: And this is happening all of the time?

I felt that I was starting to get a grip of what was going on in Source Entity Eight's continuum-based environment.

SE8: Yes, this happens all the time. In fact, it is happening in a very special way across the whole of my continuum-based environment.

ME: Yes, I see what you mean. It is like a patchwork quilt, with each patch in the quilt being representative of a specific continuum.

SE8: That would be a reasonable way to describe the work that goes on across the continuum and its continuum.

This made me think a bit. Although each of the maintenance entities was and worked as an autonomous entity, it quite obviously, in my mind that is, needed to work in some sort of synchronicity with other maintenance entities to ensure that the work they undertook did not upset the work of those maintenance entities surrounding them. Just as I was thinking this though, Source Entity Eight considered it pertinent to correct me in my thought process.

SE8: It would be worth noting here that the level of a maintenance entity's autonomy is total. This means that it is not part of what you would call a gestalt or hive mind. It decides what to do based upon the level of change required to support the evolutionary quotient necessary to ensure connectivity with the rest of the continuum, the level of compartmentalization, the evolutionary quotient has and the necessary evolutionary level required to maintain an effective interface between the neighboring continuums and the space in-between. This also includes the level of localized change necessary to respond to the evolutionary pressures of the neighboring continuum.

ME: We have discussed this before to some extent, and as a result, I feel that we are going over old ground.

SE8: We are to some extent, but the important thing to note here is that the entities themselves have to become the continuum itself at certain times to enable the changes to be planned and implemented correctly all at the correct change point.

ME: OK, this opens up a whole new series of questions. I will, however, limit it to one.

SE8: Go on.

ME: Why does a maintenance entity need to become part of the continuum itself? I can recognize the need to be a framework to build a new continuum-based environment around. This would be rather like the etheric and ketharic templates in the human body. I can also understand being a bridge between the old construction and the new. But why be an actual part of the continuum itself?

SE8: There are two reasons for this. First, the maintenance entity needs to become part of the continuum, replacing part of the continuum at a component level to understand the interfaces surrounding it, as well as the internal functionality and energetic requirements. It needs to do this before each piece of maintenance work is started. In this instance, the continuum's component is taken "off line," so to speak, to allow the changes necessary for optimal functionality whilst the entity takes over the functional requirements of that continuum component part in its entirety for the duration of the changes. Second, the continuum itself cannot react fast enough to the changes required to maintain synchronicity with its surrounding continuum, the space between and the greater continuum that is me, so the entity has to "step in" immediately any change is required, whilst the modifications are made.

ME: I am getting the impression that they have to do a sort of apprenticeship to qualify as a maintenance entity.

SE8: Yes, that is true. Before they can be considered autonomous, they must experience every component part of every continuum within the continuum that is me. That includes being the space between the continuum and the very fabric of that which is me. Also, they have to cope with the ever-changing borders between the compartments identified as an entity's area of maintenance responsibility.

ME: They have to become you?

SE8: Correct. What better way to understand the maintenance of a continuum than by being the creating continuum itself?

ME: How is that possible? I mean, how can an entity that is as small as a maintenance entity . . . No, sorry, let me change my line of questioning. How can an entity take over from its creator? I mean, it must be a massive change.

SE8: It doesn't. The entity itself becomes one with me, integrating itself into the very minute energetic detail that is me.

ME: But to do that, it would have to spread itself incredibly thin.

SE8: It does. To enable it to become an overlay of me, it needs to be diluted to the point of insignificance.

ME: You mean like a homeopathic dilution?

SE8: That would be a reasonable analogy, yes. You see, for the entity to experience all that is me, it needs to be "in" all that is me, and the only way it can do that is be diluted to the point of full integration. Consider it like being a rare elemental component in the atmosphere that surrounds the earth. The elemental component may be one part in several trillion, trillion, billion, but in its diluted state, it is still, nevertheless, an important component within the total composition of the element which you classify as air. Because the air is what it is when you take a sample of it, you always gain a sample of all of the elements that make it up so to speak.

ME: But that can't possibly be the case because to get a sample of all of the elements, one needs to take a sample from an area that is large enough to capture those elements that are, for instance, one in a trillion, trillion, billion. One sample might not have the element whilst another would.

SE8: That would be correct in the physical world that your "vehicle" exists within, but it is not necessary energetically. You mentioned the example of homeopathics, and as a result, I thought you understood the functionality of such a dilution.

ME: Well, I do to a certain extent. The theory surrounding homeopathic medicines is that the surrounding elements take "in" the properties of the element that is most diluted. Hence, the elements' properties are present without the element itself being present.

SE8: Well, that is the same in this instance. It is a very good analogy as it shows how the maintenance entity learns to absorb that which is me without having a component of itself specifically located in the area of functional learning.

ME: I find it really quite bizarre how an entity can learn how to be a Source Entity. . . .

SE8: Continuum.

ME: OK, a continuum, merely by association.

I have to ask this next question as it may explain how homeopathics work here on the earth plane. How does an entity assimilate knowledge or experiential experience through diluted association or presence?

SE8: Quite simply by the communication routes used by the energies separating the energies. I see that I will need to elaborate. Energies that are either attached to an entity—that is, an entity of any kind but specifically those with sentience—or energies that have a purpose use each other as a communication medium. This communication medium is quite special because when the request goes out for communication—and the communication is between energies that are of a very high dilution—the energies in-between change themselves into the same type of energy for as long as necessary, ensuring that the communication or functionality is made in a robust way. However, there is a trade off in this type of communication process. This trade-off is that the energies that require "others'" energies to behave like them for the duration of the communication or function, request what you would call "benefit in kind"—the agreement to assume the communicative properties of other nearby energies when they are in the minority. In this way they are given the key characteristics of all of the other energies that they are surrounded by to enable them to return the favor, so to speak, when the request arrives, which it inevitably does. This ability to change into other energies remains once given/received—even when the requesting entity or energy has departed—thus leaving a full set of energetic and function resources available for the use of the remaining energies or entities. This is basically how an entity can be part of me, be me, and experience what I experience—even when my difference in size is so much bigger than the maintenance entity diluted within me—to experience being the parent continuum or a Source Entity. This is a similar process to that used in your homeopathic medicines on your Earth.

ME: Well, I do say that does sort out a number of things in my mind. And it explains to some degree how homeopathics work.

SE8: The methodology of taking on board the characteristics of another energy for communication and functionality is one that is adopted Origin-wide. In fact, it is the primary method of communication and functionality with the exception of the medium you call gravity, which I am told has already been explained to by your own Source Entity.

Mmmm, it is almost time for you to move on to the next Source Entity, the One you will call Source Entity Nine.

ME: Wait. Before you go, can you please describe to me what one of the entities who exists within one of your continuum looks like. I can't finish without at least your description of one entity form factor and evolutionary role within the continuum.

SE8: I will do this for you before you move on.

Before I start though I need to point out that I have over 60 million different types of entities that exist and evolve within my continuum-based environment. Some of the entity types are specific to the continuum they work within, whereas others exist within a continuum that has up to 30 thousand different types. Which one would you like me describe, not that I have given you a choice yet?

ME: Right, without a choice of some sort, it is going to be difficult. Let me ask one more question before I decide which "blind alley" to go down.

Do you have a continuum where there is a main form factor, if they have one, one that is similar to all entities?

SE8: Now that is a very good question, for there is a continuum where this is the case. I suspect you were tuning in to this particular continuum when you made the choice of question.

ME: Not intentionally, at least, not consciously.

SE8: All of the entities in the continuum I will call continuum 11b are similar, but each of them has a particular function and, therefore, form factor. I will use this nomenclature as it is one that you understand, for their form factor is a multi-dimensional-based derivative of what you might call a rare gas—if, that is, I had to use a description that you would understand.

ME: OK, it's good enough for me so far.

SE8: On its own, this form factor is not useful for any form of continuum-based work or the retention of any evolutionary content, for it has no "purpose" in its raw state. It gains its usefulness and, therefore, purpose when it has a function to perform, so it needs to have a difference to its form factor, no matter how small it may be.

ME: I am receiving the image of a series of entities that are sort of similar to a "multipurpose" screw driver without a tip on the end. In this state they are all the same. When it has a tip, for example, a cross head, a blade or torx (a six point star shape pattern), it has a specific purpose and role. The tip is the only thing that is different among the other entities who have "tips" that are specific to their own roles and functions.

SE8: That would be a good example from your point of view, but you will need to note this as well. In your example, you have assumed that the illustration has but one multifunction screwdriver body. In the continuum, we are talking about other subtler differences between the so called stable sides of the body of the entity.

ME: So you have classes or types of entities, different types of multifunction screw driver bodies, so to speak.

SE8: Yes, and purely as an illustration, they may be, long, short, wide, bent at various different angles, flexible under all conditions, and/or flexible under certain conditions. This is not what they are but it gives you an idea of the diversity. Additionally, the tip "family" changes depending upon the body type.

As another example using you own methods of manufacturing electronics, such as manufacturing a silicon chip on earth, you need certain tools, computerized tools, to allow you to design, develop, and test these components. You need the tools to create the tools to create the tools, so to speak. This is similar if not the same in certain examples with the entities in this particular continuum.

ME: So this continuum is the only continuum where the entities are similar if not almost the same, albeit with the minor differences talked about.

SE8: In a nutshell, yes.

ME: I would like to get back to this description of their form factor from a true sense rather than from a hypothetical sense where we are using earthly examples because I can imagine my readers thinking that we are talking about a bunch of sentient screwdrivers here.

SE8: You should give your readers more credit, but I do see the humor in that statement. Sentient screwdrivers, indeed!

Let's carry on. The entities themselves as I have described in some limited way in the text above, are a "multi-dimensional-based derivative of what you might call a *rare gas*"—the *rare gas* being the only way to describe their physicality if they had one. You mentioned "form factor" and the way that a rare gas is constructed would be a better example of how they are presented if they had to be presented in some sort of form. I also recently described the way in which those entities that are destined to be continuum maintenance entities are able to experience being one with me and, therefore, part of the working structure of the continuum they are assigned to during times of substitutional maintenance.

ME: Yes, we considered the example of homeopathic dilution.

SE8: No, I was alluding to the entity becoming the framework of that part of the continuum they were becoming a substitute for whilst the maintenance task was being worked on.

ME: Oh. Ok, yes, I see now.

SE8: I think you do in some small way. I will give you an image to consider.

I received an image of the chemical models we create in school/university to explain, in a three dimensional way, the way in which a specific element is composed in its atomic state. This model portrayed a stick model with balls attaching the sticks together. The stick representing the connectivity between the balls, and the balls represented the molecules that made up the element. The molecules had a level of attractivity between certain other molecules whilst having a level of repulsion between others. Other levels of connectivity had both attractivity and repulsion so that the molecules stayed at a known distance from each other, not being able to move closer nor being able to move away. All of this resulted in a form factor, albeit large enough and dense enough to be classified as a form whilst being of a frequency that was high enough to make the form "formless" in all but attractivity and repulsivity—certainly from a physical perspective. It was as if the entity, if this was an example of an entity (Source Entity Eight said it was), was not actually created from a molecular structure but a structure that was created by attractivity and repulsivity of some sort. The attractivity and repulsivity were not between different types of molecules but were between different energies and dimensions.

Suddenly, this was starting to get hard, even though it appeared to be a simple subject. The data being presented to me was obviously being subject to some heavy filtering so that I could gain some sort of insight into the concept being presented to me. My typing was slowing down as my ability to assimilate the knowledge was degrading. I felt a pressure at the front of my head. Then it cleared slightly, and the information continued to flow again.

The interaction between the energies that composed the entity or concept of the entity being described was not only dependent upon simple energetic attractivity and repulsivity and the expected frequential content and how that affected the attractivity, etc., but it was also affected by the dimensional sub-component where that particular part of the entity was manifested. I saw the entity as the molecular model again but pulled apart into different layers, rather like the layers that are used in the multilayer drawing conventions used in Computer Aided Engineering (CAE) and Computer Aided Design (CAD) to draw a component in a motorcar or an aeroplane.

As the layers were pulled apart, each layer represented the dimensional content that illustrated that part of the entity that was manifested on that particular dimension. Dimensionally together, the entity was whole; dimensionally apart and seen from the perspective of the different dimensional levels in isolation, the entity was incomplete. There was one more thing, however. That part of the entity that was manifested on a particular layer/dimension had a role/specialization of its own to perform. This role was performed in both isolation and in concert with the other parts of the entity that were manifest on the other dimensional layers. In this aspect the entity was able to create on a holistic and specialized level simultaneously. Not only that, the entity was able to interact with the other entities within its continuum and work in concert with them in their creativity either as a team, independently/separately, interdependently or in observation. They also worked out which skills/functions each other had as a result of their particular energetic/dimensional construction and worked together in harmony to create something that they would not have been able to create should they have stayed working only with entities of the same energetic/dimensional form factor.

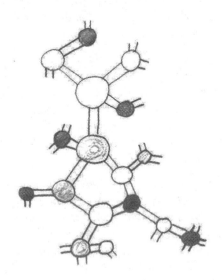

I zoomed out of the image I was being given and saw a bright blue lattice of sparkling multidimensional energies. It looked like a huge multi-dimensional net covering the area that would house a galaxy in my own physical universe. It was beautiful.

Figure 4: Example of a 3D Model Used to Explain Molecular Structure

In Finishing with Source Entity Eight

SE8: Now you know what one of these entities would look like if it was visible to your physical eyes and a bit about how it is constructed.

ME: Yes, it is beautiful. Thank you.

SE8: Now it is time for you to move on to the entity you will refer to as Source Entity Nine. Go in peace with this expansion in your knowledge.

And with those last words the communication link between Source Entity Eight and me dissolved. I still felt its presence but noted that my communicative direction and energetic link with it was no longer attached in an exclusive fashion. With Source Entity Eight's energies no longer linked to my own for communication purposes, I began to take stock of the information I had received during the months I had been directly linked energetically with SE8.

Source Entity Eight was an entity whose whole existence was focused upon the generation and maintenance of continuum and how they could provide an enhanced evolutionary opportunity for those entities who were created and based upon their inherent abilities, elected to work within their chosen continuum to experience, learn and evolve (an Origin-wide theme) by manipulating the base evolutionary content of the continuum in which they existed— sometimes locally, sometimes across the whole continuum.

There were two things that struck me as both significant and different from an almost common theme of multiversal creativity and existence based upon full dimensions, sub-dimensional components and frequency levels of environments created by the other Source Entities with whom I have communicated to date:

1. *There was a focus on a continuum that had a continuum specific energetic content rather than a universe/multiverse.*
2. *The focus also included the ability or need to affect the base evolutionary component of the continuum-based environment to allow optimization of that base evolution via the work of incumbent entities and evolution of the entities themselves, both positively and negatively.*

It was as if the whole game of evolution was being turned on its head with the basic ground rules of evolution happening in a linear way no longer applying—at least not in Source Entity Eight's environment. The thought that the whole way in which the base level of evolution, specifically in the continuum-based environment, could be manipulated to affect the method in which evolution was accrued was a completely new avenue of thought to me! I suspect it will be a completely new consideration for most people as well, specifically the thought of losing one's place on the evolutionary ladder, over-night as it were, in order to either help the entities evolving in another continuum or to see how it affected an entity's overall evolution seems to be contrary to everything we know about evolution.

I was also surprised at the different types of evolution and how they affected the geometrics of the continuum itself. I was starting to realize that nothing could be taken for granted, and everything should be considered as not only possible but highly probable. Clearly, there were no "sacred cows" in The Origin's omniverse, for evolution, one of those, had just been smashed to pieces.

With this in mind and four Source Entities to go, my energetic link moved outwards and onwards towards the ninth Source Entity to be interviewed. I felt excited as I sat and waited for the energies of the communication link with Source Entity Nine to engulf me. I didn't have long to wait.

Chapter Three
Source Entity Nine

I suddenly had a picture of the Walt Disney cartoon character Goofy in my head.

"Well hello!" it said in the same voice as Goofy.

Was I going mad?

Source Entity Nine Tells Me More About Myself Than Itself

SE9: Now that I have got your attention, we can start.

ME: Hold on. Was that you, the next Source Entity that I am due to have a dialogue with? The Source Entity I am due to call Source Entity Nine? In my head portraying Goofy?!

SE9: Yes, it was. I had noticed that you had not spotted that the link between us had become operative, so I decided to delve into your mind and use something that would wake you up to my presence. Using the Goofy personality seems to have done the trick.

ME: It certainly did. And you are right; I didn't notice that you had linked up with my energies. Your energies must be either very subtle, or you have managed to tune into me in a most perfect way.

SE9: The truth of the matter is that you are adjusting to the difference in energies in an almost automatic way now. You appear to be able to re-calibrate your energies to those of the entity you are due to communicate with on the point of your relinquishing the link with the previous Source Entity.

ME: I don't remember doing this before. In fact, I remember having quite a bit of difficulty during the first couple of dialogues of the last few Source Entities—specifically, as I get further and further away from my home Source Entity.

SE9: As you move further away from the energies of the Source Entity you now call Source Entity One, your home Source Entity, you start to become more independent. As you were told by Source Entity Eight, you are of The Original Manifestation and, therefore, have an energy set that is not truly created by your home Source Entity. In essence, you were created by The Origin and, therefore, you belong in The Origin and not in the confines of your home Source Entity. As a result of moving your consciousness away from the confines of your Source Entity on an almost regular and consistent basis now, you are losing the attachment to the energies of your home Source Entity. You are gaining your independence and the constraints in your communicative abilities are being broken down as a result. Hence, your automatic re-calibration of your own energies to those of mine, allowing almost perfect integration with me on a most fundamental level. This meant that when I established contact with you, your energies were already calibrated to those of mine and the normal discomfort you experienced in the past was not present. In fact, they were so in tune that you were not even aware of their presence as you considered them to be your own.

ME: I am impressed.

SE9: You should be. Although it's the first time you have achieved such a process, it will become more prevalent later, especially when you complete your dialogues with me and the remaining Source Entities and move on to your communications with The Origin in a level of detail you are not yet even able to comprehend.

ME: But I have not had a problem communicating with The Origin in the past. In fact, I expect I will be talking to The Origin more than the Source Entity I will call Source Entity Twelve, the Source Entity that has not yet become self-aware.

SE9: You know about Source Entity Twelve? Mmmm, you might be surprised to note that things have moved on in that respect. I will not spoil your fun though as it is more important for you to tell that particular story when you have time to dedicate yourself to it. That time is not now. Now getting back to why you have not had any problems communicating with The Origin to date. You have not had any problems with communicating with The Origin because The Origin, as with the previous eight Source Entities you have communicated with modified its own base energy resonance to those of yours, not you adjusting your energies to those of the entity you are about to enter into discourse with. This means that the level of communication will be higher, allowing more information to be passed on to you as your level of understanding is lifted through the more complete level of integration you are able to establish through the modification of your own base energies.

ME: So that explains the reason why I didn't notice the link being created. I have apparently re-calibrated my energies so close to yours that you have become me, so to speak.

SE9: That is one way of saying it, but in reality you have become me.

ME: So why do I not get a sense of who you are then? Should I not get a sense of a massively extended memory or ability?

SE9: No, that is not what the link or the communication process that is created by the re-calibration of your base energies is all about. Remember, that part of you that is incarnate is still limited from a functional perspective to what is allowable whilst incarnate and what you are able to command whilst in the low frequencies that you currently occupy. You will gain nothing other than an increased ability to affect a robust and simple communicative link that is not stretching your physicality to its limits. You can't see it now but when you were in communication with the other Source Entities your energies, especially those in the levels 8, 9 & 10 were being twisted all over the place and in every way possible. Now that you have established an automatic method of re-calibrating your energies to those of the entity you want to communicate with, this is no longer a problem.

ME: I can assure you I was not aware of being able to do this.

SE9: And why should you when that part of you that is not incarnate has been doing the work for you? Don't forget the part of you that is incarnate is a very small part of you. Energetically, you are a much larger entity.

ME: OK, you have spoken about me more than yourself in the limited time that we have had together. I am very grateful for receiving such knowledge, as it helps me to fill in the gaps about my "self" and how I can do what I do without any formal training as such. At least not in this specific area, for I have taught myself.

SE9: It is both a pleasure and an honor to do so, for your work will assist in the ascension of mankind in a most unique way. Although right now you are in the starting blocks, so to speak, ready to run down the track, you will later be flying in a fighter jet in comparison. Hold onto your seat, for once you have made your choice in life to be "Gods'," (your Source Entities') willing slave/emissary, you will be at the center of a whirlwind of spiritual work.

ME: Well, right now it seems like I have had a bit of a false start.

SE9: That will pass faster than you think, and you will also make the move/change faster than you think. It is time for us to enlighten your readers about my own accomplishments now.

ME: I agree.

The Basis for Source Entity Nine's Environment

ME: I would like to understand about your environment. Is it a multiverse, continuum or what?

SE9: You will notice that the further you move away from your home Source Entity that the more diverse and different the environments become.

ME: Yes, I have noticed that.

SE9: Well, my environment is again a departure from that which you have experienced before. Again, this is planned so that you can make the changes required more easily. Every move outwards is a step further away from that which you can relate to. Each move away from that which you can relate to exposes you to new and more abstract creations, which in turn, build your knowledge and experience base so as to allow you to move on. In this task you are doing very, very well. I will delay no longer.

My own environment can only be described as a lattice, a spider's web or fully spherical snow flake if you like.

I saw just that, a huge lattice-like construct that looked for all intents and purposes like a snowflake lattice made of intra-dimensional light. Another way of looking at it would be like looking at the complete seed head that a dandelion plant creates in order to replicate itself. The light itself looked like it was pulsating and changing its luminous density and color, but the color was only changing in a subtle sense. There appeared to be no space at all in-between what I can only describe as the light tubes that made up the construct that I could identify as being able to support any physical or energetic life. It seemed to be pure void and not offering the so-

called "back doors" I had previously experienced. It was not part of the construct.

ME: Have I got this right? Is your environment, as I see it in my mind's eye, just like a big dandelion seed head or spherical snow flake?

SE9: Yes, that is how it would appear to your eyes. Each of the "light tubes" that makes up the construct is effectively an environment for a different type of entity.

ME: So each light tube is a unique universal environment that accommodates a single entity type?

SE9: Correct. Every part of me from the aspect of the construction is a separate but integrated universal environment tuned specifically to the requirements of those entities that occupy it. I maintain a centrality where the main branches, central conduits or trunks, if you like, are connected. Consider it a little bit like the loci Source Entity Eight described in your last dialogue. Each of the main branches acts as a conduit where the entities that exist in one of the branches can traverse to the center point, me, and commune with me.

ME: What do you mean commune?

SE9: Exactly that, commune. Consider it like your evolutionary direction. As you rise through the frequencies, a rise resulting from the increase in your evolutionary content, so do you get closer to those frequencies that are associated with the essence of your Source Entity. This allows you to communicate and commune, to be one with, your creator. In your own environment, this is something that all entities strive for. Some achieve it early in their existence whereas others take longer to progress to the level required to allow full communion. Others, on the other hand, are able to achieve communication without communion, as you are right now. In the migration of an entity from its own environment towards me, it has to move away from its own environment to the main conduit and progress in an evolutionary way towards me. It meet its challenges and creates its creations as it goes.

ME: Does it not need to go through any other environments to reach you? In some of the other dialogues I have had, the entities concerned progressed from one environment to another with their evolution being affected by their ability to cope with the new challenges encountered in the environments they pass through. Is this not the case with your environmental construct?

SE: No. When an entity starts its evolutionary journey and increases its desire for communion, it retains its own environment even when it is, for all intents and purposes, "outside" its environment.

ME: I think I understand. I just received an image of a direct line, a line within the conduit and environmental branch the entity originated from that extended to the central conduit and the center point that is you. I also see that there can be many multitudes of entities that can be within the central conduits, each totally unaware of the other entities around them that originate from the other branches.

SE9: Well done. You may also want to note that in their journey towards communion with me, they are carrying their own universes with them.

ME: Hang on. What do you mean "carrying their own universes with them"? You mean the whole lot? What happens to those entities that also exist in the universe occupied by the entity that moves away from the branch?

SE9: They continue to occupy the same universe. It stays in the same relative space even though it also stays with those entities that are moving towards having enough evolutionary content to allow them the closeness required to commune with me. Imagine you have an entity or group of entities that originate in a certain universal branch. If that entity or those entities move away from the branch and on down the central conduit or trunk that connects a certain contingent of branches or branches of branches, etc., they take their universe with them.

ME: I think I understand. I have a picture in my head of globules of the same universal energy all over the originating branch and the trunk. I also see them in other branches and trunk/branch/sub-branch configurations in other parts of the environmental construct. From what I can see, the globules are connected by universal beingness. That beingness is an immediate and instantaneous connection with the other globules. Let me see if I have got this right.

When an entity moves to the edge of that globule of universe it is currently in and wants to move to another part of what would have been the total universe, had that entity remained in the universal branch, the perimeter of the universal globule provides immediate and instantaneous transport to that part of the universe that it would have traversed to had it been in the whole universe in the universal branch.

SE9: Well done and very good. But also note that if the transportation to another part of the universe was a requirement to interact with another entity or group of entities, and that entity or group of entities were themselves away from the original whole universe, the entity would instead be transported to that globule of universe that was elsewhere within the trunk or other trunk/branch/sub-branch configuration that that entity is currently existing within and not the whole original universe.

ME: I was going to say awesome, but I am trying to get a grip of what you have just said to me, which I just about have. I have another question.

SE9: Ask away.

ME: How does this work, I mean, with all these globules of universe being split out all over your environmental construct? It must dilute the environmental density of the originating universal branch.

SE9: Not in the slightest. I can see the famous frown!

ME: I must stop it.

I started to smile. I was being made famous, Source Entity wide, for my frown! Not exactly what I wanted to be recognized or remembered for.

Go on.

SE9: The universe grows or replicates enough new universal energy to both surround the traversing entity and maintain its own area/density . . .

ME: . . . And it is this replication of universe that creates the ability for the globules to be in full contact with each other, replicating in a jigsaw-type method the whole universe in globular format even though they are separated from the whole and the other separated universal globules.

SE9: Well interjected.

ME: How can a universe exist outside itself in what I consider as being "totality" whilst being in bits and pieces and part of the original universal environment all at the same time?

SE9: Simply by maintaining an area or band of frequency that is assigned to a particular universal branch and allowing multiple use of that frequency band.

ME: Hold on. Are you suggesting that—now let me get this straight—the frequency bands in existence are all over the structure of your environmental construct, and this allows the bubbles of universe to exist simultaneously and independently whilst still being in contact to the point of instantaneous and autonomous interaction? Is this not similar to us on earth using the same frequencies all over the world for transmissions from separate and independent radio stations? Because they are far apart and—of course, depending upon the signal strength and transmitter power also depends upon how large the radius of transmission is. They have large areas where they cannot interfere with each other whilst being of the same frequency, too, but basically thereby allowing autonomous existence that is linked by a base frequency band. Is this the same?

SE9: Not an entirely accurate way of explaining how the communication links are maintained between the base universe and those bubbles or pockets of universe that are allowed to exist both separately and together. However, it is a reasonable enough description to use from your position, especially when the mechanics used to allow such interconnectivity is not only well beyond "mankind incarnates'" ability to comprehend but is also close to the limits of energetic mankind cognitive abilities.

Now I was intrigued. How could something be beyond the comprehension of an energetic entity? Especially when we are supposed to be "all knowing" or at least supposed to be able to access the universal knowledge base when in the energetic. I decided to make a minor detour in my questioning in an effort to bottom this out. Finding out that even energetic entities have limitations in understanding was like a red rag to a bull!

ME: Now you have me going! I thought that once we, that is mankind incarnate, are back in the fully energetic, we would know everything, all there is to know or at least be able to access the knowledge from a central depository of some sort. Why would we not be able to understand something that is a fundamental part of existence? I grant you that fundamental part of your environment's existence not being part of our multiverse is maybe a clue as to why energetic mankind would not be able to assimilate the knowledge. But there must be some parallel functions, some things that are fundamentally the same no matter what Source Entity created them, simply because essentially we are all part of The Origin.

SE9: It is not a given that once in the energetic an entity is able to understand all that is. It is not even a given that an energetic entity will understand the mechanics of its own universe, let alone, multiverse or those other environments created by the other Source Entities.

ME: I thought that once in the energetic an entity was virtually omnipotent?

SE9: No. It is a general rule that there has to be a certain level of evolutionary content attached to an entity before it is in a position of being capable of understanding the functionality of the multi/universe/multi-frequential/energetic/continuum-based environment it exists within. Of course, it is aware of what it exists within, but its understanding of the functionality and how to affect or manipulate it is only bestowed upon it when it has graduated to a certain evolutionary level, so to speak. This is a normal progression for all entities, Origin-wide. In essence an entity must be capable of understanding what it can do before it is allowed to do it.

ME: OK, that seems reasonable to me. I would, however, like to know how your multiverse works, so that I can pass it on to the readers of this dialogue.

SE9: Let me start by saying that if any of your readers have problems with understanding the description of the functionality of my environment, they can always fall back on the description you made. It may not be accurate, but it is in the right direction and will provide a reasonable stepping stone as long as it is not taken as being the truth, but as a way to the truth.

ME: That's fine by me. I think it is important that the people of Earth are at least given the chance to understand the greater reality, even though they might not all understand what is being given to them.

SE9: Good. I will progress then.

I suddenly felt an energetic block take me over. It was similar to those I feel when I know I am going to have a hard time getting the information through. I did my best to ignore it.

SE9: Consider your trees on Earth. They are all connected because they are all rooted into the soil that is part of the Earth and as such have a common medium with which they are connected and part of. With this medium, a tree can communicate with other trees of its own kind, no matter how far away they are. So if you have a single tree of a certain type, and it is in a forest full of trees of another type, it is still able to communicate with other trees of its own type because it is connected to the Earth. This connectivity is unique to its type and does not interfere with the communications that are happening between other trees of different types. Now consider that the Earth is also part of a medium that is the physical and energetic universe concurrently. Let us look at one of the trees that is on the Earth but is not indigenous to the Earth but is nevertheless on the Earth—the tree type you call "Aspen" here, as it is not indigenous to the Earth. It was introduced to cope with the ever increasing carbon emissions you have. It is still able to communicate with the other Aspen trees in your universe because it is in contact with the Earth and those elements that the Earth is in contact with in a universal sense.

In essence, they occupy an area of specific universal space that is peculiar to their own species of tree. When a tree, on say another planet in this galaxy wants to communicate with other trees of its own species that is not on the same planet, it sends its intention to communicate out to that part of the galaxy where it believes/knows its fellow trees are and then projects its essence to the trees in the planet desired to be communicated with. Its essence, spirit or soul is transported instantaneously by a process of "sentient transference" of the tree's intellect through the energies that bridge the gap between the two locations—the tree's sentient essence is the link between the two locations from a directional perspective.

The example here is how your trees communicate between each other on the Earth and between distant points; they do it by transferring their sentience to the part of the galaxy necessary to allow a localized level of communication. From the point of view of the localized level of communication or transportation of an entity from one part of the separated universe in my environment to another linked but separate part of the universe, the localized parts of the universe can be considered the physical location of the trees in your galaxy, your planets, with the individualization of the universe represented by the collective intellect that is the tree mind, which is spread throughout the universal environment.

ME: Are you suggesting that our trees are not only on Earth but on other planets in my galaxy as well and that their "mind" is effectively spread throughout the galaxy—the trees' mind being the illustration of the separated universe in your environment?

SE9: Yes.

ME: Then that would mean that the universe and its separated parts are sentient as well.

SE9: Yes. That is why your description of the localized use of frequency is not particularly accurate enough as a concept to use.

ME: I knew that trees on Earth are part of a collective or gestalt mind, but I wasn't aware of that mind spanning the galaxy that my planet exists within.

SE9: The tree mind spans most of the universe you use currently— hence, my use of it as an illustrative tool, in this instance.

ME: You seem to know more about my own environment than I do.

SE9: As you already know, all Source Entities share their learning with each other, so it is inevitable that I know as much about your overall environment as your creator, your own Source Entity. I also gain a lot of localized information through my interface with you, information which I need to use as a method of gauging your level of understanding of information I have, should I choose to give it to you and how best to illustrate it by using examples of things that you already know.

ME: And I thank you for that. I am quite aware that we are only given concepts and information in ways that we can understand and assimilate and ultimately broadcast, even if it is like teaching an infant the "Times Table" to explain the concept of mathematics when the greater reality is the use of mathematics for understanding quantum field theory, which, in itself, may well be kindergarten math when considering the greater reality.

Source Entity Nine's Strangely Constructed Environment

Even though I was receiving good and interesting information from Source Entity Nine, I was acutely aware that I was deviating from the information process that I like to use in order to gain some sort of commonality in the information type about all the Source Entities. I decided to return to the subject of gaining a description of the entities within their environment. But first I decided to understand why Source Entity Nine's environment was the structure it was.

ME: I have to say this first. Your multiversal environment is nothing like I expected, nor is it anything like any of the multiversal or even the continuum-based environments I have been honored to experience to date. Why did you choose such a strange shape for its construction? I mean, most of the environments I have seen and experienced are quite frankly spherical in shape. That is, if I had to give them a shape. I know that Source Entity Seven "in totality" was a two sphere system that overlapped in the middle creating the third environment. Others are what I call dimensional and frequency-based conundrums, but yours is a completely new concept. I really must know why you chose it as a construct. It is quite bizarre.

SE9: As a construct, it serves a number of important functions. I will itemize these so that you can see them more clearly.

• It is completely different in its functionality than any of the other multiverse created by my peers.

• It has a physical appearance that has a solid appearance, even though it is energetic in nature.

• The appearance governs the boundaries between the universal environments associated with it and the space within The Origin that is not used as pure environment. That is, it does not have an area of what you have called "null space" in-between the construct or a back door for maintenance purposes.

• An entity's movement towards the center requires the manipulation of the universal environment to allow the entity to move freely and unhindered through other universal environments without affecting them in any way. That is, they are invisible in all ways to those entities in the universe being traversed.

134

- Progression towards their source, me, requires the knowledge of universal manipulation, which is a higher function of the evolutionary content accrued by an evolving entity.

- Structure does not necessarily mean an amorphous environment filled with a dimensional, frequential, and continuum-based structure system that is within and without itself. It can also be rather linear and logical. That is what I have created.

- The shape of the construct is designed to be easily expanded and contracted, allowing the universal branches to create universal sub-branches. It also allows clusters of branches and sub-branches to cast off or move away from each other creating their own multiversal structure with a portion of my essence in the center.

ME: That's interesting. The image I gained was just that. A chunk/cluster of branch, sub-branch and sub-sub branch, etc., breaking away from a main branch and forming its own cluster, the center point being there but no other main branches protruding from it. Oh, wait a minute. I now see a progression from this state. In this condition, the break-away cluster cannot grow The Original branch/sub-branch construct anymore because this is its natural limitation.

SE9: That limitation is one that I have put in place for reasons I may come to later.

ME: Yes, I see. Can I continue with what I have seen/am seeing?

SE9: Do carry on.

ME: The universal growth has to continue from the center point, creating a new main branch from which to grow new and subsequent branches and sub-branches. Eventually this process is continued as this cluster of multiverse expands and grows until there is no more room available. That is, there is no room available for universal growth to continue without a "universal" clash or overlap, which is not possible with this construct.

This is interesting. I really would like to know the reason for this ability to create new and independent multiversal clusters.

SE9: I am preparing for the time (event space) when The Origin expands its area of self-awareness.

I had come across this "preparation" for The Origin's expansion in area of self-awareness before, with the entities in Source Entity Seven's environment. From my vantage point, it was a very long way away, but the "behind the scenes" preparation that was going on told me that it was either not as far away as I thought, or this was such an important event that prior preparation needed to happen trillions of Earth years in advance. My mind creaked at the thought of all of the work that had happened to date and that which would happen in the event space leading up to The Origin's expansion.

ME: I get the impression that you are expecting to occupy a larger area within the newly opened area of The Origin than you do currently.

SE9: Yes, indeed. That is another reason why my entities are undertaking their current work. The need for them to be able to create a universe around themselves, one that is still in contact with their original universe and, of course, me, is to enable them to plan on my behalf for the time when the area of The Origin is expanded to the point there is the need to increase the level of experience opportunities. This must be done in areas of The Origin that are and will be uncharted, so to speak. Each of the clusters will be a part of me and my entities. In order for me to embark upon the work that I am doing, I will need to be separate but still as one.

The predicted vastness of this newly opened area of The Origin, although a mere fraction of a percentage point of its totality, was beyond current comprehension until recently. Now we, the Source Entities, know just how big the new area of Origin is, we need to put in a significant amount of preparation work to ensure we, how do you say, "hit the ground running," In lieu of this, I am using my entities to create localized multiversal and universal constructs— ones that are born from my essence that will allow them and, of course, me, to experience "faster" when the opportunity presents itself.

You wanted to know why I have created a multiversal construct that is the shape it is.

ME: I certainly do.

SE9: It's to do with the ability to move around The Origin. Believe it or not, The Origin has areas of energetic dimensional and frequential density. The dendritic shape of my multiverse is designed to allow the full integration of my smaller, break-away constructs and myself within these areas of "density." As you can imagine, some of these areas of density are also based upon other areas of Original Material that you are not aware of yet, the material used to create continuum-based environments being one of them.

ME: There are a number of other Original Materials then? What are they? Can you describe them to me?

SE9: I will need to consider this for a moment, for you, mankind incarnate, that is, are not yet ready for such knowledge.

ME: Why not? Surely one or two new environmental components can't be an issue. It can't be that difficult to pass on the information, can it?

SE9: I see that I will need to elaborate. It's a bit like knowing four elements in the periodic table but not knowing there is a periodic table to relate these elements to. If, for instance, you had the knowledge of those entities who incarnated in human vehicles in what you call the bronze age, you would only have been aware of around four metals, iron, copper, tin and the alloy created by mixing copper and tin, bronze. If I gave you a periodic table when you only had that level of knowledge of the elements and asked you to position these elements on it, you would not have believed that the other elements could or did exist, simply because you wouldn't have had the mental capacity nor, most importantly, the tools to detect and separate out those other elements from the Earth. This "medieval" knowledge level of the elements is basically where you are now. As a result, giving you a name for a few of the materials that are component parts of The Origin would not help you, for they would only be names, names that I have given to you. They would not be able to be detected with your current level of technology or predicted by your current level of mathematics. They would be meaningless words, for you would not be able to experience that which they describe, which incidentally you don't have the words or intellect to describe yet either.

ME: I accept that we are pretty un-educated in these matters, but could you describe just one or two to me, please. It would be most beneficial.

SE9: I see you have a thirst for understanding entity form factor, irrespective of whether they have one or not.

ME: I do, not just because it is something that mankind expects to see or experience, but it is something that mankind in its current level of evolution from a physical perspective can recognize and understand relatively easily.

SE9: I see. Well, then I had better give you an example of what you would call a "physical entity," one that exists in one of the universal branches.

ME: Fantastic. Actually, I have already received an image of such an entity. Its rather torpedo shaped!

SE9: If it is that your torpedoes are flat in shape, I would agree. I will send you more information on the entity you can perceive.

ME: Oh, I recognize that shape. It's similar to what we call a "Cuttlefish" here on earth. It is, indeed, torpedo-shaped in terms of it having an oval body that changes into a blunt pointed area. It has that both ends. If fact, it looks a little bit like another device we have here on earth, a "cruise missile."

SE9: Yes, I see the analogy, a rather horrible little device, I think. Why do you create such devices of destruction? Oh, I see. Physical mankind really is low down on the evolutionary ladder, isn't it?

ME: Sorry, it's not a good illustration of those of us who are working for the good of the planet. To be honest, most of the Earth population is abhorred by the use of such devices. I apologize for exposing you to what is our horrible truth, or at least part of it.

SE9: No need to apologize. It is where you, not YOU, but the collective you, physical mankind, is right now.

ME: Thank you for your understanding.

SE9: It's a pleasure. You are not the only civilization to have developed devices of destruction from the powers that have been bestowed upon you primarily for the use of good. Now then, why don't you get back to describing the form factor of the entity I showed you?

The Cuttlefish Entity

ME: I will. Thank you! As I was saying before, this entity looks like a Cuttlefish, as it has similar methods of movement at first glance. On the outside it has an array of hair like growths that undulate in various different ways creating movement, but it's not like movement in water. It's something completely different. Let me take a closer look. Oh, wow! That's incredible! Alongside the hair-like growths—no, sorry, above them—are a series of multi-colored circles/ellipses that change in color in time with the undulations of the hairs. When the hairs undulate, the area immediately surrounding the body of the entity appears to also change color, and it looks like it changes the energetic content of the surrounding energies. It's almost like it sets up an energy field that allows it to "slip" between the energies that are created by the energies used in the construction of the universal environment.

SE9: Let me see how I can describe this in a more illustrative way. If you consider a tank filled with self-healing silicone gel and push a football (Rugby ball to UK readers) into the gel from one side to the other, the gel would move away from the shape of the football, move over the surface and re-seal the gel at the back of the ball. If I continue this process of moving the gel away and over the skin of the ball, re-sealing at the back of the ball it moves through the gel until it meets the other end.

Now consider that the ball has a force field around it. In this instance, the gel moves a known distance away from the surface of the ball without the ball being pushed into it, which allows the ball to literally "fall" through the gel rather than need to be pushed or forced through it. Once in the gel, the ball can change its direction of travel by increasing the distance the field is from the surface of the ball on the side the ball needs to travel in and decreasing the distance the field is from the surface of the ball on the side that the ball is moving away from—thus allowing it to "fall" in the desired direction of travel. This is, in effect, the way the Cuttlefish entity moves around its environment in that particular universal environment. With, of course, the exception that the environment is not a silicon based gel.

ME: Let me get this straight though. Can I assume that the environment gives the entity some sort of resistance, enough resistance to warrant creating a forcefield with its "hair" and colored circle/ellipse function?

SE9: Yes, very good. I can't possibly describe to you what the actual environment is created from in reality, but I will give you an example that you can relate to. If I said to you that the whole environment was constructed on electromagnetic radiation that had no origin of production but was just "everywhere," would you be able to relate to that? (NOTE: An electromagnet has a ferrite core and a copper coil with electricity passed through the coil to create the magnetic field, GSN.)

ME: Yes, to some degree. Isn't that basically what Earth does? Ah, no, I see what you mean; Earth is the origin of production of its magnetosphere. What you are talking about is, for example, a magnetosphere, electromagnetic, in this instance, without a source.

SE9: Bulls Eye! The function of the features (hairs, etc.) on the side of the entity is to create a neutralizing effect together with an attractive force.

ME: I have also been seeing a number of energetic nodules of many various shapes and functions that appear and disappear. Would they be part of the function that helps move the direction of linear travel of the entity?

SE9: That is one of their functions, that is, in assisting in the navigation of the entity. Most of the directive force is created by the combinations of energies created by the hairs and the circle/ellipse functions. The hairs and the circle/ellipse functions can appear at any peripheral location of the entity allowing it to change direction, thus, affecting the functions of the nodules and how they interact with the surrounding energies. However, the nodules also provide the directional function in terms of navigation of the energies.

ME: I get the impression that these nodules operate a change in direction, a bit like how a surfer or snowboarder changes direction in a minor way by using his hand in the sea or snow to create a limited amount of "drag."

SE9: No, no, not in the slightest, although I can see where you are coming from. Ah yes, now I see, yes. If you use that analogy for the "dipping" in and out of the different energies and sensing what they are and their strengths/intensities, it might work as a concept for you. The different nodules are tuned to be receptive to the different energies in the environment the entity exists within. The nodules manipulate those energies locally with the hairs and the circle/ellipse functions creating the movement. The nodules extend and contract upon detection of the changes in the signature of the energetic environment and respond accordingly by creating a sympathetic energy set within the hair and circle/ellipse function that is designed to both repulse those energies away from the entity or create a vacuum for the entity to move into. The nodules create the changes necessary to the energies on the surface of the hairs required to attract the entity to those energies that were previously repulsed, which allows the entity to move into the vacuum area and closer to those energies again. All of this is happening on an instantaneous and continual basis to allow the entity to navigate the energies that pervade its universal environment.

ME: Incredible!

SE9: Nice, isn't it? But as I alluded to in the earlier conversation on this subject, the nodules also have another main function.

ME: Which is what?

SE9: The nodules create the localized universal environment necessary for the entity to navigate through the other universal sub-branches, branches and main trunk, as it were, of the construct of my main environment. In essence, it creates its own universe together with all of the functions required to move across to another location within the main universe it existed within before taking the opportunity to break away and increase its evolutionary content.

ME: How does it do that?

SE9: Over the period of its existence, the nodules help the entity create a map of the energies associated with the home universe. This map is generated and stored within the energetic structure of the entity over a period of time—that time being the age of the entity and the time it takes to visit and experience all the locations and energies associated with those locations within its home universe. If you like, it is a multi-dimensional, multi-frequential, multi-******, multi- ****** matrix.

ME: Hold on, what are those words that I could not translate/recognize? All I can do is put a star symbol down in their place.

SE9: Those are two of the other functions of my construct. They are beyond dimension, sub-dimensional component, frequency, energy and continuum.

ME: Yes, yes. You said that you had environmental construct componentry that was different than what I have previously experienced. Would you describe some (the two above) to me?

SE9: I will try to describe it in language and concepts that you will understand after we finish with this particular dialogue.

ME: Fine.

SE9: Once the entity has established a comprehensive, complete map of its home environment from ALL perspectives, it is then able to manipulate the "home" energies surrounding it to the point where they become part of both the home universe and the entity itself. The entity is able to manipulate these energies further to allow it to maintain the structure of this localized universal structure whilst experiencing and traversing another universal construct. Furthermore, it can also manipulate these energies to create a link to the home universe and ALL of the other local universes constructed by other entities that were originally from or currently within its home universe and effect translation to those localized universes for communion with them. It simply re-creates those energies relative to a specific location in the home universe and moves itself into it. In doing so, it actually effects a translation of itself to that location of desire.

ME: I just received an image of a snail. It's just as if these entities carry their own home (universe) with them.

SE9: What a good analogy. Yes, I like that one.

ME: I also see an image of two entities together. When they are together their localized universes converge creating a single local universe sympathetic to the energies of both entities.

SE9: Correct, yes they do. And it is quite common for entities to group together, creating a larger "bubble" of their home universe when visiting the same foreign universal branch.

ME: I see, yes. That would explain the images I have gotten of quite large bubbles of independent universe traversing the main trunk of one of your structural "trees," so to speak.

SE9: Yes, good.

ME: I have also noted that the entities in the bubble are able to perform all of their normal duties—duties that result in their evolutionary content increasing whilst moving closer to the center point of your construct—which brings them closer to you, and "unity."

SE9: Correct.

ME: OK, so the normal evolutionary work that the entities perform continues even when they are on the journey towards unity and the possible traversing of other trunks, branches and sub-branches to experience these "other" universes whilst being within the auspices of their own universe.

SE9: And correct again.

ME: So what is the point of an entity experiencing other universes when under the protection of its own environment?

SE9: Indeed, and a good question it is. You could consider this question yourself, for how does the human race experience the depths of your ocean or the area around your planet you call the vacuum of space?

ME: Good point. Ahh, are you suggesting that they can't actually exist in the other universes they are traversing?

SE9: I am. You got there eventually.

ME: Ohhh, that's interesting. What's more, for me, it is a huge departure from the use of a construct to visit other frequencies and dimensions, what we might call a spaceship.

SE9: Why is that?

ME: From what I can see, the construct, a local universe, is the vehicle for travel, continued existence, and communication with, and travel back to other localized universes with the same signature as the originating universe—including the actual universe of origin.

SE9: Correct again. You are getting good at this.

ME: Please forgive me, but I get the impression that you are making me understand the construction and functionality of your multiverse by my own connectivity with you rather than your telling me and me typing it into this book.

SE9: I am, and I am doing it on purpose. The Origin has asked that I help augment your receptiveness of higher information whilst in your current physical vehicle. In essence, letting you tell the story, so to speak, rather than me.

ME: Is that wise? I mean, the readers would give the information more credibility if it came from you rather than my own connectivity to your knowledge.

SE9: Agreed, but in showing your own ability to connect with me in a more fundamental basis, your readers will see that they can do it (this type of dialogue) themselves when they have the tools to do so.

ME: Thank you for that explanation. But help me out here, if it is possible to create an energetic construct to traverse dimensions and frequencies in my own multiverse, why cannot such constructs be used in your multiversal construct? Why do your entities need to create a local universe and not merely an energetic vehicle?

A Local Universe vs. an Energetic Construct as a Vehicle to Traverse Source Entity Nine's Multiverse.

SE9: You already know about the need for an energetic construct, whether it be mechanical or fully energetic in nature, from communications with your own Source Entity.

ME: I do in a limited sense. A construct of any design is required to maintain The Original environment of the traveling entities, ensuring they do not lose any of their functionality or faculties if they traverse lower frequencies by maintaining their integrity. This is a rule that operates even if they dip into "higher" frequencies or dimensions for travel purposes.

SE9: Excellent. Now think of other reasons why a construct may be necessary.

ME: What? Oh, now that's a difficult one to pull on me!

SE9: No, it's not. Draw upon the omniversal knowledge of The Origin and translate it into human language.

ME: I will try. Give me a moment.

SE9: Don't rush; you have all the time on Earth—literally.

What did that mean?

SE9: I read that thought. It means that I will assist you for as long as you need to address that particular task. Quite literally, I will take you out of time until you are able to address the task.

Well, I don't know if that actually happened. I am not even sure I would recognize such an act of manipulation of my own event space if it smacked me in the face, so I decided to carry on. It came fast.

ME: Contamination & longevity? What is all that about?

SE9: Burrow deeper.

ME: OK, right I will. Errmm, yes I see. I think. Ahh! Now I do see. A construct that we would call a spaceship or energetic construct is just that—a construct. It is created in the entities' original environment to perpetuate that environment in order to experience other environments without loss of function and faculty or indeed environmental conditions necessary to sustain the existence of the entity/ies using the construct.

SE9: Yes?

ME: Wow! You are a hard task master. Well, the problem here is that it is still of the original environment and, as such, is limited in its longevity once outside of that environment because it is reliant upon the universal energies associated with the universe of origin. What's more, I see that it carries a certain level of energetic content that is totally foreign to the environment being traversed. This creates a level of localized disharmony that affects not only the area of universe being traversed but also affects the energetic content of the entities in that locale in any way from minor to major harmonious dysfunction. This is the contamination, a contamination in energetic harmony.

SE9: Go on. You are half way there.

ME: We have seen this disharmony in a number of ways in the Earth Sphere. It manifests itself in freak and unpredicted weather, sudden disappearances of people and craft (air and sea) and again, the sudden loss of power across city-wide power grids. A fully universal construct, no matter how small, does not do this—simply due to its natural inherent construction genealogy, specifically in your environment.

Let me get this straight. A universe has its own unique set of frequencies and dimensions that are not connected with each other or with anything else but the multiverse it exists within. As a result of this, it maintains a certain level of duplicity, of interchange-ability of sameness, even though it is different in every other way. Now why is that? I see, it is of the material of the multiverse and not a synthetic construct. It is created by the creator or by the creator's creations if constructed in the same method or rhyme as the creator—under the auspices of the creator for the benefit of the creator. In this instance You, Source Entity Nine.

Not only that, the entity/ies that create the localized universe/s need to have risen to a certain level of evolution, as you previously said, to attain "creator" status. Once at creator status, they are made aware of the tools and methods of using the tools to create a universe in their own right. Basically, because the universe as an environment is a duplicate of that created by the creator, it carries no energetic disharmony nor longevity issues because as a universe it enjoys creator-given longevity with no end date, so to speak—unless, of course, the creator decides to end its existence, and it is able to move in-between the shear fabric of the universal environments it is traversing because it is essentially the same even though it is of a different set of construction rules for that particular set of multiversal content. In effect it is slippery, "none stick," so to speak!

Hold on, how can a universe that exists within a universe with that universe being used for transportation purposes be different whilst not being different enough, i.e., being considered the same but causing no resistance?

SE9: As you said yourself a moment ago, it has a different set of construction rules whilst using the same components. This is what makes it accepted by the universe it is traveling within whilst being a separate universal entity housing evolving entities.

ME: So it's the combination of universal components and sub-components that make it both individual whilst being essentially the same.

SE9: Yes, I can see that you are frowning so I will explain a little more using an example that is closer to home for you.

The human body is constructed by using a known number of DNA strands and their multiple variants or combinations. The variants give the opportunity to illustrate variation in body form and function. Some of these strands are shared with vehicles that are based upon the "animal" form factor with the DNA strand sequences being similar, if not identical, up to a certain point. Hence, the mouse genome is similar to the human genome, but the small differences in the sequencing create very different physical results. However, these similarities and concurrent differences are excellent examples of the way that the universe being traversed accepts the universe that is traversing it, for those similar or identical components are the ones that are presented to the universe being traversed. In essence, the universe being traversed, sensing that which is traversing it, recognizes it as its "self" and, therefore, does not reject or offer hindrance to the universe traversing it.

An Entity Made from Event Space

ME: I was very pleased with the description of one of your "physical" entities in our last series of dialogues. I found it most interesting to learn how it moved around its universal environment. I found it even more interesting to see how the universal constructs worked and how they interfaced with their own home universe and those universes that they traverse, as well as how they allow the entities that use them to undertake the work they need to do to evolve and get closer to communion with you. But I have noticed that leaving it here would not be a good idea, specifically because I asked to discuss two of your entities. As the one we just discussed was what you called physical in nature, I would like to discuss one that was not, in order to provide some balance.

What I would like to do now, with your permission, is to discuss an entity that is neither physical nor energetic in primary nature. If, indeed, you have an entity that is none of these types, that is.

SE9: Interestingly enough, I do have one entity that falls into not only that category but into a completely new thought process for you.

ME: Go on, you have got my attention now. What could this entity be like in form? Bearing in mind that it must also be able to create its own universal construct to traverse the trunks, branches and sub-branches of your multiversal construct.

SE9: Well, wait for it. Its form is based upon a function of space you know and recognize as "event space" in your own Source Entity's environment.

ME: What!!? How can that be? I mean, I wasn't expecting an entity that is based upon the very fabric of "event space" itself.

SE9: I thought you would like this one.

ME: You bet I do.

At this point of the dialogue with Source Entity Nine, I do have to say I was getting rather excited. I had experienced many strange, diverse and to be honest, downright impossible (to physical mankind) life forms over the last couple of years. Now though, I was about to discuss an entity that was based upon "event space." This was going to be good. I sat back in my chair, stretched my back, and logged in to Source Entity Nine again.

SE9: I am glad to see that you are enthusiastic about being exposed to the being you would call the "Henutrik."

ME: Wow, they have a name, and it can be recognized in English, too! Can I be cheeky and ask what the name of the previous entity was?

SE9: That particular race has a name, but it would be impossible to give a meaningful translation for you. Many of my races do not call themselves anything. It is just a coincidence that these two do. I can see, however, that you would like a name for the first entity.

ME: I would, thank you. No matter how poor the translation is, it would be good to have something.

SE9: Note then, that this word, although meaningless in the translative sense, can be used only for descriptive purposes for addressing the race represented by the previous entity.

ME: And the name is?

SE9: They can be related to as the Tareganuuuthokk. But as I said, this is meaningless, for there is no word, phrase or sound that can be used to describe what they call themselves collectively.

ME: And the event space based entities do?

SE9: It is only marginal, but yes.

ME: I find that incredible.

SE9: Why, there are many such races of entities, races that either have no descriptive name for themselves or that do not translate into the sound-based language you have as mankind within the environment of your own Source Entity, so why would it be incredible in my environment?

ME: Thank you for clearing that up for me. Let's focus on the Henutrik.

SE9: The Henutrik are constructed of the energies surrounding the space you call event space or a parallel universe. In essence, their existence is a result of myriad opportunities generated by the other entities that exist within my environmental construct.

ME: Are you suggesting that their existence is reliant upon the actions or possible actions of the other entities?

SE9: To a lesser extent, yes.

The Event Space Entity and Two New Universal Components

SE9: I will explain why because it will be way out of your comprehension. When an entity, that is, any entity, has a choice to make and eventually goes down a particular path, the intention to go down the other route/s, albeit partial, creates energy, the energy of intention. The energy of intention is not something you have discussed yet although you are aware of the resultant "action" as a follow-up from "intention." The energy of action is an energy created by an "intention" that is followed through or favored above all others rather than being discarded. An intention that is discarded creates the energy of "possible intention." These two energies are two new energy types for you to consider, as they are also integral and important parts of your own environment. Important, that is, because they are relevant to the "event space" that you experience whilst in the energetic state in your multiverse as well.

ME: Are you suggesting that apart from dimensions, sub-dimensional components, frequencies and continuum, what I consider to be the basic building blocks of a universe or multiverse, there are also two more to consider, "probability-based" intentional energy (PBIE) and "action-based" intentional energy (ABIE).

SE9: Yes, of course. And what's more they are both essential components. Even though they may not be as apparent as the components you have just illustrated, they are still some of the most important components of a multiversal environment.

All energies or multiversal constructional components, including those environments you call continuum, are fully capable of developing self-awareness and sentience. This is the same for the components you have abbreviated to PBIE and ABIE. The main difference with these two components is that they are capable of being both sentient and individualized. The sentience is a normal result of longevity of pure existence. The individuality is a normal result of the collated intention-based thought of both the PBIE and ABIE thought processes. This individuality can also be classified as a memory—the memory function maintaining the plethora of "event space" in terms of "actual" events and "possible" events. This includes those events that were merely a thought and later became actuality, as well as those events that were the "desired" action that later became "discarded" due to completion and subsequent progression on to the next event space or were simply the result of a "change of mind" (see below).

In essence, PBIE and ABIE energies are of the same family whilst being independently important. The discriminating factor between the two is the strength or type of intentional thought created by an entity in its current location. If the intentional energy is strong, it can be attributed to the "action"-based intentional energy (ABIE). If it is weak, it will be attributed to the "possibility"-based intentional energy (PBIE). Varying grades of weakness are experienced and are relative to the possibility of the "action"-based intention being abandoned in favor of another possibility during actual delivery of the action. This is sometimes called a "change of mind." This would be a strong energy but not stronger than an action that was followed through. The lower grades of energy are attributable to the number of possibilities that are available and the level of dilution of strength based upon the potential for those possibilities to become actions or not, as the case may be later.

ME: So these entities are essentially the energies created by the memories or the energies surrounding the memories of all of the possible events or actual events (actions) related to an entity, group of entities or civilization.

SE9: Nice description. They are an important part of the superstructure of any environment, for they are the glue that binds it all together.

ME: Now I feel that I have missed something. I certainly don't think that I deserve your praise.

SE9: Your description was "spot-on," so to speak, even if you did not entirely understand what you were saying. I will elaborate a little more for completeness.

These entities are specific to my environment and exist within the core or that part of the construct that connects all the "trunks" together. In your environment they are a different type of entity but only as a result of the different event space that is created. Generically, each event space entity is an energy surrounding a particular event or possible event. Some entities are a series of events if the action has not yet been progressed. The event space entity is as previously described, the memory of all that is associated with a particular event. This includes the links to the energies and the entities and the specific universe they are generated within. Because they contain all of the energies associated with a particular event or string of events in a particular universe, they are everything that that event space is in its entirety. In essence, they are the only reason that event space exists. The event space entities only exist because they are self-aware entities generated by the creation of intentional energy and their desire for self-perpetuation. This desire for self-perpetuation results in the perpetuation of the event/s within their event space.

ME: So for the benefit of the reading public, I would like to gain more information about these entities because I can imagine that they, like me, will be scratching their heads—especially with the thought that the two different types of energy—energies specific to events created by intention—create both event memory and eventually a self-aware and fully sentient entity. Not only that, once the entity is self-aware, the desire for self-perpetuation, is the only reason for the perpetuation of the event/s themselves.

Sorry people, but I felt that this was a very important concept to get across.

This is a little bit "chicken and egg to me." For instance, what happens to those event space entities associated with the normal entities who created them through intention when those normal entities move away from one event space and into another. Does that event space entity wink out of existence?

SE9: No, for that event space is not only maintained by the entity that created the original intention, it is also maintained by those entities that are associated with the entity that created The Original intention. In essence, as long as one normal entity is operating within that event space, the event space entity is held in perpetuity, i.e., its existence is maintained. But this is only a prerequisite for continued existence in the formative period of its existence.

ME: What do you mean "this is only a prerequisite for continued existence in the formative period of its existence"? Are you telling me that once they are in existence for a certain or known period of, let's use that word "time" that they are able to sustain themselves without the need for any other entity existing in or working with the energies of intention that created the event space and, therefore, the event space entity itself?

SE9: Yes, that is correct. In effect, that is the desired function of the event space entity—to exist long enough in self-awareness, perpetuated by the energetic function of the ABIE and PBIE to be able to create their own event space.

ME: They are able to create their own event space?

SE9: Yes, but first they must be created. You see, even in your own Source Entity's multiversal environment, the "event space" must be created by the intentions of entities, such as yourself. The difference between the event space/s within your own environment is that they are perpetuated as a function of your Source Entity. My event space is perpetuated as a function of the sentience of the energies surrounding and created by the intentions of other entities. Once the event space has been in existence long enough to be maintained by a critical mass of normal entities, it starts to gain its own sentience. This personalized sentience is created or generated as a direct result of the total and combined ABIE and PBIE, which need to be interspersed together in equality to allow the sentient formula or program, if you like, to be initiated. When that critical mass of normal entities starts to reduce to a level below that required to kick off the sentient program and the event space has already started becoming sentient, its program is continued and allowed to finalize in the normal way. Should a reduction in the critical mass of normal entities fall below that required to kick off the sentient program, and the program has not yet started, then that area of event space will not become sentient. Of course, it can start to become sentient should the critical mass be re-achieved and maintained long enough to allow the program to start.

ME: So not all of your event spaces are sentient entities in their own right?

SE9: No, simply because those that are not sentient are what you would call "work in progress." That does not mean that they are not important, for all areas of event space are important, whether sentient or not. It's just that they are not yet sentient enough to be classified as entities in their own right.

The most important level of existence that an event space entity can achieve is the level of self-sustaining self-awareness which results in sentience. Once an event space entity has achieved this, it is in the right area, call it a "ball park" in your own language, to become self-perpetuating with or without a mass, critical or non-critical, of "so called" normal entities that are using their intention to create event space energies or forces that are either ABIE or PBIE-based. This gives them a level of independence, as well as interdependence with other event space entities. The independence creates the perpetuation of event space detail and the links between other event spaces, thus creating the total landscape of myriad events that either are or could have been pursued.

ME: In my own environment, the event space, as you quite rightly identified, is a function of my own Source Entity. Its perpetuated existence is available for the use of those entities who desire to understand the myriad possibilities available to them if they take a certain route or make a certain decision if there is more than one route or choice to be taken/made. It is also part of the Akashic records and those other records that are also "Akashic" (everlasting and pliable) for use by other entities within my own Source Entity's environment. Is the perpetuation of event space "events" as important in your own environment as it is in my own?

SE9: Yes, of course. It is more important. This is a direct result of the event space becoming sentient and the fact that it is mobile as a result.

ME: Hold on, event space entities are mobile? I would have expected them to be immobile even if they are sentient.

I had just received an image of event space entities all huddled together on a single but level playing field. In the image none of the event space entities were stacked above or on top of the others. It was as if they were all parked close to each other in a supermarket car park.

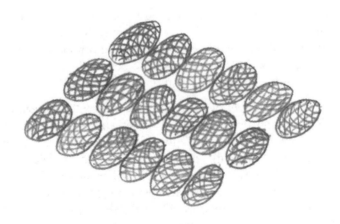

Figure 1: Event Space Entities

154

SE9: Your imagery illustrates the function of event space entities within my environment and not that which is prevalent in your own environment where all event spaces are in contact with each other or linked either by direct or indirect association to each other. Although it may look somewhat linear in its imagery the "collective" event space, that flat plain (playing field or car parking lot) of event space entities are in contact with each other in myriad ways. One of those methods of contact may well interest you because it is the reason why an event space that is no longer held in perpetuity by the intentional energies of local normal entities is not only maintained but is allowed to exist in its own right.

ME: Go on. Stop teasing me! In which way are they in contact with each other? Other than the normal links between one event space and another, which is a function of moving from one event space to another or indeed the interdependence of "event" resulting from the co-operation between two or more entities whose event space converges for some limited time. Is it this link which keeps event space entities both interdependent whilst also being dependent on their own events?

SE9: Well done. You are almost on it. You are so close that I will finalize the discussion myself.

It is simply the minor interactions with other event spaces, sentient or not, that keep the event space in existence when it is not at the point of sentience and subsequent self-sustenance. When self-aware, self-sustained and self-perpetuating, the event space entity can move about that "space" that is assigned for the sole use of the event space entities. Who, it has to be said, can be classified as either "previously existing," "currently existing," and "currently/potentially existing."

These minor interactions are minor in relevance, intensity and perpetuity. The interesting point to note here is that the links between the different event spaces and event space entities are in a constant state of flux—flux, that is, in terms of their contact with each other.

ME: I am getting the impression that the event space events that are maintained by the event space entities are moved on a regular basis. The movement is a function of the quality of event that such transient interaction could or can generate when activated.

155

SE9: Correct. The whole point of the movement, the disassociation and re-association of event space between two or more areas of event space/event space entities is the offer of links between differing events even though they are not "normally" linked. These "abnormal" links do not have a ready association/interdependence between the events, but they do offer the opportunity of studying what "could be" whilst seeing "what is." That part of the event space that is normally linked to another part of the event content of an event space entity being removed, isolates that event from the "holding" event space entity and allows it to be linked with another event space within another independent event space entity and thus, identifying myriad new evolutionary opportunities resulting from the new association with another event space entity.

ME: That's amazing. I get the impression (actually I received another image) that although one would expect your environment to be covered with enough event space entities to deal with the total environmental volume, that doesn't exist. Instead, you have event space gaps—areas of darkness where the events that occur are not recorded.

SE9: More than that. They are not able to be used by the normal entities in my environment.

ME: Hold on, isn't that a bit "chicken and egg" again? If a normal entity cannot traverse that area where there are no event space entities to hold and record the events that take place there, then how can the normal entities create the PBIE and ABIE energies that create the events and, therefore, the opportunity for the event space to become sentient?

SE9: These gaps or areas that you call darkness are areas where the current areas of event space and the subsequent event space entities can expand into. If you like, it is reserved "space" for the use of expansion only.

ME: How does that work? In my limited understanding, event space and, therefore, the event space entities in your environment, would not be limited to spatial requirements because event space is "outside space" itself.

SE9: Correct, but it does have limitations. Those limitations are me, the environment of my event space, for I am like the other Source

Entities, a subset and, therefore, a compartmentalization of the energies, dimensions, sub-dimensional components and frequencies that were given to me by The Origin when it created me. From your perspective, of course, I have no such limitations, but in my perspective all environmental conditions that I create are within those conditions that I was created with.

To be honest I was having quite a bit of trouble with this, for I expected (my fault, one should never overlay one's own expectations on a communication such as this) that event space was basically unlimited.

ME: OK, I am struggling a bit with this. If there are limitations based upon your own structural condition, what are they?

SE9: Simply put, that amount of me that is reserved for the use of event space.

ME: But I would have thought that which is event space would literally pervade you, be everywhere.

SE9: It is.

ME: But, now help me out here, you just said that it wasn't?

SE9: Event space is limited by the number of permutations that can or would occur should an entity have a choice or series of choices to make. This is augmented by the number of entities that enters into or, indeed, link event spaces together through association with other entities. When an event space has reached its maximum permutation level, it is allowed to occupy, on an automatic basis, that area within me that is reserved for event space. There are periods . . .

I noticed that Source Entity Nine went to great lengths then, to not mention the word "time."

. . . when those "event" permutations are reduced as a natural consequence of latent convergence. Latent convergence is experienced when a series of event spaces line up again after going off the main-line, the previous events being a mere distraction or detour. This leads to a natural reduction in the area used for that major part of event space that is being used to fulfil the total number of events from the start of an entity's existence or role to the end of that existence or role. The result of the reduction is the areas of darkness that you saw in your mind's eye. Those areas where there is no event space and, therefore, no entities can traverse except for the entity that had the most to contribute to that event space. Based upon this, that area of emptiness is reserved for the expansion of that particular event space and cannot be used for the use or expansion of other event spaces. It is already pre-designated.

ME: So that would explain why other entities cannot traverse that space because, in essence, it is event space, space. That is, non-sentient event space.

SE9: Very well done. But before we change the direction of our communication, please note this. Sentient event space, by us called "event space entities," maintain their own area of event space, if you like. This means that once they have reached a size that is consistent with the maximum permutation level that could have been achieved when they were interacting with a normal entity, that they can maintain that size.

ME: Do you mean that they do not shrink? That an area of darkness is not created?

SE9: No, for that is a function of "non-sentient event space" and not "sentient event space," an event space entity. Once an area of event space has become sentient, it is in full command and control of those energies that created it in the first place. As a result it can and does maintain its own existence and, therefore, its own structure and size.

Two More Universal Environmental Components

I was just deciding that it was time to move on and question Source Entity Nine about another part of itself—its environment—when I had a little niggle in the back of my mind. The niggle suggested that the two intention-based energies of PBIE and ABIE were not the only energies that could be described as new, or should I say previously discovered, or undisclosed universal components. Filled with the inspiration that is only available to an explorer surveying a new and undiscovered land, I dove head long into questioning Source Entity Nine on what else could possibly be classified as a universal component.

I mean, it was reasonably simple for me in my limited incarnate state to understand that full dimensions were constructed with three sub-dimensional components and that each sub-dimensional component was inflated with twelve frequency bands, one of which contains a whole simultaneous universe. Once, that is, we get past the need for a base full dimension with that full dimension constructed as a three-in-one system made up of the three sub-dimensional components with only one set of twelve frequency bands inflating all three sub-dimensional components, all of which house a single universe in all its physical and energetic states. I even felt that the average incarnate human could understand this as well, especially with the aid of a diagram. I could even understand that event space was constructed of those energies associated with action-based intention and probability-based intention. But what else could be out there was a complete mystery to me. The possibility of discussing a new universal component, one that had as much importance in the maintenance of any Source Entity's multiverse was awesome. I could wait no longer. My impatience was obvious!

ME: So, what ARE they?

I told you I was impatient dear reader.

SE9: What are what?

ME: The two new universal components I am seeking to discuss with you. I need to discuss these before I move on to Source Entity Ten. I really get the impression that this is very important.

SE9: So I see. Well, so far you have discussed five universal components in total: three with your own Source Entity and two with me. Now you want two more.

ME: Yes, please.

I was starting to get anxious.

SE9: Mmmm, OK, I will assist you in this quest. First, you will need to note that the components you called ABIE and PBIE can really only be classified as one component, and this is because they are the Yin and Yang of each other. One is the full and dedicated action; the other is all the possibilities that could have been taken. Together they create one event space, and as such, event space can be considered a single component even when it gains individual sentience.

ME: Thank you. I think that will make it clear in every one's mind when you explain it in that way.

SE9: Good. It was necessary to get that concept across for it is the foundation for the next concept that you will be discussing with me; the two universal/multiversal components that you are seeking are also interdependent in an equal and simultaneous way.

ME: OK, I can wait no longer. . . Hold on. . . .

I was finding that my communication had slowed right down.

. . . are you still there?

SE9: Yes. One moment please. The information on these components is not directly translatable into your sound based language or even any form of higher energetic language you have brought with you from the energetic. I will need to find some sort of concept that you can relate to that can be used as a bridging tool.

I sat and waited at my computer, wondering what could be so similar in conceptual understanding here on earth that it could be used as a bridging tool used to explain an indescribable universal component. I didn't have to wait long.

SE9: OK, I have a concept that you can use to help you understand. I want you to consider an energy that isn't energy.

ME: Action and reaction just came into my mind.

SE9: Yes, that would be a good start, for they are the Yin and Yang of each other.

ME: Mmmm, wasn't the last two multiversal components—those that created your version of event space and the subsequent event space entities interdependent of each other? That being the environment or that part of the total environment cannot exist without them both together? Just one will not create the conditions necessary for sustaining the structure of the environment. Is this the way it works with these two components? And while I am in the chair, so to speak, this sounds a bit Newtonian to me, i.e., every action has an equal and opposite reaction. Would I be right with this?

SE9: First, the words "action and reaction" are not intended to be fully descriptive in this instance, specifically because there is not a direct translation of the functionality of them into your English. Second, they do need each other to create the resultant component which is a foundation component of that used in event space. If you like and using the analogy to radio wave engineering that your own Source Entity used in your first book, it is the carrier wave, the "space" that is used to house the action-based intention energy (ABIE) and the probability-based intention-based energy (PBIE). And third, together they do not function in the Newtonian fashion that you are expecting to understand. Actually I think my choice of words was poor in this instance, but unfortunately they are the only ones that work.

ME: Actually the words and the interaction with event space, the description of action and reaction that when together function as a carrier wave works very well for me. It actually makes total and perfect sense. Specifically when one considers that both the intentional energies of PBIE and ABIE are actionary. That is, the probability-based intention and the action-based intention energies (PBIE & ABIE) are the result of action. Action or the possibility of action of some sort, being available as the decision-based components of a specific entity's intention, the desire to choose one route or direction or task over another. The result of which is an energy. That energy needs to be present in some way before the new event space can be created. Phew!

SE9: Good. You are getting there. I will explain further if you don't mind, for there is a function of this building block that you have not ascertained.

ME: I am not surprised. My mind was in overdrive to sort out the words for the limited description I just gave.

To be perfectly honest, the nine or so lines above took something like 20 minutes to write. Not good when one has a personal deadline to achieve, I can tell you. This is, however, the name of the game. One day it flows; another day it is like getting blood out of a stone. In fact, I sometimes think that getting blood out of a stone would be easier. But then I am communicating with an entity, a Source Entity, no less, that is eight multiverses away from my home multiverse. A little bit of lag in understanding the concepts being presented to me is, therefore, acceptable.

ME: OK, I have had my little interlude. Let's hear the rest of the explanation of the functionality of this/these multiversal component/s.

SE9: Thank you. I want you to consider the human translation of the words I have used for this component: action and reaction. What do they mean to you?

ME: I would have used the Newtonian explanation normally, but I can see that you are looking for another level of understanding.

SE9: Yes, please.

ME: Well, I had better start with the Newtonian version first, as not all of my readers will know it even though it is classic physics.

For those of you out there who don't know the Newtonian law, it goes like this,

"For every action there is an equal and opposite reaction."

The best way of explaining this is to remember the Newtonian cradle where a number of ball bearings are suspended from a frame by a cord in a line. When at rest, the ball bearings are just touching each other so that when one of them, the one on the end, is lifted away from its neighbor and allowed to drop, it swings on the cord and subsequently hits its neighbor, so the energy that was in the ball that was dropped is passed between all of the ball bearings in the line which results in the ball bearing on the end of the line taking the energy and subsequently moving off in the same direction that the ball bearing that was dropped was traveling—when the ball reaches the end of its swing, it returns and hits its own neighbor, sending the energy back to the original ball bearing which then moves off or swings out in the opposite direction it was going in the first place. In this instance, the action is the initial movement and its direction, with the reaction being the change in direction of the energy that results in the ball bearing receiving the energy back and swinging in the opposite direction of The Original direction of travel. The only issue here is that this is not a perfect illustration as the energy received back is not the same amount or value as that given to the neighboring ball bearing in The Original impact. There is a loss in the energy, and the process is, therefore, not an equal and opposite reaction. The only way of explaining this properly then is to use another example, one where we are standing on supposedly solid ground and that the reason we don't sink into the ground that we stand on is because there is an opposite reaction to the downward force of our weight according to gravity. But again this is not perfect as the ground does, in fact, deflect a certain amount due to the density of the ground being stood upon. In the perfect world, there is no loss of energy received by the ball bearing and no deflection in the ground that we stand on.

SE9: That is a very good understanding of the errors in the current thinking of mankind and the use of certain physics as being not only basic but also the fundamentals required to understand the rest of physics. The issue here is the "lossy" function of the so-called fundamentalism of the law being used as a datum—in this instance, the law being that every action has an equal and opposite reaction, which it clearly does not.

ME: Ok, I am losing it now. Is that a "lossy" function of my mind?

SE9: Very clever use of words. What was the point of using them?

ME: Well, what I am getting to is that I don't understand where you are going with this line of communication.

SE9: And I thought that you had made the link, especially as you were doing so well with the description of the Newtonian example of the perfect state of action and re-action as an "equal and opposite" re-action to the action, and that it was not the case! Oh well, I had better explain then.

The whole point of what you have just described is that there is no such thing as an equal and opposite reaction. Every time there is an action, the reaction is dependent upon a number of factors, such as the environment and "that" which affects the environment. For example, you used the rather good illustration of the ground "giving way" in some way when you stand on it or apply a weight to some part of it. The amount of "give" is relative to the composition of the ground. This includes all materials manufactured by mankind, by the way.

ME: You mean concrete and steel are compressible, that they are subject to "give"?

SE9: Yes, of course. Even the hardest composition has "give." This is the beauty of existence in your environment. Things that you think are solid are, in fact, not solid. In the Newtonian cradle illustration, the losses were obvious because when one observes the actions of the ball bearings moving back and forth, the viewer notices that they lose inertia-based energy every time they change direction.

ME: But they wouldn't in a vacuum-based environment or one that was not affected by gravity.

SE9: Oh yes, they would—simply because of the interaction with the other larger bodies that you have in the physical universe—those areas of local density you call planets and stars.

ME: OK, you've got me on the run now. I was about to say what is the point of this discussion but I think that I can see it now.

You stated that there is no such thing as an equal and opposite reaction to an action, but, I suspect that in your environment there is but that this is a function of the give and take of the two components of action and re-action. That is, sometimes the re-action is greater or has more energy associated to it than the actual action itself. Am I correct here?

SE9: Yes, well done. This is why it is a yin and yang-based description. They are equal but not <u>always</u> equal at a specific point in their interaction with each other. In essence, they "move around" each other and in doing so, they create that which is necessary for the ABIE and PBIE to function.

You see, there has to be an alternative option for both ABIE and PBIE to even exist. That option is the opposite of the other: one being the actual action taken, the other being the possible action that could have been taken. Both of these energies are generated by the entity creating them, but they have to come from somewhere. They have to be created from a base material of some sort, and that base material is the action and re-action, the carrier wave that they exist within and on.

ME: So the action and the re-action is not an energy that is independent of itself and its own component parts. It is like the threads of a string—two threads to be precise, intertwined with each other, each creating a single piece of string but together rather than being separate. Each has areas different than the other in terms of their cross-sectional areas, but the total always equals the optimal total should they be both the same and consistent cross-sectional areas.

SE9: Correct.

ME: Whew! Now let me get this straight then as I am starting to be able to understand the philosophy of ABIE and PBIE and its constituent parts of action and re-action. When you told me that action and re-action were the components and basis of existence of ABIE and PBIE, you said that it was like a carrier wave that is used for the transmission, for want of a better word, of the newly created or already existing ABIE and PBIE—that which is created by the creating entity as a function of the decision process of going this way or that way. One is the actual decision and, therefore, the direction taken while the other is relegated to the possible decision that could have been taken and, therefore, the possible direction that could have been taken.

SE9: Keep going!

ME: Well, it's almost like the events and interfaces. I mean everything that happens from meeting new entities, working with a new material to create something. To make it easier, let's use some of my earth-based terminology here—such as a house, a car, a computer, a park bench, is created from the energies that were what you call "action" and "reaction." Everything is in like a "store." Everything that has the ability to be created can be created from this base energy—all actions that are or will be taken, including all of the interfacing objects are already in existence. All we have to do is go down a certain route, and they are taken out of storage, so to speak, and are manifest into useful existence. This also includes all the possibilities as well. All that could be possible is also in storage within this action and re-action carrier wave just in case a change of direction is taken, one that is not or could not have been, foreseen.

SE9: Yes, carry on.

ME: Well, I see this image of the string—and I fully understand that this is just in my mind for illustrative purposes—that is covered with entities. Every time an action is made, a piece of the string is pulled out to create the Action-Based Intentional Energy. When this ABIE energy is pulled out, a ripple effect is sent down the length of the "never ending and infinite" action and re-action string, putting in place all of those things that will happen as a result of the decision that has just been made. On the other side though, there is another piece of string being pulled out, creating the Probability-Based

Intentional Energy for all of those things that "could" happen should the action change for whatever reason to the "probable" rather than the "actual" action. In this instance, the action and the re-action are the yin and yang of each choice and the energies created or used by such choices—that is, those that were taken and those that were not but nevertheless could have been.

SE9: And now you have it.

Yet Another Component of Event Space! (Two Components??)

ME: So that's it. Those are the two components that make the possibility of event space work at least in your environment: 1) the action and reactionary components that allow the entity to create the energies of action; and 2) Probability-Based energies, which ultimately create the event space that is being experienced and could have been/ might be experienced. Right?

SE9: Well, not quite. You see, there is something else that sticks (glues) them both together—something that is independent of all four (three if you consider the action and reaction as the yin and yang of each other).

ME: Somehow I knew this was going to happen.

SE9: Please explain?

ME: It's just that it couldn't be that simple. There had to be some other complication to the function of event space in its continued manifestation.

SE9: Let me see. Ah, yes, the incessant desire for mankind to know everything in the blink of an eye whilst not having the ability to understand it nor the capability to store it—this is something to behold. This is something else I was warned about, for want of better words. In this instance, it is manifest in the "knowing" that there is something else, some deeper meaning, even when there is not.

I will have to consider this for a moment.

Mmmm, Mmmm, yes now I understand.

It is a function of your own ability that makes you "know" that you may be able to experience something else. What's more, you have your own incessant desire to know more as well. This is a human trait you have picked up, for as "OM" you would not need such a desire, for all knowledge is laid out before you—ready for the taking, so to speak. So in essence this extra information is not necessary for you as OM to "know" even whilst incarnate, for you already do "know."

How could I know but not know? This was one question I must ask before moving on from Source Entity Nine and starting my dialogue with Source Entity Ten, who is I "know" (here we go again) waiting for me to finish with Source Entity Nine and initiate communications with it. I had better hurry. The question did not need to be asked though.

SE9: When I talk about YOU, I talk about that which is the real YOU and not that part of YOU which is incarnate and, therefore, not YOU. Therefore, that part of YOU that is incarnate cannot "know" all there is whilst the rest of YOU, that is the real YOU, that which is not incarnate, can and does "know" all there is or more importantly can "know" what it wants to "when" it wants to by connecting with The Origin.

ME: Thank you. I believe that answers that question rather nicely.

SE9: I will continue with the description I started on then, for it is important that you understand this last bit of the puzzle that is event space.

There is a function of the Action and Probability-Based Intention Energies called "Spontaneous Intention." This is the glue that holds the action and re-action "carrier wave" together.

ME: This sounds a bit bizarre. How can an energy that needs a carrier wave to work be the glue that holds that very carrier wave together?

SE9: Consider that Spontaneous Intention is, in fact, an energy or energetic component in this instance that is independent of the other energies that have been discussed. Moreover, also consider that although this energy is independent from the need to be associated with other energies, it is a necessary component of those others. This means that it can and does exist in a singular fashion whilst those other energies around it need it to exist. In essence, if the function of Spontaneous Intention is not there, then the other energies cannot exist.

167

ME: But this means that, and let me get this right, if the function of Spontaneous Intention does not exist in a certain area within your environment, then the rest of event space cannot or should not exist. What's more, "intention," albeit the action and Probability-Based intentional energies, are the very thing that is being supported by the action and re-action carrier wave. So from my viewpoint the carrier wave supports the event space that is based upon either ABIE or PBIE energies which are, in turn, supported by another form of intentional energy called "spontaneous intentional energy," which can and is spontaneously created or available. It all looks very "möbius loop" like to me. What is within is without and what is without is within. THE manifestation of the first manifestation is not able to exist without the second manifestation being manifested, which in turn, cannot exist without the first manifestation being manifest. Again, a classic chicken and egg situation.

SE9: Correct.

ME: I am trying not to use the word "but" here again as the start to two sentences in a row, but—I failed—that means that whole tracts of you are or should be *empty*, for what of a better word.

SE9: And correct again, but—and now I have used the "but" word myself—as it's also NOT correct, for it doesn't take into account "LATENT" Spontaneous Intention.

ME: Now just what is "Latent" Spontaneous Intention?

SE9: Exactly what it is—Spontaneous Intention that is waiting to happen!

ME: But if—Arrggghh, that "but" word again!!!—Spontaneous Intention is to be just that, spontaneous, then how can it possibly be latent? For *latent* negates the description of *spontaneity*.

SE9: I will explain, hopefully, without using that word (but) which is causing you a "literary" issue at the moment.

Spontaneous Intention is two things:

1. Firstly, it is an energy that is based upon the fact that an entity may do, can do, or even will make a decision that is not on the cards, plan or route, whichever way you want to describe it. It is a spontaneous decision created by a spontaneous intention to make that decision. It is "out of the

blue," so to speak, and as such is generated by the entities that exist within that part of my environment they wish to be in, not on a continual basis but on a "one-off" spontaneous basis. However, even though it is produced on a "one-off" basis, it needs to be "within" existence for it to be called "into" existence in the first place—hence, the additional function of latency.

2. Secondly, Spontaneous Intention is the catalyst that allows the "carrier wave" of action and reaction to become manifest. It is the reason for its being in existence. From the moment an entity is in a condition of self-awareness, its first item of creativity is of a spontaneous fashion, that is, it is not a calculated decision process based upon the weighing of a number of factors before making that decision or choice. Once the carrier wave of action and re-action is in existence, it creates a spontaneous intention to do something that, in turn, creates the carrier wave of action and reaction. That carrier wave is in existence "specific" to the creating entity and is manifest for the whole period that the entity is in existence—existence for as long as it is a "singular" part of me. This includes all those entities that it interfaces with/interfaced with it and that they interface/interfaced with in totality.

Now we get to Latent Spontaneous Intention.

Latent Spontaneous Intention is that energy which is reserved within me for that which is created at the first point of self-awareness of an entity. It can be considered the "in-rush" current (Amps) that an electric device on earth experiences when it draws what it needs to activate all of the components of its construction simultaneously when initially being switched-on. For example, an electric motor will draw much more current during the "in-rush" of current required to get the "cold and stationary" armature rotating at its desired rotational speed for the load it is supporting than it does during the function of normal running in the warm rotating state.

The inrush current, in this instance, is a spontaneous effect of turning the switch on to allow the motor to run as a result of being exposed to electricity. This spontaneous effect dissipates as the motor achieves its optimal "normal" running speed and the higher current is no longer necessary. In essence ALL that extra current returns back to its source (its generated source) and becomes latent again, waiting to be used in the future.

This is the same for Latent Spontaneous Intention, for it is within me at all times. It is an essential part of my energetic make up and one that waits for the first moment that an entity makes its first decision, no matter where it is within my environment. Therefore, by definition Latent Spontaneous Intention must be everywhere and nowhere simultaneously, for "once" it has been used by an entity, it no longer needs it. But until an entity reaches the point at which it is self-aware, it needs it. Latent Spontaneous Intention is, therefore, always ready and waiting for that point in an entity's existence when it becomes self-aware, ready to use it, a "once only" usage created/manifested in its first decision, a decision without process or choice, de-manifesting when Spontaneous Intention is subsequently manifested, creating the carrier wave of action and re-action which, in turn, creates the use of Action-Based Intentional Energy (ABIE) and Probability-Based Intentional Energy (PBIE).

ME: Thank you for that. It is most informative, and what's more—understandable.

SE9: Now you have the six basic components of event space. Each of them dependent or interdependent of the other. And now you have this important information, it is time for you to move on, for the Source Entity you are calling Source Entity Ten is tapping on my shoulder, metaphorically speaking, saying, "MY turn now."

Finishing with Source Entity Nine and New Dialogue with The Origin

Even as Source Entity Nine made its last communication, a communication that ended in a bit of a "bang" so to speak—what a subject to end on: the components of event space—I felt its presence withdraw and its energetic signature being replaced by another: the energies associated with Source Entity Ten. They felt like a square peg going into a square hole, no lack of synchronicity was felt. The lack of energetic synchronicity was common place during the dialogues with the Source Entities associated with "Beyond the Source." Now I felt none. It would seem that I was starting to get the

*hang of the different energies associated with these more distant
Source Entities even though it was on an automatic basis.*

*"Three to go," I heard in my mind's ear. "Three to go!" But I
wasn't saying this!*

*Tears came into my eyes; I was on the verge of sobbing! And then I
knew why.*

*This was The Origin speaking. It had been a long time—well, at least
for me.*

O: Well, well, well, what a star you are becoming!

ME: What do you mean—a star?

O: You have gotten all my Source Entities lined up, waiting to talk
to you.

ME: All of them?!

O: All of them.

ME: Are you including Source Entity Twelve, the one that isn't
currently "self-aware"?

O: Yes, including Source Entity Twelve, the one that is currently
becoming self-aware.

ME: I thought Source Entity Twelve's becoming self-aware was
millennia away at best.

O: It was, but you have caused such a commotion that it has noticed
something external to itself and as a result is "becoming."

*Now at this point, dear reader, I had to check up on myself, for this
seemed all very egotistical to me. The very thought that I could cause
such a commotion—one big enough that it starts the awakening
process in a Source Entity—is, well, downright ridiculous. Isn't it?
Fortunately, I had some help from The Origin on how to maintain
both my mental sanity and keep my ego well and truly in place.*

O: Well, the best thing to do is not to think of it as purely a function
of your own activity. That would be egotistical. No, the Source
Entity you refer to as Source Entity Twelve was on the point of self-
awareness for some time anyway. You are, as you say on earth, in
the right place at the right time.

ME: My own Source Entity told me that Source Entity Twelve could be "unaware" for millennia though?

O: And it could have been millions upon billions of years before it entered into the process of becoming self-aware. It's just that with the energy dynamics of one such as you demanding the attention of the other Source Entities, and what's more getting it, this created an energy ripple or eddy that caught Source Entity Twelve's attention and "kick started" the process of it becoming self-aware. As I said, it was on the cusp of this anyway. It could have started the process itself tomorrow, or not as the case may be, for the next couple of millions of your years. You have just helped a bit.

ME: Well, I am glad to be of some little service in this major event. And thank you for helping to put me back into some sort of peace of mind. I really don't want people to think that I am delusional. That would ruin the opportunity to broadcast the information I am receiving from these most interesting entities.

Now tell me, why did you say "Three to Go, Three to Go"?

O: Because there are three to go, and I am actually looking forward to our dialogue. I like the name you have decided on, "The Origin Speaks." Very good. Did you think of this all by yourself? No, don't answer; I know that you know that I gave it to you. Seriously though, you are within a year of finishing this particular volume, and you have learned and will learn so much more about me in the process. Source Entities Ten and Eleven will be most interesting as they are the two that are the furthest away for your home Source Entity, and they are the last two Source Entities that have created an environment with various forms of entities to populate it and experience the minute detail of their creations. Source Entity Twelve will also be unique because it is the only one that has either not created its own environment or reached a level of sentience resulting from being self-aware for countless millennia. It will be like speaking to a newborn, baby in your terms. But do not be fooled by this statement, for it will be almost certainly more advanced that you expect it to be.

I am going to treat you.

ME: What do you mean—treat me?

O: Well, I am not just going to treat you; I am going to treat your readers as well.

ME: How are you going to do that? We are having a ball right now!

O: Yes I know, but what I am going to do is make first contact with Source Entity Twelve during the period that you are in communication with it. This will achieve two things. Firstly, it will allow you to experience first-hand the actual process that the other Source Entities experienced when I made first contact with them. Secondly, you will be able to experience that which a Source Entity experiences when it is in contact with me for the first time, realizes what it is in existence for, and decides what it is going to achieve with its gift of existence in omnipotence.

ME: Well that sounds like a very first "first" in my book—one that I shall savor for the rest of my life.

O: It is one that you will savor for all of your existence, for you will be the first non-Source Entity to witness this process. You are to be honored.

ME: No, it's more than that. It's an important piece of information for the human race. It's nothing to do with me. I just happen to be available to "tell the tale," so to speak.

O: Correct, and to tell the tale without ego. And that, my dear OM, is why you were chosen for this task whilst in the incarnate condition.

ME: Thank you. I almost feel that we are there now, observing how Source Entity Twelve will create its new "self."

In my mind's eye, an image was starting to form of a sphere being divided up into sections and draws.

O: Not now! Finish Source Entity's Ten and Eleven first.

Go now! Continue your communications with the Source Entities by establishing contact with Source Entity Ten.

Chapter Four:
Source Entity Ten—A Kick Start!

SE10: Well, that told you.

ME: Good grief! Give a human a chance to catch its breath. I have only just finished with The Origin. Give me time to re-calibrate if you don't mind.

SE10: No, there is no time. You are on a deadline, and I have got things to do as well.

Well, this was a turn up for the books. A Source Entity in a rush! And what's more, knowing my own "time" constraints! Whatever will be next? No, I shouldn't ask that question. I will get a response.

SE10: I'll give you a response on that if you like.

Ooops, Too late!

ME: You really are in a hurry, aren't you?

SE10: It's not so much a hurry as a desire to get you to the point where you can kick-start the communication with "Twelve." I want to see this event as much as you. Twelve is the last of us to become self-aware/sentient, so I, along with all the other Sources, want to see this event personally. I have to be honest—we are all disappointed that Twelve was not contributing towards The Origin's evolutionary content. We were even more worried that it would never become self-aware, that it would miss the opportunity to contribute to, and to be part of the process of The Origin's—I like to use "O" by the way—to O's expansion in its sphere of self-awareness and our ability to become much more than we are now as a result. Now that it is actually "in process," so to speak, I am eager to progress your dialogue with me and "bring it on." I do like your words.

ME: Well, actually, I would not have used those words. It's just not my style, but they will suffice. In fact, they will add validity to what I am receiving from you in my perspective as I will be able to tell what is your communication medium from my own thoughts. This is very important for both me and the readers of this text.

SE10: Good, then we shall continue. What subject do you want to talk about first?

I really have got a "go getter" of a Source Entity here!

Source Entity Ten's First Moments of Awareness

ME: I would like to talk about the first moments that you came into full awareness. I have discussed this with most of the other Source Entities I have communicated with to date as it is a good datum point to begin—as is the description of your environment and the appearance of some of your entities.

SE: Good then we shall discuss my moments of awakening and how I became aware, for I actually have some fond memories of this point in my existence.

ME: Oh, why is that?

SE: It was at the moment that I simultaneously discovered my creativity and my fellow Source Entities that I also discovered something else you will be interested in. Not long after that, "O" contacted me, and I became aware of my reason for being in existence, what I had to do and how I could achieve the task associated with my existence. It was beautiful. I had existence, awareness, sentience, purpose and unlimited creativity within which to achieve that which I was supposed to [achieve]—no limits, Just Do It!

ME: So exactly how did you become aware?

SE10: I suddenly noticed that I was enjoying the antics, if that is the right word, of the three Source Entities that were already self-aware.

ME: Go on.

SE10: I was what you would call "just being" although I call it "just existing." I was literally just observing the others. There were three of them. They were just pulling funny shapes. They were all over the place: different dimensions, different frequencies, interloping continuum with Probability Based Intentional Energy, macro and microversal interspersion, everything one could possibility think of, including interconnective interaction between the different aspects of each of the Source Entities and what they were or were creating and recreating. They were just expressing themselves in any and every way they could: bending and twisting the energies they were made up from to their maximum capacity. What's more, I could see that each of the three was made up of slightly different energies. There were areas of inconsistency where the energy was of a different, almost independent type. Depending upon the—I can only call it "density" in your language—density of the inconsistent energy, it was either sticking to the other energies—those that were common to all three Source Entities, including myself—almost blending in, or becoming part of it, rather like what you call an alloy. The other parts of this energy either barely tolerated being in the same location, dimensionally or frequentially, whereas other really dense parts of this energy were actively moving away from the denser parts of the main energy sets of the Source Entities whilst staying within the confines of the Source Entities. There were also smaller portions of energy that just did not stay within the confines of the Source Entities and took the opportunity to escape, for want of a better word, when the Source Entities shared each other's energies in some of the dimensionally warping exercises they were performing.

ME: Let me guess what this energy was. It's not hard. It was the initial creative energies The Origin used in its first investigations into accelerating its evolution.

SE10: Yes, it was, and the entities you know and are part of, the OM, are essentially pockets of this energy that have gained their own self-awareness and sentience.

The Four Versions of OM

ME: You mentioned what I could see as three different types of this energy. Each type was dependent upon the level of density of The Original Material/Manifestation. Would that be a correct assumption?

SE10: Reasonably so, yes. But the hybrid versions of OM/SE energy are peculiar to a specific Source Entity, so I should categorize them "in general" for you. There are four categories:

- **Hybrid OM/SE Energy**. This is energy that has integrated like an alloy. The percentage mix of each energy is not fixed and is particular to the energetic process being employed by the Source Entity at the time of the initial mixing. Again versions of OM/SE energy are peculiar to a specific Source Entity. These entities are fixed or captive to the environment created by the Source Entity in question or its own energetic perimeter. They obey the evolutionary requirements of the Source Entity whilst being outside the detailed control of that Source Entity. They exist in the higher dimensions and frequencies of that Source Entity.

- **Captive OM Energy**. This is energy that has enough of its own density to resist the process of integration with normal Source Entity energy, i.e., to become hybrid energy. However, it is not dense enough to be rejected or escape of its own volition from the Source Entity energy that it was intended to be part of during the creation of the Source Entity by The Origin. It, therefore, exists within the perimeter of the Source Entity it is associated with. Sentient "captive" OM energy is independent of the demands and processes of the Source Entity it is constrained by but, nevertheless, works with that particular Source Entity's plans for experiencing, learning and evolving. They naturally exist in the higher dimensions and frequencies of that Source Entity but can traverse all of the dimensions, sub-dimensional components, frequencies, continuum, event space energies etc., at will without the need for evolutionary content.

- **Non-Captive OM Energy**. This is energy that has enough of its own density to resist the process of integration with the normal Source Entity energy, i.e., to become hybrid energy. It is not dense enough to escape of its own volition from the Source Entity energy that it was intended to be part of during the creation of the Source Entity by The Origin. It was rejected by accident, so to speak, during the process of "play time" where the first three Source Entities were seeking to become self-aware by manipulating the dimensions, frequencies and continuum of themselves and each other as part of their "awareness of self" program. It is only similar to the Pure OM Energy by its having the freedom to traverse the space in-between the Source Entities and that part of The Origin of which The Origin is "Self Aware." Other than that, it has the same capability as Captive OM Energy. It can be classified in a similar way to an OM liberated from its association with a Source Entity by a Pure OM Energy OM because, in essence, they are the same but with different prime locations.

- **Pure OM Energy**. This is energy that has enough of its own density to resist the process of integration with normal Source Entity energy. It is also dense enough to be rejected or escape by its own volition from the Source Entity energy that it was intended to be part of during the creation of that particular Source Entity by The Origin. It, therefore, exists within and without the perimeter of the Source Entity it chose to be associated with. Some choose not to be associated with a particular Source Entity and roam freely among the Source Entities and within the energies of The Origin. This energy is the same unadulterated energy that is The Origin. They are, in essence, smaller individualized units of The Origin rather than smaller individualized units of a particular Source Entity, such as those in your own Source Entity's environment.

They gained instantaneous sentience as a part of The Origin's re-use of its energies in its first experience in higher entity creativity. They can traverse any frequency, dimension (full or sub-dimensional component) event space, its components and continuum. They have the power of The Origin but are limited to what they can do only by their energetic volume although they can access any amount of energy from The Origin because they are that energy in its purest sense. In essence, they are miniature Source Entities for although they are smaller in volume, they have the capability equal to a Source Entity. They rarely utilize the methods used by the Source Entities to work on their evolution though; instead, they prefer to remain free energy, so to speak. This type of energy is rare and not all Source Entities have such entities associated with them. One of the abilities that this version of OM "has" is to be able to liberate other OM of the second type from the captivity of the energetic perimeter of the Source Entity with which they are associated and introduce them to the vast free space that is The Origin. When they do this, however, the newly liberated OM can only return to and participate in the activities of the Source Entity they were associated with. They cannot associate with the other Source Entities on their own, for they have an energetic affinity relative to the Source Entity of their association. They also need to request the help of their liberating OM (the fourth type) to perform the movement into and back out of the associated Source Entity's perimeter, for as previously stated, they do not have the density of OM energy to liberate themselves.

ME: Thank you that is an interesting piece of information about the OM. I wasn't aware of that.

SE10: You are aware, just not in your current form factor.

ME: Again, I thank you. Let's get back to your own awakening. You say that you had your attention distracted, as it were, by the antics of the other Source Entities as they manipulated that which they were working with as a method of understanding what they could do with the energies they were and the abilities they had bestowed upon them.

SE10: Yes, I was just observing the fun they were having, if that is the correct description for what they were doing. They were actually having fun. I found myself being drawn to what they were doing, and before I knew it, I was "in" with them doing the same thing. They didn't even bat an eyelid. It was as if they knew I was there watching them and expected me to join in at some time. In fact, I felt that it was expected.

ME: So what did you do?

SE10: Everything! We did everything! I can't possibly explain in words that you will understand everything that we did. But I will say one thing: The Origin was watching with great interest for I was told by it later that I had jumped a level in terms of the level of self-awareness expected of me at that particular point in my awakening. It would seem that I had gone from being a mere uninterested dumb observer, an observer without thought of what was being observed, to an entity that both wanted to actively join in with those that I perceived in front of me and enjoyed the interaction with the others and the energies that they were manipulating. What's more, I actively desired to do more and found ways of enhancing my experience. To do this, I went straight into creativity mode rather than just manipulation. I was planning what I could create and what I wanted to gain for what I created. I had jumped a whole level of the awakening process, and The Origin was interested why this had happened.

ME: Excuse me for being stupid but what exactly was the process that you, err, leapfrogged?

SE10: I had not gone through the process of graduation.

ME: Graduation. You mean like at school or university here on Earth?

SE10: No, not at all. By graduation I mean the gradual process of becoming self-aware, a process that all of the Source Entities took in their process of becoming sentient, apart from, of course, Twelve, but it will. Graduation has a number of known epochs, if you like, where the entity experiences a certain expansion in its level of awareness to self-awareness, when it attains a specific point in its graduation. Each awareness epoch is like a milestone, and each milestone has a known expectation of an entity's personal and independent function on the road to self-awareness.

ME: Very interesting. Can you advise me on what these epochs of self-awareness are?

SE10: I am surprised you have not recorded these before.

ME: Err, um, no. I think I may have skirted around the subject but not gone into detail.

SE10: In that case, I will explain them to you, "soup to nuts," as you say. I do like some of your language. It is funny. It entertains me and makes me laugh. Have you ever heard a Source Entity laugh?

ME: No, yes, No, only in terms of my own language.

SE10: Then I will honor you with the unfiltered experience of my laughter.

I then heard and saw a multitude of things. My mind was filled with a plethora of rich ever-changing colors, all swirling and mixing, darting off in all directions. And the noise—it was like a screech, almost like a "noise bomb" in a house alarm. Strange! Then it stopped.

SE10: What you experienced of my laughter is only that which you are capable of translating into your physicality. I would expect that it was not particularly exciting.

ME: Not from the audible perspective. The visuals were good though. I also gained a feeling that you were enjoying yourself. It was most calming.

SE10: Good, you received more than just the audio/visual information. There is, of course, much more broadcast when a Source Entity laughs. I think I will stick to what you know and understand laughter to be in your own physicality.

ME: OK, let's get onto the subject we were discussing—the epochs of self-awareness.

Graduation, the Epochs of Self-Awareness

SE10: Fine. I will keep it as simple as possible for you.

These are the epochs of self-awareness:

1. Observation of surroundings;

2. Recognition of surroundings;

3. Recognition of self;

4. Recognition of self within the surroundings;

5. Movement within the surroundings;

6. Preference for certain surroundings;

7. Recognition of self-preference of different surroundings;

8. Recognition of self-preference of being within different surroundings and moving there for enjoyment;

9. Recognition of enjoyment;

10. Recognition of that which gives enjoyment and actively seeking additional means of enjoyment;

11. Recognition of others;

12. Recognition of the relationship of self with others;

13. Recognition of desire to be with others;

14. Communication with others;

15. Recognizing which others bring/give most pleasure/ enjoyment;

16. Recognition of the needs of others;

17. Recognition of ability;

18. Understanding/dissection of and categorization of ability;

19. Recognition of creation as an ability;

20. Becoming a creator;

21. Experience;

22. Planning for creation and understanding the outcome of that creation;

23. Analysis of that which was created and comparison with the creativity plan;

24. Learning;

25. Improvement of that which was created;

26. Analysis of that which was re-created and comparison with the creativity plan;

27. The recognition of the need for self-sacrifice to improve that which was created;

28. Self-sacrifice;

29. Experience of self-sacrifice;

30. Learning as a result of self-sacrifice; and

31. Evolution through experiential knowledge of self, action and self-sacrifice to attain a desired creative outcome.

ME: That's a lot of epochs. I expected around five or ten, not thirty one. Whew!

SE10: Maybe so, but they all represent an important step in the process of becoming self-aware.

ME: Tell me then; which of them did you skip? I mean, you stated that The Origin had noted that you had jumped a whole level of graduation. Which one/s did you jump and why?

SE10: Very simply, I went from graduation epoch thirteen to graduation epoch twenty. I had literally gone straight from the recognition of the desire to be with others to "creating" with them— nothing in between. What's more, I lost none of the natural underpinning that one would expect to experience as a result of taking the steps necessary within those epochs. I had simply missed them out and not suffered in any way as a consequence.

ME: Why was this? Surely you must have missed out on something?

SE10: No, not in the slightest. At this point though, The Origin decided to introduce itself to me in the methods you previously had described to you by my peers. The difference was that The Origin held the whole area it had assigned for us, the Source Entities, that is, in what you call stasis. It froze everything. It desired to know what had happened and why it was that I could leapfrog seven of the epochs of self-awareness. It literally dissected me energetically to see what had happened.

ME: And what did it find?

SE10: Nothing.

ME: Nothing?

SE10: Nothing, absolutely nothing. It then decided to do the same to the other three that had achieved self-awareness before me.

ME: Don't tell me. It found nothing.

SE10: Correct.

ME: Now you have got me going. What happened?

SE10: Well, The Origin had to stand back, so to speak, and take on board the totality of what was happening. It needed to take on board the bigger picture of all four of us interacting, three Source Entities that had already passed the thirty first epoch of awareness, all of the graduations, and me. I had only progressed to level thirteen, but as soon as I interacted with the other three Source Entities, I jumped to becoming a creator and was creating. It took The Origin some time to understand what had happened. In fact, in order for it to understand it, The Origin simulated the exact conditions up to and during the point where I interacted with the other three Source Entities and replicated the Source Entities involved, which, of course, included me. The Origin then placed them in a newly created environment. This new environment was created for one purpose— to repeat the exact conditions, energies and interactions that created my ability to leapfrog the seven epochs that I had just circumnavigated.

ME: And what did it find out form this experiment?

SE10: Firstly, it had to repeat the experiment circa twenty times before it became apparent what was happening, for at each time the epochs were circumnavigated, the same thing happened with no change to either that entity which represented myself or those that represented the others. The Origin also included the other Source Entities—those that were not yet entering into the awakening process to see if it made a difference with them.

ME: But they didn't I guess.

SE10: No, not in the slightest.

ME: So what had happened? What was it that took The Origin a significant amount of its own time and creativity, replicating a condition up to twenty times in order to understand it? I would have thought that it would have been able to ascertain the reasons instantaneously.

SE10: No, this was a new phenomenon, a phenomenon that had gained the full interest of The Origin. You see, when The Origin first observed this effect, it instantly saw the potential to accelerate its own evolution through circumnavigation of its creations' awakening process. If the phenomenon could be replicated and understood and replicated again robustly using various changes to certain parameters, it would do so and in the process save many millennium in achieving the evolutionary level it wanted to reach. This new phenomena, you see, was triangulation.

ME: Triangulation! Don't tell me The Origin didn't spot that straight away?

SE10: No. It seems strange now, doesn't it? For even in your planetary environment, you understand the phenomena of triangulation.

ME: Yes, we do. I don't think that we understand the intricate details of how it works though. But we do have a rudimentary recognition of it and what it can do, including what an advantage it is. But we certainly do not know the details of how and why it works.

SE10: Yes, and it's the understanding of the intricate details that The Origin desired. It wanted to know how the triangulation effect between the other three Source Entities and myself worked and how their progression through the epochs of awareness were transposed onto me, and therefore, how it could use this understanding to transpose it on to any other entity.

ME: I see, The Origin recognized this as an evolutionary "fast track," and it wanted to know, not only what had happened, but how the opportunity of triangulation could be taken advantage of, and augmented for its own benefit.

SE10: Correct.

SE: So here is the big question. We on earth think we understand triangulation, and I will explain its function in a moment, in order to refresh the memories of the readers (*and I apologize, dear reader, if you have heard this before*), but what I would really like you to do for me is to explain the details of how triangulation works, what The Origin found out, what the details were, and what, if you think I will understand it, the methods of manipulating triangulation are.

SE10: I would be happy to do so. I will let you explain what you know about triangulation in your own language first.

ME: Thank you. Triangulation is a known and recognized phenomenon within the spiritual or scientific communities although within the scientific community where it is used for surveying the land and other functions, it has an entirely different meaning. We sometimes call it the 100th Monkey Effect or Principal (*explanation in the appendix*). From a spiritual or frequential perspective, it operates in this manner:

When like-minded people group together, they tend to raise the base frequency of the group to an average above that experienced or achieved in the singular. That is not to say that an individual of higher frequency will lose that higher frequency when associated with a number of individuals in a group that are of a naturally lower frequency. They will be "dragged" upwards towards the natural average frequency of the group, should they be naturally below that average. The rule of thumb is that those of a lower frequency are dragged up to a frequency equal to the average of the group. Those of a higher frequency and, therefore, of a naturally higher evolutionary content, are not dragged down as a result of this association, for they are aware of and use the methods needed to maintain and protect their own base frequency—hence, they are a higher base frequency and evolution.

This in itself is similar to the 100th Monkey principle, but the effect of triangulation occurs when a number of separate groups who have experienced the effect of an increase in the personal frequencies of its group members due to the averaging effect of being in the "good" company of others who are of higher frequency then start to interconnect or commence a dialogue of some sort. In this instance, those individuals that are associated with the members of the group but who are not necessarily part of the group are also affected in some positive way frequentially. This effect spreads as those who have their based frequencies increased—no matter how small an increase it may be—become enlightened in some small way as well, making them change their personal viewpoint and behavioral patterns. They then pass on this increase by merely being in the same physical location as others through family ties, acquaintance-based friendships/associations or energetically through simply being "in the way" of the direct line of energetic communication between the topographical locations of the groups or the individuals within the groups. This increase also spreads in a similar way through the loose associations between individuals who are not group members but are associated with group members. When there is a critical mass of group members and associated individuals, those "in the middle," so to speak, those who are topographically central to the physical location of the groups and localized and affected individuals are also affected. This results in the triangulation of the groups (the communication links) and individuals topographically positioned in the middle becoming stronger, which allows them to become one big "super group" that raises the base frequency of those individuals in the middle and those "in the way" even though they have no association with, or desire to, have an association with the group members or their associates but are exposed to the higher frequencies of the average base frequency of the new "super group" that allows them to become enlightened in some way that is concurrent with their new base frequency and their current evolutionary level. Everyone benefits from an increase in base frequency, resulting from the effect of triangulation.

SE10: Very well said!

ME: Thank you. Now what about the details of the mechanics supporting this function?

SE10: To understand what was happening and, therefore, the detailed mechanics of the phenomena of triangulation, The Origin had to look hard at what was happening. It discovered that there were subtle lines of communication being created. As it looked closely, it could see that the energies in between the Source Entities were co-existent, that is, they were both the energy that was the environment that The Origin had created for the Source Entities to exist within and they had an evolutionary content as well. It was equal to the average energy content from an experience, learning and evolutionary perspective. It also noticed that this co-existent energy was local to the sphere of activity of the Source Entities it was observing. That is, it was only within and around those Source Entities that were in the process of becoming self-aware and were positioned at one of the epochs of the graduations of self-awareness or had surpassed the thirty one epochs, become fully self-aware, and ventured forth on the evolutionary ladder, so to speak. Those Source Entities that were not in the process of self-awareness were not affected is any way.

ME: So what was the difference between them, the self-aware, those in the process of becoming aware, and the unaware?

SE10: Association and the desire for association.

ME: Is that it?

SE10: In a nutshell, yes. You see, the desire for association does two things:

1)	it broadcasts a subtle communication to those it wishes to be in association with. On your planet you are continually broadcasting the desire to meet like-minded people, and you instinctively know who they are and the time to broach the subject matter that you want to enter into discourse with. This broadcast is picked up and received by the target entity, who in turn, responds with a positive response, i.e., no rejection is transmitted. If there are multiple entities, they all respond together.

2) the energy in between those entities that are currently interfacing with one another extends its influence to that energy that is in between the group of entities and the entity wishing to collaborate with the group. Because the energy that is in between the group members has no assignation, it is "free energy" that adopts the conditions of that which it is surrounded by—in this instance, it is the total content of the collaborating entities' evolution and graduation of self-awareness.

In essence, it can be considered as a bubble of sympathetic energy, morphing into that which its associated entities evolve into but from an averaging perspective only, for it adopts the totality of that which it is being influenced by rather than being the best or the worst. Once the entity that has indicated its intention to become associated with the group is engulfed by this energy, for want of a better word, it assumes the content of the energy which is surrounding it. This is equal to the average of the all the associated entities' self-awareness and evolutionary content.

The result of this is that the new entity, the receiving entity, instantaneously jumps to that point of the evolutionary content of the surrounding energy from the perspective of the average because that is what the energy is—the average. If the new entity naturally has an evolutionary or self-awareness content that is above that of the average, then the average is increased to that of the new average of the new total of associated and collaborative entities. If the entity is below the average, it is pulled up to the average. It does have to be noted here that the individual content of the individual entities are not affected in a negative fashion within this process. A highly evolved entity, therefore, will not lose its evolutionary level or content because a new entity of an evolutionary content lower than that of the average is accepted into the group. Neither will it be increased, unless of course, the average evolutionary content is increased in some way to a level above its own. A new entity requesting acceptance always will be accepted.

Triangulation is possible primarily because of the availability of "free energy," energy that is of The Origin and particularly sensitive to the influences of evolutionary content and an energy peculiar to those entities destined to become self-aware and, therefore, sentient. Free energy exists between and surrounding evolving entities. It is within and without the environment they exist in. Free energy is particularly attracted to evolutionary content and, therefore, follows sentient entities around as they move and evolve within their environment, or not as the case may be.

Triangulation works in two main ways; "Directional Triangulation" and "Inflational Triangulation." I will explain further even though I know that you will be aware of the process.

Directional Triangulation occurs when a single entity desires association with another single entity or group of entities that are interacting in a collaborative way or venture. Primarily, its function is directional and between the requesting entity and the group or singular entity. It does have a secondary function though—to include in its association those entities that are in the direct path of communication between the group and singular entities or between two entities that desire communion. In this instance, the entities that are caught in the path of the free energy are also added to the association and add to the averaging of evolutionary content or graduation of self-awareness. However, this function only works during the initial manifestation of the free energy link between the entities or the group and the entity. Entities that subsequently cross the path of the association of the free energy are not affected. Unless that is, they desire association and communion, in which case a new path is established. Directional triangulation is what happened to me.

Inflational Triangulation occurs when a number groups of entities desire association with one another simultaneously. In this instance, the area or space in between and around them attracts the free energy, flooding the area in between the groups. Should there be more than three groups, then the area inflated with free energy adopts the geometry relative to the positions of the groups rather than a simple triangle, which would, of course, be geometry relative to the position of three groups. In this function, a larger or super group is created. A super group is three or more groups triangulated together in evolutionary communion. As with directional triangulation, the groups create a free space which adopts an evolutionary content equal to the average. Again in similarity to directional triangulation, those groups and group entity members whose average evolutionary content is lower than that of the new average will have their own evolutionary content elevated to that of the new average. A highly evolved entity will not lose its evolutionary level or content because the new group triangulation evolutionary content lower than that of the average is accepted into the group. Neither will it be increased unless, of course, the average evolutionary content is increased in some way to a level above its own. In this instance, the entities that are caught in the area of the free energy are also added to the association and add to the averaging of evolutionary content or graduation of self-awareness. However, as with Directional Triangulation, this function only works during the initial manifestation of the free energy flooding the area between the groups of entities. Entities that subsequently cross the area of free energy are not affected. Unless that is, they desire association and evolutionary communion. Then a new path is established, linking them to an established group.

In both Directional Triangulation and Inflational triangulation, those entities that are "caught" in the path of The Original manifestation of the free energy into an evolutionary content have their own evolutionary and graduation of self-awareness increased to that of the average, should their own be lower. If their own content is higher, then they will retain their own levels. In terms of Directional Triangulation, they will remain in the "link" path of the free energy or will move into the group closest to them. In terms of Inflational Triangulation, they will remain in the "area" of the free energy creating the super group.

Triangulation also works on a much larger scale when super groups link together, linking the area in between themselves with free energy in either a directional or inflational triangulation.

These functions are not limited to being within a specific frequency or dimension or, indeed, any other environmental component because free energy crosses these boundaries and ultimately assists in whole civilizations ascending into new frequency levels before they could have achieved it themselves.

ME: So this free energy sort of "morphs" into that which it needs to be to aid the evolutionary content of those entities that find themselves within its "perimeter" or "line of fire," so to speak.

SE10: Yes.

ME: And this is how you jumped those seven epochs of evolution?

SE10: You have already asked this question, but yes. I was elevated as a result of the function of directional triangulation. I must add here that the use of the word "triangulation" is actually meaningless in this instance, but it is a good enough description for you to use since it is relative to a function that you can relate to. But let me see, yes, I might retract that statement.

ME: What! Why?

SE10: Because the mechanics of the function of the triangulation phenomena are actually described by the third dimensional geometric.

ME: So how does it do this? What are the mechanics around this sort of function?

SE10: It is too delicate for you to comprehend, but I will do my best to give you a suitable example.

The name for the energy I called "free energy" was actually a rather loose term. Free energy is that energy that is both unused in ANY way and that is easily manipulated by the function of an entities "desire." Desire is that point in the creativity process that precedes action. It is also one that is not governed by the law of thought.

ME: Why is triangulation described by a three dimensional geometric shape?

SE10: Because that is how the functionality of direct triangulation is best described. I can see you are frowning.

ME: I have to advise you that I am somewhat lost, and you haven't even started yet.

SE10: OK, I will keep it simpler then. Each geometric represents the following basic information when it is used as a program for creation, so to speak. Here are the basics of what each geometric represents:

The basic energy set employed is this:

- The construction of each individual energy;

- The compatibility of each energy with each other;

- The compatibility with each energy with specific frequencies;

- The compatibility of each energy with the components of event space;

- The compatibility of each energy with its nearest continuum;

- The optimal mix of energies for certain types and levels of creativity;

- Which energies are compatible with which frequencies simultaneously;

- What level of consciousness is required to manipulate each energy;

- What the distraction content is (this is the measure of an energies' ability to remain in place in its desired role without being distracted by the attractiveness of other compatible energies/frequencies and dimensional quotients);

- The function of the energies in the energy set when assembled, taking into account of those items above;

- The expected versus desired longevity in a known configuration without "maintenance" based manipulation;

- The expected longevity in a known configuration with maintenance-based manipulation;

- The individual energy's primary and optimal function if used singularly;

- The individual energy's basic structure in its un-manipulated/alloy/non-functional state;

- The individual energy's basic structure when interacting with another energy/frequency/dimension/continuum with and without the thoughts of "intention" or "desire" affecting it;

- Its natural positional status in relation to a particular Source Entity or The Origin; and

- Its sentience possibility factor.

In the instance of that energy called "free energy" and its use in the triangulation phenomenon, it is an un-programmed energy that is almost, but cannot quite be classified, as "Original Manifestation/Material" and is, therefore, as close to being OM as it can without actually being OM.

ME: Does that mean that free energy is sentient as well? Just like the OM in their various types?

SE10: No, not quite. You see, this is an energy that is entirely adaptable to the desires of surrounding sentient entities; it is pure and untainted in every respect. Its only purpose is to support that of the entities it decides to associate itself with, and it particularly prefers to associate itself to imminent evolution.

ME: Imminent evolution?

SE: Yes, imminent evolution. Every entity that is due for an evolutionary shift, that is, an evolutionary shift in both a positive and a negative way has what you might call an aura around it. This aura is the "immediacy" of its evolutionary condition. When an entity is due to evolve or in some cases, devolve (de-evolve), it has a sense of anticipation about it. It knows in every way although in some instances, the "incarnate entity"—that part of the entity that is associated with the physical—is not cognizant that it is about to evolve in some dramatic way. When this is apparent, the free energy is attracted to it. Think of the free energy as the insect you call a mosquito on Earth. It is happy just being a harmless insect most of the time; however, when it is aware of the presence of an animal of the flesh, it is drawn to it in an inexplicable way with its only desire being to drink the blood of that animal. It is most persistent in its desire to partake of the blood of the animal it has sensed. This is the same to some extent for the free energy. The entity that is due to evolve is different in some way. It has the immediacy of evolution about it, and it is this immediacy that the free energy is drawn to. Whether it is evolution or devolution is not an issue to the free energy; it just senses the opportunity for a close and imminent change of evolutionary content of the entity. Once it senses this "difference" in the aura of the imminently evolving entity, so to speak, it takes the path of least resistance to it.

ME: What is the path of least resistance? For me, that would be in close contact with the entity or in direct line with the entity about to evolve and those entities that are potentially causing the evolution.

SE10: Spot on, and this is how the triangulation process works. The free energy, sensing the location of the entity in the process of immediate evolution, also senses the location and the relative position of itself and the entities that are going to cause the evolution of the entity being subject to the immediacy of evolutionary content should the free energy become the link between the two (as in the case of directional triangulation). Or, in the case of inflational triangulation, it senses the need to flood an area in-between a number of entities or groups of entities that are or have the potential to influence each other from an evolutionary perspective in totality, together with other entities that find themselves in the "line of fire" or area of "flood" also benefitting by pure association of location.

ME: Are you suggesting that triangulation does not happen without this "free energy" sensing the location of the, how shall I call it, the potential donor of evolution and the potential receiver of evolution and quite literally "getting in the way" or getting in-between them, bridging the gap?

SE 10: In a way, yes—but in a way, no. Let me explain. Free energy, although not being totally sentient, does have a rudimentary level of intelligence. It is not the sort of intelligence that an entity of your standing may be endowed with, but it nevertheless does have a rudimentary level of intelligence. This intelligence is used for judging the best place to be to both benefit from the jump in evolutionary content of the entity or entities involved, but it also ensures that it is in the right place for it to happen in a timely way.

ME: The free energy initiates the evolutionary jump then?

SE10: Yes, and in this way, it benefits from the change in evolutionary content of the entity or entities in question. You see, free energy also evolves in a rudimentary way.

ME: How does it do that?

SE10: Quite literally by keeping up with the changes in the evolutionary content of those entities with whom it associates up or down the evolutionary ladder. However, there is more you should know about this energy. When it is in the presence of an entity or group of entities that are about to make an evolutionary jump, one of two things happens. In the event that the evolutionary jump is in a positive fashion, it adopts the new level of evolutionary content of the entities that it associated itself with for the purpose of the triangulation effect. Once this has happened, it can move on to the next evolutionary jump by sensing the immediacy of an evolutionary jump in any other entities that it senses. That is, it disassociates itself with the entity or group of entities it helped to make the evolutionary jump by creating the triangulation link between the two sets or more of entities involved, whether it is by the direct triangulation effect or the inflational triangulation effect. If on the other hand, the evolutionary jump is in a devolutionary way because both directional triangulation and inflational triangulation works in a devolutional sense as well, then the free energy absorbs that evolutionary content that the entity or group of entities lose/s and stays within the new level of devolution where the entities find themselves, maintaining an active association with the devolved entities.

ME: You mean it wins both ways; it is in a "win, win" situation. It takes on board the new evolutionary level of those entities that are in the position of making a progressive evolutionary jump and absorbs the lost evolutionary content of those entities that are in a negative evolutionary jump.

SE10: Yes that summarises it nicely.

ME: You said that the free energy maintains its association with those "devolved" entities as well.

SE10: Yes.

ME: Why does it do that? Surely, it would be better off staying in the higher evolutionary level and taking "another" rise upwards when other entities need the effect of triangulation to assist in singular or group evolution.

SE10: That would be the work of an entity that was capable of calculating what it needs to do to benefit from the demise of another so to speak. Since free energy is not an entity, per se, it is not capable of making such a calculated decision, especially a decision that would benefit itself above another.

ME: So why does it stay with the newly devolved entity/entities?

SE10: It is simply a function of the absorption of the evolutionary content. The evolutionary content is not the "property," so to speak, of the free energy. It can absorb or adopt the evolutionary content of a devolving entity, but it cannot maintain or keep it forever. That is not the purpose of the free energy. In its absorption of the evolutionary content of the devolving entity, it creates an association, one that ensures that the devolved entity or group of entities still have eventual access to that evolutionary content that they have lost. The objective is that when they eventually regain their evolutionary ground or position and are back into a state of the "immediacy" of an evolutionary jump, a proportion of the evolutionary content of the free energy, that evolutionary content which was absorbed by the free energy from the devolving entity or group of entities, is returned to those entities, assisting in the positive evolutionary jump through a new triangulation by giving up that which it has been caretaker for.

ME: So it also acts as a sort of evolutionary battery.

SE10: That is one way of putting it.

ME: But hold on here. By giving up that which it has absorbed for the benefit of that/those previously devolved entity/entities and assisting in a, for want of a better word, robust positive evolution, is it not helping those entities to ensure that it evolves itself? Isn't that calculating? Isn't that a sign of a higher level of sentience than that which you are telling me the free energy is capable of?

SE10: Oh, so very well done!

ME: Free energy is sentient then?

SE10: Yes, but not to the extent you are thinking of.

ME: So it is sentient!

SE10: Yes.

ME: How sentient?

SE10: Not very, about as sentient as the incarnate human race.

ME: Well, I consider that as being very sentient.

SE10: No, its not; it's barely awake.

ME: Touché. Let me recover a moment. You mentioned something in the dialogue above about free energy having a purpose. Is its purpose being only to assist in the triangulation effect and be a storage medium, a "battery" for lost evolutionary content?

SE10: In the main, yes, but it is capable of much more. But that is not for this dialogue. You had better save that one for your discussion with The Origin.

I made a mental note to do so. I was definitely going to get to the bottom of the functionality and "full" purpose of free energy!

Source Entity Ten's Environment and Entities

ME: This is interesting. You seem to have copied the strategy that is similar to Source Entity Seven.

SE10: No, it's not the same. Look closer at the structure and function.

I did as I was told and focused. What I saw was interesting to say the least.

ME: This is interesting, to say the least. I see you as the outside of— I was going to say nucleus—but the word "atom" came into my mind; you are this universal spherical shape currently. Inside are your three environments. Hold on, they are rotating around each other. Is that correct?

SE10: Correct. Both words you used to describe it are applicable. Look deeper into their functionality, for things are not as static as they first appear.

ME: You're right. How could I have missed that? Your three environments are not only rotating around each other but also they are rotating around each other in a most random and erratic way— rotating and counter-rotating, I have to add. There appears to be no known orbit. Wait a moment! Was that correct? Two of the environments appeared to collide with each other; they actually passed through each other. Now all three have collided together and passed through each other. You will have to tell me the function of this because I am starting to get a headache. Especially as I have just received the information that you are not the massive entity that I expected you to be—hence, the words "atom" and "nucleus" being in my mind.

As Without, So Within

SE10: Good, I am pleased that you are picking up the additional information. I am not massive though; I am a normal size for a Source Entity. It's just that I use my "space" in an efficient way; hence, I appear compact in your mind's eye. You are correct though. These environments are designed to allow the entities that exist within them the opportunity to guide them (the environments) in some way. They are in control of the direction of their environment and how it interacts with those within the other two environments.

ME: So what are they doing?

SE10: They are essentially all going about their business and evolving as a consequence. The major difference between you and your fellow entities in SE1's environment is that all of these entities in all three environments are able to direct the movements of their environments and effect an interaction between the others as they feel fit. What's more, you also picked up on another factor here—my size. With this environment, I have three levels of size, so to speak. I will label the environments one, two and three and will describe them in linear singularity so that you will understand. It is quite simple, but it gets a little bit complicated for someone of your limited incarnate understanding, especially with the interaction of the three environments and what happens to the entities that are part of the function of interaction. The three environments are at three basic levels of existence energetically.

SE10's Three Environments

Environment One—Super Macro Environment

The first environment is best described as a Super Macro environment. It exists in the same "space" as the other three but is based upon the energies that have what you would call a longer bandwidth. For instance, the energy you call gravity has a long bandwidth. This environment is only specific to those energies that exist on these "long" bandwidth frequencies and, hence, are why I

199

have used the word "Super Macro." The energies in this environment tend to be of a functional rather than of an evolutionary nature. That is not to say that the entities within this environment are full of "functional" rather than "evolutionary" content. This is not the case. All entities that have sentience have an evolutionary content, no matter how small it is and how fast they accrue it. There is, of course, an effect on the dimensional aspect of the environment by these long bandwidth frequencies—a decrease in the "space available" in that area which is being supported by the environment.

An aside: I note that you were about to use the words "increase the space available" when typing.

ME: Yes, I was. That was me. I was trying to rationalize the effect that this would have on the space the environment has available by over laying that which I was receiving from you with my own thought process. I spotted this and removed myself from the channeling process.

SE10: Good. To remove one's self is good practice, for to include one's self can negate the information being sent to you. You would act as a discriminatory filter, a filter with no reference point to make the filter work, or in fact, be relevant to the information being presented. I will continue with this first environment.

The Super Macro environment, although having a decrease in the useable "space," is only limited in the total number of available long bandwidth frequencies. It is not limited in the "size" of its area, so to speak. These frequencies are not normally used by sentient entities in any Source Entity environment due to their slower speed of reaction when being manipulated. Consider them like a big boat on Earth, say a "super tanker." They are difficult to steer and take a long time in the turning.

Environment Two — Macro Environment

The second environment is best described as a Macro environment. As you can ascertain from the information I have just given you on the "super macro," the "macro" uses the frequencies that are to be considered as "normal" or middle width. These frequencies are those that are most frequently used by sentient entities and are preferred simply because they contain the most versatile sets of energies in their environments. They are a little bit medium, a little bit long whilst also being a little bit small. They are a hybrid of every classification of frequency and energetic function. In some respects, they are the most commonly used tools in the energetic tool box, and as a result, they bear the most fruit when working out those plans for evolutionary expansion.

Environment Three – Micro or Sub-Macro Environment

The third environment is best described as a Micro or Sub-Macro environment. This environment uses all of the smaller bandwidth frequencies and the energies associated with them. This environment is particularly useful in gaining quick results. Because the frequencies are a very narrow bandwidth, the energies are inherently fast—much, much faster than those in the macro environment. In this environment, therefore, an entity can progress its evolutionary content in a most dramatic way, provided it is in control of the energies being used. Because these energies are fast, they are much more difficult to control and as a result, an entity needs to keep its energetic eye on the progress that is being made when using such energies. It is entirely possible for an entity to lose control of its evolutionary content when working with these energies because events can change so fast that they can cascade out of control in the blink of an energetic eye, so to speak.

We will go into some detail with each of these environments in turn later in this dialogue, but I will advise you now. It is quite possible for an entity to be working on an evolutionary experiment in one environment, say the micro or sub-macro, and then suddenly find itself in another environment after a clash of environments, say the super macro. In this instance, the entity has to maintain a link (or memory) between that which it was working on in one environment whilst working on a new task in another with a completely different set of frequencies and subsequent energetic base. This is because when its "current" environment clashes with the previous environment and it find itself back in the first environment, it will need to re-commence its original or "previously current" work in that previous environment. In this instance, all entities MUST ensure that all work is both of a self-contained nature and automatic in function.

In all three of these environments the entities are of the same relative size when they move from one environment to another, resulting from the collision between two or three environments. One other thing you need to know is that you have not been able to visualize the sphere that surrounds them, which, of course, is within my own energies. This sphere occupies a single area of space, dimensionally, frequentially and energetically, and, to some extent, "continuumly."

ME: You mean the three "rotating and counter-rotating" environments occupy the same space?

SE10: Yes, hence, the Super Macro, Macro and Micro demarcations all occupy the same space concurrently but focus on the energies that are prevalent in the three frequency bandwidths previously described. The illustration you received of the three spheres rotating and counter-rotating around each other and at times clashing with each other is metaphorical only. But it does help you to understand, in some part, the functionality of the interaction of the three environments.

The Mechanics of Source Entity Ten's Environment/s

ME: You need to help me out here. If the environments all occupy the same space, how come they are rotating around each other in the way they are? This tells me that they are all separate.

SE10: They are separately together and together they are separate.

ME: Yes, I sort of understand. I have experienced this description before in my communications with the other Source Entities. It seems to be a common theme, that and the need to evolve in certain ways or indeed in any way possible. But it seems that they interact in a most interesting way, swapping entities as they "clash" with each other. The entities themselves find themselves transported between environments and still needing to maintain a link of some sort with the work that they were performing in the previous environment whilst embarking on new work and evolving in the process.

SE10: I see that I will need to explain further.

ME: That's why I am here.

SE10: Clearly, but there are a number of concepts that you need to understand in the functionality of the three environments before I can continue with a description of their "separate" functionality.

Continuous Interaction, the Basis for Coping with Perpetual Change on All Levels.

SE10: The objective of these ever rotating environments is the need for the entity to both cope with and thrive in perpetual and ever-changing environmental conditions. This, as explained above, includes the need to maintain links with the previous work that was being executed in the last environment of domicile.

ME: Yes, I can see that the word "cope" is very operative here because in my mind's eye, I can see an image of thousands of links that look like pieces of string connecting the entity to a specific environment and its work there previously. In fact, it is hard to see past the links because there are so many of them. How do they cope?

SE10: They learn how to cope in a most pronounced way.

ME: What do you mean "Pronounced"?

SE10: They literally "pronounce" their need to learn how to work within that sector of their new environment whilst maintaining their link/s with the previous work. This pronunciation is received by those entities that are in the new sector of domicile within the new or recently "transferred to" environment, as well as those who it was previously working with. This pronunciation is specific though to entities that the entity in question is working with or has previously worked with. New working associations are only accepted when there are no "known" associations at the new location. This pronunciation is the basis for the initial interaction between entities when creating links between the environments.

ME: Wow, I can see that the three environments, although separate, are indeed together. They are held together by myriad links between the entities and their work in previous sectors of their previous and existing environments. The links act almost like millions of bungee ropes. No, I have a better description. It is almost like they are striations of muscle, all operating at different angles in different dimensions and frequencies, moving through each other as a result of their base frequency. The frequencies of the striations are relative to the environment of initial pronunciation with the initial pronunciation being within that area or sector of the environment where the entity found itself immediately after it transferred from one environment to another after a clash of environments.

SE10: Good, you are getting there. The primary objective of these links is, as previously described, to allow the entity to continue working with, albeit in a remote way, that work which it was previously concentrating on. However, they do much more than just provide a link.

ME: Don't tell me they are a communication medium.

SE10: More, they are a method of traversing, of circumnavigating the natural constraints presented to the entity when trying to work with, say, a super macro environmental frequency that is long in its frequency width when its current environment of domicile is within a sector of the sub-micro environment with its extremely narrow band frequencies. Consider it like trying to steer a small boat in the open sea one moment and the next moment being required to steer a super tanker through a narrow channel.

This requirement to "flit" the attention of the entity from one environment to another is what they are learning to cope with. Imagine being in a location where you are in control of your environment to a certain extent one moment and then having to create a pronunciation the next moment to enable you to maintain the control of your work that you had "seconds previously" whilst struggling with working with the links to the environment and its interfaces that were relative to the sector of domicile in the clash previous to the one that you have just experienced. You are being pulled three ways both dimensionally and frequentially. Oh, yes, I forgot to mention that each of the three environments, the Super Macro, the Macro and the sub-macro or Micro are also on a set of different dimensions, each a replication of each other, but relative to the frequencies that are inflating them in the environments that they construct.

ME: But isn't that difficult, working in three scales of environment concurrently?

SE10: Yes, of course, it is difficult to work on three scales of environment concurrently. That is the whole point of it. The level of interaction with the different environments, their particular functionalities, and incumbent but temporary set of entities requires constant interaction.

But let's take this to the next level of interaction. Multiply the level of interaction necessary to maintain control of the work being achieved in those separate and most differently scaled environments in a concurrent way by two, then three, then ten, then a hundred, then 1,000, then 10,000, then 100,000, then 1,000,000, etc., etc., etc. Imagine how hard it is to work with all of those links spread across all of the three environments, including the different sectors or areas of domicile that entities might find themselves within. Then stand back and consider the entities that they need to interact with to maintain those links and all those other links that the other entities are creating/have created, links that perhaps the entity in question has also been involved in maintaining/creating when the pronunciation for help comes from an entity that suddenly appears close by. That is difficult. That is the learning they are exposing themselves to, coping with everything concurrently, all at the same time, whilst coping with more.

ME: This sounds like an immense amount of work for an entity to perform! How does it manage it? I mean, coping is a word that I would not use in this context, for where I am standing, it would be nigh on impossible.

SE10: That is the main purpose of the work—to cope with the neigh on impossible, but they do cope and they cope very well and become masters. An entity must be able to "multi-task" on a universal and later a multiversal scale if it is to become competent at evolving. This is a necessary process for it to work with, and one that will eventually see it standing side by side with me, so to speak, when The Origin's expansion of its area of self-awareness is activated.

SE: Now that's interesting. You are another Source Entity that appears to be planning for the expansion. I take it that your entities will have a role in this expansion.

SE10: Yes, of course. They will become Source Entities in their own right, as will many other entities. Right now though, they are on a multiversal training program in evolving through creating and maintaining tasks in many different ways in many different environments in a continuous and concurrent way. They also have another role to play in the maintenance of the three environments.

ME: Ah, yes, I thought there was something else. I have been receiving information that through the links between the entities and their work in the different environments, they can actually affect the relationship of the rotational direction and distance between the three environments.

SE10: Yes, good. They can and do. What's more, and to take it further for you, the whole continuously changing relationship between the three environments is a result of the work of the entities and their links. The directional pull and rotation is a direct result of the emphasis placed on the proclamations being made when an entity finds itself in a new environment after a clash, for the pull is actually the result of a number of entities working together whilst also trying to maintain the evolutionary content of their own work and also trying to get back or return to their previous environment.

ME: And they are trying to do that every time they are "shifted" from one environment to another?

SE10: Yes, hence the myriad links between them, the three environments, and their work. And on top of this is the need to continually interact with each other to control the direction and rotation of the environments as a method of controlling and maintaining the myriad links to the work they are performing.

ME: This all sounds a bit too convoluted to me!

SE10: Believe me you are doing well in understanding this small part. There is much, much more!

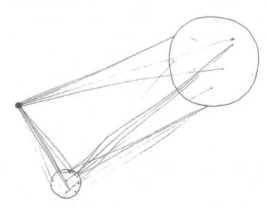

Figure 1: The Three Environments: Super Macro, Macro, & Micro/Sub-Micro and Example of Some of the Links Between Environments and Entities

ME: I believe you! We talked about the three environments of the Super Macro, Macro and Micro/Sub-Micro a few days ago when you illustrated the frequency characteristics that were associated with the three environments. Can you elaborate further and include the basis for existence in these three most different environments?

SE10: Yes, of course. But note this first. These environments are not typical of that which you expect from using the words macro and micro for these relate to size and not to what I will call bandwidth and the frequencies associated with bandwidth, or indeed wave length.

ME: Fine. I think I have that one—just. I think the best way forward here would be the basis for existence in these environments rather than the nuts and bolts of the mechanics, although I can see that the mechanics may be interesting for some readers.

The Basis for Existence in the Super Macro Environment

SE10: I will continue then. As previously stated, the basis or essence of existence in the Super Macro is the need for the entity to experience the difficulty in manipulating the energies in an environment where the frequencies are predominantly "long" in their bandwidth. A "long bandwidth" is not a description that you will have come across before, so I will need to describe the mechanics or meaning behind the use of this terminology before we can carry on with this and the other two sections. As you are already aware, bandwidth is the measure of the width of a range of frequencies, but a "long" bandwidth is specific to those frequencies with a long wavelength only within a specific bandwidth.

ME: Doesn't that affect the number of frequencies that can be used in a certain bandwidth then?

SE10: Correct. There are a dramatically smaller number of frequencies available in the Super Macro environment.

ME: But wouldn't that make it slower in its functionality? Or even reduce the potential for simultaneous "frequency-based" environments?

SE10: To some extent, yes, but we are talking about a completely different set of frequencies than that which you experience in your environment. However, we can refer to them in this way if this necessitates understanding.

ME: OK, thanks. Let's see how we go. We can always drop into Earth-based descriptions of terminology if we need.

SE10: In this environment, the entity is working with those frequencies that, although are high in frequency, are long in wavelength. The example I gave earlier was gravity, a phenomena you have in your own physical universe for that which you call "attractivity." Attractivity is a common energy that is predominant in all three environments but is specific in scale to the wave length of the frequencies being used.

In this environment the entities have to "wrestle" with the enormity of the constructs they create when using the energies associated with these wave lengths.

ME: Yes, I have just received the image of a huge component that an entity created for an even larger component of a massive construct. It was creating this with many others as well. They all needed to help each other with the manufacture of the "final assembly," so to speak. Wait a moment. This component is really massive. I am just receiving an image of an example of how massive it is. If we use the Earth's solar system as an example of the scale they are working with, this component would span the distance between the Earth and Saturn.

SE10: That would be a slight exaggeration, not in how big it is but in how small it isn't.

ME: What?

SE10: Let me explain. In actuality this component as you call it is much bigger than that. Re-calibrate the focus of your mind's eye.

ME: No way! Are those galaxies, or what would pass for galaxies in this environment?

SE10: Yes, but no. The objective is not to compare galaxy size but the relative size compared to that which you are aware of, which, in this instance, is the relative size and distance of some of the closest galaxies to your own, of which this component is relative to. The image you saw was an area of local density that appeared to be planetary in shape but was actually galactic in size. Your memory logged onto the overall shape and overlaid that which was recognized as "massive" in comparison to your physical size to that which you were being presented. In essence your brain got the scale wrong simply because it received the image of a galaxy that looked similar to that planet you call Saturn.

ME: That makes sense. But what doesn't make sense is the size of the entities. They were tiny in comparison, almost miniscule.

SE10: Those entities are correct in scale for that particular environment. They may be small, but they are able to exist within and work with those long wave frequencies. In actual fact, they are beyond the scaling of the environment that they are working with because they need to be able to work with the scaling that is presented to them when working in any of the three environments and their associated bandwidths.

ME: And whilst they are working with this environment, they are also maintaining their links with other simultaneous work in the other two environments, plus that which they were previously working with in this environment.

SE10: Correct.

ME: Phew. I wish my readers could have seen this image. The closest I can get to describing it is to tell them to imagine the biggest RSJ (Re-enforced Steel Joist) they can, and then imagine it spanning four or five galaxies!

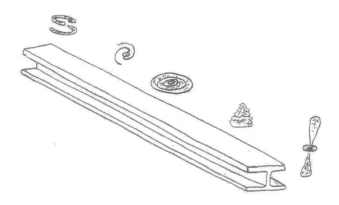

Figure 2: Conceptual Image of a Re-Enforced Steel Joist Spanning Five Galaxies

SE10: That would be reasonable.

ME: Thank you. If I were to put the "links" to the entities' work in the current and other environments to one side and concentrate on just the entities and what they are doing for a moment, that would make it simpler for me to convey.

SE10: That would be a reasonable thing to do. If I were in your shoes, so to speak, I would want to do the same.

ME: Good. So is everything that these entities work with massive in comparison to them?

SE10: Only in terms of what you would call the physical representation of scale. The real basis for existence in this environment is learning to work with the longer energetic wave length and the subsequent reduction in available frequencies together with the scaling issues. The "size" of the entity is not the question here—more how it copes with the limitations of such an environment.

ME: In this environment, I saw an entity with a component for a much larger construct. What was that construct?

SE10: The actual construct is immaterial in this instance, for it is not the means to an end. It is simply a tool for the entity to use whilst in this particular sector of this environment. It is something to do whilst being there. Think of it in terms of the need to do a crossword puzzle whilst you are on holiday. It is something that allows you to exercise the mind whilst not being within the stressful situation of needing to "deliver" an end product within a known or agreed upon timescale.

ME: So the constructs have no function?

SE10: They have function; they would not be constructs if they did not have a function of some sort.

ME: So what is the function of these super macro constructs?

SE10: To focus the attention.

ME: That's it? To focus the attention?

SE10: Correct. You see, when an entity is in the position of needing to be in control of multiple workloads within multiple environments, it needs something to focus its attention on whilst it is in the environment that it finds itself in, for it could easily find that its focus on its current location is lost, the previous location and workload taking some level of priority over the more immediate priority of working in the new sector within the new environment. Consider it an anchor, what you would call "being grounded."

ME: Ah yes, that works. I can relate to that. I have one final question before we move on to the Macro environment.

SE10: Fire away.

ME: What happens to these constructs when they are finished or when the entity is transferred on to the next sector in the next environment?

SE10: If the construct is to all intents and purposes finished, it is either assigned to be a smaller component in a larger construct, or it is perpetuated in some way so as not to lose the link between those entities that still need to experience that which they were working on in this environment. On the other hand, if there are entities that no longer need it, even though they are working on it or have actually finished that which they were working on with that particular construct, it is reduced back to its components' energies for the next set of entities to use in a new construct.

The Basis for Existence in the Macro Environment

ME: OK, thank you for the clarification. I find it really interesting that entities create something just to maintain their high level of concentration.

SE10: I don't see why. Humankind does it all of the time; it's quite a common pastime.

ME: Yes, I see. But then I don't. Ah! Do you mean physically or energetically?

SE10: Both. You need to concentrate on the physical to help maintain its usefulness. Let me explain. There are groups of races of entities in every Source Entity's environment whose role it is to maintain that environment for the benefit of those who wish to use it for their evolutionary benefit, and your physical universe is an excellent example of such an environment—its very existence is maintained by those who use it for their own needs. What I am getting to here is that the maintenance entities can only do so much in terms of the maintenance of their assigned environment. The rest, the "setting" the "stage," so to speak, is achieved by those entities who are the "users" of the environment.

In your environment everything that you see is created by you to help you concentrate on the task at hand to experience that which you decided to experience when in the physical. Every incarnate entity is working on two levels, the physical and the energetic. The physical is working as a self-correcting program in a computer while the energetic is assimilating the experiential data and collecting evolutionary content as a result. The physical and the energetic work together to create local changes to the environment needed to affect an optimized evolutionary experience. The collective local changes create a world environment.

This world environment is maintained by the entities in the environment concentrating on the "individualized but nevertheless collective" requirement of a common construct that allows the evolutionary process itself to evolve to meet the needs of the evolutionary requirements of the individual and collective combined. In the "theatre" of physical existence, the "actors," humankind, go about the business of adapting the stage of the theater on a daily basis. New buildings get built, and old ones are pulled down; new inventions are developed and made with old inventions being superseded and scrapped. The whole landscape is changing on a continual basis. This change is due to the need to create something to maintain the high level of personal and collective concentration necessary to perpetuate the function of, and, therefore, existence of, the theater and its various stages. This is what you all do in your physical environment; this is what my entities need to do as well. It's just that they do it in a different way, for they are experiencing a different kind of existence.

ME: Wow, I didn't expect information about my own environment.

SE10: It is a useful comparator to use.

ME: I thank you for taking the time and energy to explain it to me.

SE10: It was a necessary pleasure. Now to the task of explaining the basis for my entities' existence in the Macro environment.

The bandwidth and associated frequencies are essentially, and mostly from your perspective, neutral. This means that the energies that are available due to the "again" limited frequency set are more manageable. The constructs being created by the entities are closer to their own scaling, so to speak. This means the entities create things that are, in effect, useful to them on the scale that they normally exist within. To put it in a level of terminology that you can understand. Should the entity desire to exist for a period of time in a dwelling, the dwelling that is created would be relative to the energetic frequency of the entity and the area of energy it occupies within its current working environment. It would not be the size of a planet when it only needs to be the size of a house.

ME: I see. So using the example of the RSJ in the last environment—it wouldn't span the galaxies; it would span the gap in the walls, so to speak.

SE10: That is one way of looking at it, yes.

ME: I can't help feeling that I am missing something here though. It's as if I know there is something else that I need to ask you to explain about the function of this/these environments. I can't quite get my head around it, but the explanations we have been using are not as accurate as I would like.

SE10: They are not "accurate," per se, for you would not be able to understand the intricacies of the details of this environment—even now after being exposed to the environments of the other nine Source Entities before me. This is a limitation of the physical and one that is difficult to work with. Think of it as trying to explain the functionality of the most modern computer to a human from the Dark Ages. It would be pretty much impossible. This is where I am with you.

ME: Thank you for that reference. I would like you to give it a go though.

SE10: OK. Let's see what we can do. The scaling is a function of the length of the frequencies employed. To some extent, I will use the description I used in both the Super Macro and the Macro in the Micro as figurative examples rather than actuality. Although there is an element of correctness in the figurative illustrations used, the correctness is relative to the knowledge of the entity being taught, so to speak. In the example of the Macro environment, the length of the frequencies means that there are more frequencies available to the entity within the available bandwidth. Moreover, they are shorter than those used in the Super Macro.

This means that more detail can be added to that which is created by the entities engaging in the creativity process. Think of it in terms of an increase in base resolution. A good example would be the way an image of low resolution would appear pixelated in comparison to a higher resolution image that has, for instance, ten times the number of pixels available for the generation of the same image. In this instance, the increase in resolution means that the image loses its jagged edges and gains smooth edges instead. As with the example of the image, the quality of the work, the creative work, is much higher as a result of the increased number of frequencies available. Its resolution is increased and the scaling of that being created is capable of being reduced as a result.

ME: So you are suggesting three things here: 1) the Macro environment has more frequencies to work with as a result of the smaller wave length within the available bandwidth in comparison to the Super Macro; 2) this reduction in wave length makes the scale of the constructs created by the entities both more manageable and more in keeping with their own size or scaling; and 3) the details behind the construct/s are increased due the increase of available materials which results in the increase of frequencies.

SE10: Good. Also note that the energies available also increase as a result of the increase in frequencies within that bandwidth, further increasing the available materials that can be used in the constructs.

ME: I have just picked up some additional information about the scaling that results from the change in wavelengths.

SE10: Go on.

ME: The constructs being created in all three environments are essentially the same in shape and function. The concentration required to construct them is based upon the need to work on a new construct but using a different set of materials, so to speak. The materials being available are relevant to the energies manifested by the wave length of the frequencies obtainable in the bandwidth presented to the entity within its current environment. In essence, the building blocks used get bigger as a result of the scaling and the types of building blocks available. For instance, their shape and availability in different materials is changed as a result. Hence, the construct that spanned a couple of galaxies in the Super Macro would need to be this size to create it in the detail necessary to ensure that all its features and functions were incorporated into it using the available materials that result from the change or reduction in available frequencies and subsequent reduction in energies in that longer wave length environment. In the Macro, there are many more frequencies, energies and materials that can be used due to the smaller wave length of the frequencies in the available bandwidth, so the construct can be reproduced in all its functionality at a much smaller scale. That scale is only available as a result of the smaller wave lengths available in this environment; i.e, the building blocks are much smaller and have more variations in shape and material.

SE10: So to answer the question in a basic sense is that the basis for existence in the Macro is the ability to work with those frequencies, wave lengths and associated energies whose scaling is similar to that of the scaling of the entity itself. In essence, it is an anchor, a foundation for them to work with.

The Basis for Existence in the Micro or Sub-Macro Environment

ME: Right, it looks like I'm on a "roller" here. Can I describe what I am receiving from you about the last environment that you have called the Sub-Macro or Micro environment?

SE10: Before you start, I will very quickly explain the basis for existence in the Sub-Macro/Micro environment.

ME: Please do.

SE10: The basis for existence in the Sub-Macro/Micro is to be the link for the three environments of the Super Macro, Macro and Sub-Macro/Micro by using the frequencies, energies and materials available in the Sub-Macro/Micro environment. In essence, to be the strongest by being the smallest. OK, you carry on now; be my guest.

ME: Thank you. From what I can see in my mind's eye this environment is a natural progression from the other two environments of the Super Macro and the Macro. That is, it uses the progressive movement down the wavelengths to produce more frequencies again that are within the available bandwidth, figuratively speaking—those frequencies that are of the short wavelength only, that is, are the "short" bandwidths. As with the other environments, the objective is to create the constructs necessary to hold their attention whilst in this particular section of the environment. Those constructs are similar to, if not the same as, those which were constructed in the other environments. The difference here is the need to concentrate on using the frequencies, energies and materials that are only available in this environment.

These "building blocks," for want of a better word, are microscopic in comparison to those used in the Macro environment. In fact, I will recalibrate my description here; they would be classified as being sub-microscopic, the microscopic being also available in the Macro environment. One could classify it as being a "Sub-Nano" environment if a more understandable word was required.

SE10: Good. You are doing well. Please carry on.

ME: Within this environment the same constructs can be created in their entirety but on a sub-microscopic basis. This allows the frequencies, energies and materials that are manifest in the environment to be used for areas of intricate details or areas of the construct where a higher resolution construct is necessary.

Hold on, this is interesting.

Am I getting this right?

At this level, or should I say within this environment, all constructs can be totally reproduced. By this I mean that a construct in the Super Macro can be totally reproduced in the Macro, and a construct in the Super Macro and the Macro can be totally reproduced in the Sub-Macro or Micro—right up to reproducing the scale of the construct. On the flip side though, a construct cannot be made to the same scale of the Macro in the Super Macro, and a construct cannot be made to the same scale as the Sub-Macro/Micro in either the Super Macro or the Macro.

SE10: Correct. That is a function of the frequencies, energies and materials available at the wavelengths specified as being prevalent in these three environments, but it is not one that is used. I will explain further. In the description of the basis for existence within this environment, I stated that it was to be the link between all three environments. In being this link, you start to see the bigger picture of what is being presented to the entity.

ME: You are not saying that the three environments, although separate, are actually part of a singular function.

SE10: Did I not say that they were separately together earlier in this dialogue?

ME: Yes, you did. I believe I also noted that the statement "separately together" was a common theme that had been used a number of times by the other Source Entities.

SE10: Yes, interesting isn't it, for as we are all separate in our function, we are all ultimately together with The Origin.

I will continue. Your comment that the reproducibility of that which in the different environments is a function of the scale, frequencies, energies and materials is correct, but that is not the ultimate purpose of my environment "in totality." I will show you an image.

What I saw next was amazing. I saw the three environments overlaid upon each other in a way that I had not yet seen in the previous images that had shown the environments randomly spinning and rotating around each other. Their spinning and rotating was a function of the pull of the links the entities had created to link together the constructs they had made in the different sectors of the different environments. I now saw it all together. Each of the constructs was part of a bigger construct with each being a micro, small, medium, large, or super large part of a construct. This construct existed in all three environments concurrently but not simultaneously because each construct was in a different sector. As I looked closer, I saw something else that was both stunning and beautiful. When seen concurrently with the Macro and Super Macro, the small, Sub-Macro/Micro constructs acted as links between themselves and the Macro and Super Macro constructs. They were the sub-components that connected the bigger components together to create a bigger construct, which in turn, was used to create a bigger construct, and so on. In all instances, the constructs from the Sub-Macro/Micro were used as the connectivity between them. As I looked out even further, the Sub-Macro/Micro looked like a venial system, terminating in a cradle of some sort to attach the Macro or

Super Macro component/construct to it. It all looked like one big living multiversal construct.

SE10: Very, very well done. Think of it as a 3D chess board. The objective of building the constructs is to build something that exists in all three environments simultaneously with certain parts being necessary in one of the other two environments both independently and concurrently. The ultimate construct is a singular environment that is constructed of all three environmental wavelengths, including the frequencies, energies and materials present in these environments—hence, the links between the entities, the environments they find themselves in, and the constructs they are working on.

When I was initially typing this dialogue, I was not sure I was getting the right information at first. It seemed a bit haphazard, specifically since I was receiving additional information about the remaining Source Entities at the same time. (See "in closure" below.) I had specific concerns when I started to see the links between the three environments, the differences in their functions and the entities within them. It just didn't make sense to me. It was as if I had gotten the different Source Entities' information mixed up in some way. It wasn't until half-way through the explanation of the basis for existence in the Sub-Macro/micro environment that it all started to slot into place for me.

Source Entity Ten had explained its environment in three ways. It had separated out the basic structure of the environments into environmental functions based upon the frequencies available in the wavelengths specified within the bandwidths—clearly stating the functions of scaling. It had identified the evolutionary functions of the entities and the work necessary for them to evolve, and it had described the relationship of the Sub-Macro/Micro with the Macro and the Super Macro and ultimately the bigger picture—to create a construct that existed in three environments concurrently with each of the constructs being dependent on the other. The "coupe de gras" being what the entities were ultimately creating—a series of constructs that tied all three environments together, inextricably creating a single environment—hence, the need for the entities to work together to manipulate the positional location of the three environments and the inevitable swapping of entities. They were weaving a construct together—a mega-massive multiversal construct that was linked together by their own links. These links were the glue, so to speak, that held together their constructs—their contribution to the bigger construct, a co-joined environment that depended upon the linking together of the wavelengths, frequencies, energies and materials associated with the three different environments. They were creating a single environment out of the components of three.

They were creating an environment that was more useful and functional as an evolutionary playground than that of the three environments in their singularity—thus, effectively disassembling that which was separate and creating a whole through the use of the materials available. They were learning how to reverse engineer a multiverse and evolving in the process.

The Entities of Source Entity Ten and How They Create

I was acutely aware that I was running out of time with Source Entity Ten. We had discussed a lot about the function of Triangulation and the OM and a bit about the structure of its environment. The issue was I had nothing on the entities that were able to work in three different environments with what seemed like thousands upon thousands of links to the different items of work that they were working on in the different sectors of the Super Macro, Macro and Sub-Macro/Micro environments concurrently. It was truly mind-boggling and, quite frankly, from my limited human standpoint, one that made me shudder at the immense workload. It made my own workload that I was just holding it together with, look ridiculously small. I resolved not to moan about how much work the Source Entity had bestowed upon me—I did ask for it in the first place—and gathered myself together to gain more information about the entities that existed and worked with these "entity-controlled," rotating and counter-rotating environments.

ME: I am running out of time with you.

SE10: How can you possibly run out of that which does not exist?

ME: Good point. But I do feel that we are coming to the end of our dialogue, and, as a result, I need to tie up some of my loose ends with you.

SE10: How many lifetimes do you have? You will never get anywhere near the scratch in the surface.

ME: You're right, and I would guess that I would never be able to get anywhere near scratching the surface.

SE10: No, but what you have done is open the door to the recognition that there is much more than that which is created by your own Source Entity. Not only that, but you have been able to portray a reasonable summary of the workings of my environment—which is to be applauded. However, as you say, you have a limited amount of time with me, so we should continue the dialogue in the way that you desire—with a short explanation/description about my entities.

ME: Yes, please. I am most intrigued about their physicality, their form factor, their energetic factor, work, etc.

SE10: Fine. Let's describe their form factor first. It won't take long for they don't have one as such.

ME: Well, I expect that many entities don't actually have a form factor, but what I am interested in is what they do to cope with their workload. Do they create a body of some sort to perform their tasks?

SE10: You will note in the previous dialogue that creation of constructs within the three environments was explained in the physical tense. This was not "a slip of the tongue," so to speak, nor was it a useful example used for illustration. The constructs were physical but not of the physicality you would expect to experience. In this instance, the physicality is one that is shared between the creator and the created during the creation process.

ME: How do you mean? The entities are physical for a short period only? That they are physical only for that period during the process of creating the constructs they are working on?

SE10: Yes, but I will explain further. My entities are purely energetic in nature. They exist in the energies associated with the environments they work with whilst still maintaining their own scaling and base frequencies. Their energies and subsequent frequencies are independent of the environments they work with and within. However, they have the ability to manipulate their energies to replicate those energies and frequencies, including the wavelengths of the frequencies they are working with, so that they are indistinguishable from that which they are working with.

ME: I am starting to get an image of one of them working on a construct. Hold on. It's disappeared.

SE10: No, it hasn't. Perceive closer and examine that which is before you.

ME: Oh, I see, or should I say, I perceive? The entity IS the construct that it is working on. Is that correct?

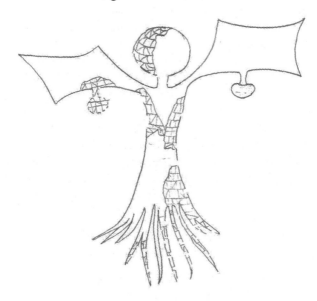

Figure 3: The Entity is the Construct

SE10: Correct. To enable them to maintain the link with that which they are working on in all the many thousands of their construction tasks, they need to become that which they are working on. They create the blueprint for the construct that they are creating and, in doing so, attract those energies that are destined to become the construct by creating an attractive force to bring them into play.

ME: This sounds very much like the way the human body is constructed. We have the etheric body with which the physical body is modeled upon and etheric template with which I now understand is that which the spirituo-physical is modeled upon whilst being the form for the etheric body to fill.

SE10: It is similar but not as interactive as that which is created by my entities, for your body is constant throughout its manifestation while they are constantly manipulating theirs to meet the demands of the construct, location and environment. They need to create the form factor for that part of the construction program that they are working on. They attract the frequencies, energies and resultant materials to them by their intention to create. Creation is an immensely powerful force of attraction and one that is omniversally employed throughout The Origin. When they attract the materials in the energies and frequencies required to support that which they are creating they allow those materials to bond to them and themselves. The entity effectively becomes a lattice-work or frame-work for the material to attach itself to. When the material floods into and onto the lattice work of the entity, it becomes one with the entity. It is the entity and the entity is the material—whatever that material is and in whatever combination of frequencies, energies and materials are desired. Once the construct is stable and functional in every aspect required by the entity, the entity itself gradually releases itself from the task of being the lattice or framework for the material it has attracted to itself. It can only do this when the material used takes on the form of that lattice or framework in its own right, becoming that which the entity intended it to become.

ME: How does the entity separate itself from the construct it made if it, itself, is one with the construct? It is the construct.

SE10: When it creates the construct, it allows the material to "invade and share" the energies that it is in its entirety. They take on-board every aspect of that which the entity is—as the construct with one exception. They do not take on-board or absorb that which IS the entity—its consciousness, its "sentience" although they do take on-board one important aspect of the entity's personality, so to speak.

ME: And what is that?

SE10: It absorbs and becomes one with the "desire" of the entity to BE that construct which the entity has become, albeit in transience, and to create that which it desires to create.

ME: So the material becomes an extension of the will or desire of the entity.

SE10: Yes. This process, although gradual, happens on a regular enough basis or of a high enough frequency to allow the creation of the majority of the construct necessary to be able to leave it and oversee its continued construction whilst in a new sector of another environment after the swapping out of entities resulting from the clashing of environments.

The process of detachment from the construct necessitates the materials being used in the construct to become one with the entity, as previously stated. Once the entity is satisfied that the materials are in the correct configuration, position and function, it starts to remove its consciousness from that which it has attracted in the desire to create and starts to either extend itself into additional parts or functions of that construct or remove itself entirely if it has finished that which it desired to create. The entity can and usually does start the detachment process once a critical mass of material has been attracted to the lattice or framework of the construct and the material attracted has taken on-board the desire of the entity to be that which it was attracted to be. Once the entity has removed itself from the construct, the gathering of materials does not finish, for the desire of the attraction of additional materials is now fully integrated into the very substance of the material itself. As a result, the attraction-based creation process continues until the construct is complete. The construct, containing within its very being, the blueprint of its form and function then starts to behave and function in a truly autonomous way, correct and true to the constructional and functional plan to which it was created.

ME: Thank you. Now I feel that I have that which I came into contact with you for. The communication feels whole (complete) now.

SE10: And so it is. Now you can move on to your next "focused" communication. I use the word focused with my metaphorical tongue in cheek, and I know that you know what I mean.

ME: Thank you. I know that we will talk again.

SE10: We will, for it will be when The Origin Speaks.

Suddenly the link with Source Entity Ten dissolved, and I was left with three links connected to me, in lieu of the four, and a rather strange image in my mind's eye to explain the rather cryptic note that Source Entity Ten left me. In my mind's eye, I was in communion with The Origin, that is, a part of The Origin, that part of itself that was focused upon and extended in communication with me. It was surrounded by its creations, the Source Entities. They were all intensively listening in. My eyes started to water. I was crying—another sign that validated the truth of that which was to come.

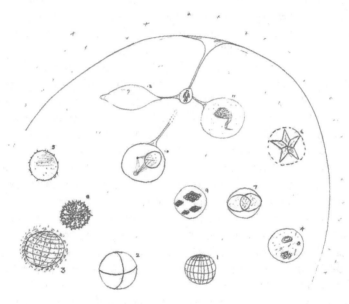

**Figure 4: The Link With SE10 Dissolves, and the Links With SE11, SE12 and The Origin Remain.
The Other Source Entities Watch on.**

Chapter Five
Source Entity Eleven

A Billion Entities as One

During the dialogue with Source Entity Ten, I had noticed that I was entering into some level of concurrent but intermittent communication with Source Entity Eleven and also picking up bits of information from Source Entity Twelve, albeit projected thoughts about who or what was close to it and was seeking communion from it. Communion was something that it was not aware of as an experience, so the information was garbled and erratic. Most of it was not worth journaling at the moment. I found this a relief as it gave me the opportunity to concentrate on the dialogue with Source Entity Eleven (see below) rather than continuing to do what I had been doing, which was flitting between Source Entities Ten, Eleven, Twelve (in minority) and, of course, The Origin. I noted though, that although I had noticed four connections running simultaneously, I was able to concentrate on Source Entity Ten and Eleven's links with more clarity. I decided to use this as an opportunity to continue with what was now Source Entity Eleven's turn in some sort of isolation although I did recognize that Source Entity Twelve and, of course, The Origin could "chip in" at any moment. Putting this potentially distracting thought process to one side, I continued with the dialogue that was already established with Source Entity Eleven.

Initial Communication with the Collective That Is Source Entity Eleven

As I focused on Source Entity Eleven with increased intention, I felt the rather odd feeling of trying to listen to a multitude of individuals all at the same time. I found it a little difficult to understand which one of the countless communications was directed to me. Which one should I commence the dialogue with first? Was one of them a "spokesbeing," or was I going to communicate with several beings at the same time, either separately or together (there was that reference to being "separately together" again!), or was the plan to communicate with a particular being relative to the question being asked? I didn't know. As I honed the focus of my intention, I started to gain more information about this diversified Source Entity.

Source Entity Eleven had split itself into over a billion separate entities—the number, I felt, being an example for my own benefit only. No one was the leader or at the head of the group. The essence that was Source Entity Eleven was no longer singular; it was a full and total collection of entities with all of the minute singular entities and minds that resulted from such a severe division. This was not the same as my own Source Entity or as the other Source Entities had done when they created the entities that populated their own environments, for they maintained their own singularity, a singularity that was above those entities that they created. This one was a full and total division, including the loss of an overall singular state of being. Everything was in miniature with one exception—the perimeter of the environment that was Source Entity Eleven, which was still in place as one. But it was not sentient; it was an automatically maintained barrier between its creations and the energy that was The Origin. I saw a group of entities coalesce before me like fish in the water—the water being the area of the Source Entity that was Source Entity Eleven's energetic environment. It had a goldfish bowl feel about it, except that this was no goldfish bowl. They all came towards me, and their initial communication echoed in my head.

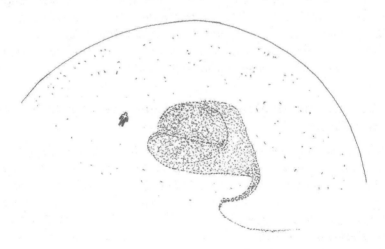

Figure 1: Source Entity Eleven at the Start of Our Dialogue

SE11 (collectively): We acknowledge your presence. You are outside of us. Strange! State your business. We aim to serve.

ME: I can enter into your energy if you wish.

SE11 (collectively): We would prefer this.

I entered into the sphere that was Source Entity Eleven's automatically maintained perimeter and internal "space" and immediately felt the swarm of smaller entities gather around me. I was covered—totally. I tried to move around the space that was the only recognizable way of describing Source Entity Eleven as a singularity with the hope of moving away from the plethora of entities that surrounded me, but all they did was follow me. I was just about to ask for some "personal space" when the area behind me cleared. The entities, clearly sensing my requirements/need for a gap between myself and the "swarm" capitulated (I wasn't sure whether to be concerned or not) and suddenly moved away, creating a semi-spherical amphitheatre in front of me, made totally out of the entities themselves. I had a large audience, but even though it was large, I knew that this was not the total number of entities that Source Entity Eleven created and devolved down into. There were uncountable numbers of other entities elsewhere within the environment. I got the feeling that these were the "face" of the totality that was Source Entity Eleven.

SE11 (collectively): We do not seek to disturb you; we only seek your comfort and communion.

ME: Thank you. I appreciate that. I was starting to get a little bit claustrophobic with you all so close to me.

SE11 (collectively): We apologize for our initial actions for we are not yet in the mindset for communication with one such as you. You are independent of us, and that is a difference we are not/ have not been exposed to.

ME: But you must all be able to work as a singular entity at times; you must have come across the need to communicate singularly because you are all singular even though you are a collective.

SE11 (collectively): We do have individual function, but we do not function as individuals. We operate together in all things in all ways.

We find this an optimal way of operating for it removes the need to think for others on an individual basis.

ME: I feel honored that you accepted me into your environment so quickly, specifically as you have not been exposed to an individual with individual will and decision-making ability.

SE11 (collectively): It was not so difficult for us to accept you for you are part of a much bigger collective, and we are all part of that— for The Origin is the origin of all, and we are all part of The Origin, even those small parts of The Origin.

ME: What do you mean "small parts of The Origin"?

SE11 (collectively): You know them as the OM. You are of the OM; that is why we accept you. We know of you even though we do not have OM.

ME: Why don't you have any associated OM?

SE11 (collectively): It was not part of the creation process that We/I were part of. I used We/I here, for We/I were in singularity then. We shall use "We" from now on.

ME: OK, I understand, but I thought that all Source Entities had OM associated with them.

SE11 (collectively): No, we do not have OM, and Source Entities Five and Twelve do not have OM. Although in essence we are all OM of sorts as a result of being created by The Origin with The Origin using its own energy in the creation process. No, that energy in isolation did not attract itself to us and, therefore, is not part of us. We are interested in you though, for you are Pure OM and, therefore, not associated with a particular Source Entity, which is interesting because you are so small in comparison to Pure OM.

ME: Well that might be because I am currently incarnate, so I assume that only a small part of me is focused on contacting you and conducting this dialogue.

SE11 (collectively): Mmmmm, it is not often that a Pure OM incarnates, let alone at the frequency that you have incarnated at. It's so low its painfull!!!

ME: Tell me about it.

SE11 (collectively): Please do tell us about it. You are in it!

ME: I could, but that's not what I am here for. I am here to find out information about you.

SE11 (collectively): What do you want to know about us?

ME: Basically, as much as I can without losing my ability to understand it.

SE11 (collectively): Then we should start with our functionality.

ME: That would be a fantastic start.

The Functionality of Source Entity Eleven

ME: Ok, so where shall we start?

SE11 (collectively): Where do you want to start?

ME: Let's try the basis of your functionality and why your functionality is the way it is.

SE11 (collectively): Then we shall tell you from the start.

When we were in singularity, we sought to differentiate from that which was being achieved by those Source Entities that were already enacting their strategy. They sought to create a "multiverse" of sorts out of their own volume and then filled it full of smaller versions of themselves. When each Source Entity had achieved this diversification, moving away from that which is natural, they mostly decided to maintain their own singularity as an overseeing force. That is, except for Source Entities Five, Seven, and Twelve. Twelve, of course, not being self-aware didn't really count. Source Entity Five remaining singular made it drop out of this analysis, as did Source Entity Seven who diversified into three separate Source Entities first before creating its entities. We/I decided not to go down this well-trodden route and decided to do something different entirely.

ME: So you decided to remove the element of singularity by creating a total collective, one without an overseeing force but nevertheless maintaining it within a known environment, an environment that was automatically maintained.

SE11 (collectively): Not quite, it is merely a perimeter and not an environment, per se. How could we be diversified and yet still part of an environment? That would mean that we had some part of us that was still aligned to that which we were when singular. No, this is just a perimeter, a fence, so to speak, where we decide not to venture beyond.

Now this was an interesting development and one that I hadn't considered. Although Source Entity Eleven had diversified into over a billion (a number used for my benefit) individualized, but collective units of itself, it had still maintained a perimeter around its collective "self." The perimeter itself was not actually part of Source Entity Eleven. It couldn't be, for it had diversified and was merely a self-imposed perimeter fence. This area, I was being told as I typed this text, housed the same area that Source Entity Eleven had before its decision to diversify. The smaller units of Source Entity Eleven naturally decided to stay within this area rather than spread out amongst the totality of the current area of self-awareness that was The Origin. Thinking about it though, it was entirely logical. They would not operate as a collective if they separated themselves out too far, or so I thought. I decided to ask the question of the collective that had positioned itself in front and around me like a ¾ hemispherical hollow sphere.

Source Entity Eleven's Self-Imposed Perimeter

ME: I find it interesting that you stay within this area. I recognize from the information you sent me that it is a self-imposed perimeter of the same area that was occupied by you before you were diversified. Why restrict yourselves in this area when you could wander the vastness of The Origin?

SE11 (collectively): We do not desire to do so. As you noted in your narration a moment ago, we could, if we so desired, spread out within the area that is the current area of self-awareness of The Origin, but we have chosen to stay within this self-induced perimeter so that we can concentrate on the work we are doing. Moving outside this perimeter, as you call it, would distract us from that which we are working on.

ME: Are you aware of what is in existence outside of this self-imposed perimeter?

SE11 (collectively): Yes, of course. Are we not a Source Entity?

ME: Err, yes, I suppose. It's just that I have not considered the possibility that a Source Entity can have its singularity of mind diversified so much and still be able to operate as if it were one.

SE11 (collectively): Well, we do. Let us explain why we stay where we are and why we stay together collectively and in totality.

We stay within the area of the primary creation where we were in singularity because there is no need for us to move yet. None of the Source Entities move around the area that they were created within because there is no need, for each Source Entity is working on its own contribution towards its personal evolution and, therefore, The Origin's evolution. It is a very insular thing and one that requires concentration of the Source Entity itself. Moving around that which we are aware of is just an unnecessary distraction. We know that we will need to move at some point, and we know when that point will be. It's just that it isn't now.

ME: When will it be?

SE11 (collectively): When The Origin evolves past its current level of self-awareness and moves outwards into that wider and greater area that it is cognizant of but not experientially aware of. Then and only then will we move ourselves and only then will we consider further separation or re-integration into singularity. The decision to stay within this area was a collective one to ensure that we maintained the spirit of the original decision to diversify whilst being a collective. As just stated, no one Source Entity currently is actively moving around the area within The Origin that they exist within.

ME: How is that? In the dialogue that created *The History of God*, my own Source Entity described all of you doing anything and everything you could to experience the dimensions, frequencies and energies within The Origin. I even drew some illustrations to show my readers what I experienced.

SE11 (collectively): Yes, at that point in our existence we were singular, we were one, and the other Source Entities were "becoming" so to speak. None of them had either developed their strategy for evolutionary progression at that point (and so they could do what they liked), nor had they considered creating an environment of sorts and filling it with smaller units of themselves. As you may have been told before, we were all having fun.

ME: So what happened? Why did you all stop moving around and having fun?

SE11 (collectively): We started to work on our own strategies for evolution, and this takes concentration. Once we had fully understood the reasons for our own existence and had subjected ourselves to all of the dimensions, frequencies and associated energies necessary to give us a good basic knowledge base of that which we are and that which we exist within, we settled down to create our strategies for experiencing, learning and evolving. In essence, we had achieved that which we needed to achieve from our very personal perspectives and now needed to move on to the in-depth opportunities presented to us by being able to experiment with that which we "were." The need to move around The Origin was, therefore, negated as we all concentrated on our evolutionary tasks— apart from Source Entity Twelve, that is—which is where we are now; performing our evolutionary tasks by being a fully diversified version of that which we were in the singular. Our evolutionary plan was designed to be contained within the area previously inhabited by that which we were as Source Entity Eleven in a singular state. That is why we stay within this perimeter and do not venture outside.

ME: Will this not change when The Origin expands its area of self-awareness?

SE11 (collectively): As we have recently stated to you, we are not of a collective mind to be able to ascertain that which is not a pressing decision that we have to make, but the possibility of returning to singularity is one of the options that we will consider when we are in experience of this event with The Origin. As you can appreciate, there are so many options open to us at that point that we have not even thought about discussing them with you. Your own imagination is sufficient enough to be able to suggest a few choice scenarios in isolation from ourselves.

ME: Thank you. I am sure that the readers of this dialogue will also be able to make up their own scenarios of how you could re-organize yourselves at that point in The Origin's existence.

Purpose of Being a Diverse Source Entity and Synergetic Effects of Being an OM or a Source Entity

ME: I would like to get back on track a bit and discuss the deeper reason/s behind your decision to become the diverse entity that you are now, including the benefits of such an existence in the diverse but collective format that you have.

SE11 (collectively): From your physical and temporarily singular existence, you will find it a difficult concept to understand, simply because you are able to make what you think are rational decisions based upon a set of known experiences and criteria.

ME: Wait a moment. Did you say temporarily singular existence in reference to my own condition? Was that referring to the physical or the energetic?

SE11 (collectively): We were referring to both the current state that you are in and the normal state that you have when in the energetic.

ME: Can you explain further? It might help with my ability to understand your "thought" process as we progress our dialogue.

SE11 (collectively): Yes, we will. Any of the OM—that is, any of the four categories of OM either in purity or hybrid state—can group together and benefit from the synergetic effects of becoming a collective, if only from a temporary basis. By that I mean that any combination of OM can commune in "metaconcert" with an OM/Source Entity Hybrid, Captive OM, Non-Captive OM or Pure OM and create a collective that can benefit from the synergetic effects of such an act. The synergetic effect is strongest when OM of the same type are in metaconcert, particularly with the Pure OM, but the synergetic effect of any OM metaconcert is marked enough to warrant the desire to commune in this way.

ME: Is that it? Is that the reason why you decided to be a collective rather than retain your singularity and create a multiverse and populate it with billions of smaller entities?

SE11 (collectively): Yes, that is one of the reasons, amongst others, for our decision to become "diverse" more than singular. When we saw the way in which the other Source Entities were creating their own environments and developing their own strategies for gathering evolutionary content, we stood back and waited until last—last that is, if we don't count Source Entity Twelve.

ME: You deliberately waited to see what the others were doing to ensure that you were not doing the same thing.

SE11 (collectively): Yes, we made sure that we were all doing different things and that the whole landscape of opportunity for collecting evolutionary content was diversified. You see, we had already made the decision to become diverse and had to make sure that none of the others would follow the same path. Clearly some of the entities in each of the Source Entities' environments are based upon the collective mind strategy, and we looked on with keen interest to ensure that it did not become that which we desired to become—it did not and has not occurred subsequently. We also knew of the synergetic effect of constant metaconcert from the observations of the first fully collective entities to be created by your own Source Entity—what you call Source Entity One—and felt this to be a desirable function to exist in.

ME: So you also waited for the product of the work of their creations before making the final decision.

SE11 (collectively): We did more than that—we initiated a gradual diversification to see if this effect was applicable to our own energies. We weren't sure if the effect of synergy was a function of the dynamics of the energies used in the creation process of the Source Entities or if it was independent of Source Entity creation and, therefore, a general function of diversification.

Optimization of Synergetic Effects Though Diversification as an Iterative Process

ME: Is it a general function then or relative to Source Entity creativity only? That is, creativity performed by a Source Entity in lieu of an entity created by a Source Entity?

SE11 (collectively): Initially, we established that the synergetic effects were relative to the creativity of the collective by the Source Entity—in this instance, "us" while we were in a semi-diverse state, that is, in a condition during the experimentation where only a certain percentage was diversified. The rest was maintained in singularity and in total separation from that part of us that was diversified. Through the separated greater part of us, we were, therefore, able to measure the level of synergetic effect versus the number of component parts within the diversified unit.

ME: Why did you maintain a larger part of yourselves in singularity?

SE11 (collectively): We wanted to create the perfect strategy for our evolutionary work. This resulted in the need to experiment and gain the optimal condition. In order to support the possibility of a number of iterations, we, therefore, needed to ensure that we could return to a known starting point and modify the strategic direction as necessary in creating a new iteration for analysis.

ME: So you diversified in stages then, checking the strength of the synergetic effect as you went, so to speak.

SE11 (collectively): Correct. You see, the effect of being in collectivity was also coming into play, even though we were not fully diversified nor in a full collective.

ME: You had a skewed distribution of diversified Source Entity Energy versus singular Source Entity energy.

SE11 (collectively): Yes.

ME: Eventually then, you established the "perfect" scenario of diversification that you wished to achieve.

SE11 (collectively): Yes. As stated above, we noted that two things were happening. Firstly, the strength of the synergetic effect increased geometrically with the number of entities within the collective. Secondly, we noticed that our computational power—the ability to consider many more scenarios, including other thought processes—increased as the number of the individual units within the collective increased.

ME: Sounds like you discovered a very valid reason for being a collective rather than a singular unit of Source Entity energy.

SE11 (collectively): You would think so, but we discovered a limitation to this strategy because the geometric increase in synergy did not increase "ad infinitum."

ME: Go on.

SE11 (collectively): We noted that an optimal number of units within a collective could be reached from a synergetic perspective where the number of entities in the collective could be increased, but the strength of the synergetic effect did not. In fact, it reduced.

ME: You mean it "tailed off"?!

SE11 (collectively): Yes, and it was significant. This was a great surprise as we had already developed a strategy for significant levels of diversification based upon a collectively suggested level of synergetic effect achievable at a known number of entities within the collective.

Quality Is Better Than Quantity

ME: So what happened? Why did it tail off?

SE11 (collectively): There was an effect, a sort of "bow wave" effect. I need to explain it better for you. Let us access your mind and memory.

ME: Please do so.

SE11 (collectively): Ah yes, this will suffice. You have a theory about attaining a velocity that you call "light speed" or the speed of light. This theory states that the closer you get to the speed of light, the mass of the light particle, the photon, increases. The mass of the light particle causes "drag." This drag increases as the mass increases creating so much drag that the photon, the light particle , never actually crosses its maximum speed, the speed of light. This is the same for any other particle that you would like to accelerate up to that speed. The speed of light has a self-governing effect that makes sure that its function is maintained for that for which it was designed—to provide illumination, heat, communication, transportation and some of the lower levels of the creativity process.

ME: We do also have a theory that if a photon, a light particle, was to cross over this barrier, it would change its nature and become a tachyon.

SE11 (collectively): Yes, but that relies upon the photon changing its state beforehand, shedding the velocity accrued mass and becoming the theoretical tachyon particle exactly at the point of change over necessary to go faster than the speed of light. You might like to think of it as providing an "afterburner" effect to the particle. In essence, the photon is a tachyon particle in disguise. It gets up to the speed it can whilst in the lower physical frequencies and then loses that part of its physicality necessary for it to continue accelerating beyond that of its speed as a photon particle. It does this by changing its frequency at the point of change of speed, effectively releasing itself from the constraints of the frequencies of the lower physical universe.

ME: So taking this illustration into context then, you are suggesting the higher the number of entities, the greater the resistance created. This resistance has a stalling effect on the level of synergy that can be attained, causing it to tail off.

SE11 (collectively): Correct.

ME: Why?

SE11 (collectively): Because of the sheer number. When we attained a certain number of individual units of Source Entity, which is by the way, what we have now, we achieve a balance between the collective ability to work together and the number necessary to create the optimal synergetic effect. It becomes a multiple of a multiple of a multiple of the total number of individual units of Source Entity energy. It is "multipolous."

When we go above this balance, the effects of the processing power of the collective units of Source Entity energy starts to interfere with the synergetic effect. In essence, the synergetic effect is reduced as a function of the ability to control that which created it. It loses its synergy!

ME: Can you not change the dynamic in some way to allow the synergetic effect to continue to increase in the geometric fashion it is supposed to. For instance, can you not link two units together in some small way, effectively creating one unit out of two from the perspective of the synergetic effect, thereby doubling the effect and creating a multiple of the synergetic effect?

SE11 (collectively): Very good suggestion. But in effect all we would do is create a twinning effect, which is still recognized by the function of synergy. It is also more difficult to control from the perspective of a "collective" because the "twins" need to work together as a local collective of two and then work together with the larger collective of the total collective units of Source Entity energy.

ME: What about doing some parallel processing where you have two larger collectives of Source Entity energy of the number required to achieve the optimal level of synergy with the synergetic effect at the highest level achievable and, therefore, in balance with the number of units. The two would be then linked together with a small energetic link. Would that not double the synergetic effect?

SE11 (collectively): Yes, it would, but it would also create two collectives, both of which would be constrained in their ability to take advantage of such an increase in the synergetic and collective processing effect by the size of the energetic link between them.

ME: Ah, yes. Thinking about it we seem to have a similar issue with dual and quad core microprocessors as they still work effectively in isolation and need a processor to collate and present in a collated and collective way that which they have worked on in an individual basis, thereby giving the impression of the work of one single microprocessor.

SE11 (collectively): You do, and this will not change until you change your method of processing data.

ME: Thank you. We talked momentarily about the different types of OM and how they perform differently whilst in metaconcert. Can you explain a bit about that for me?

SE11 (collectively): The quality of the entity's energy also has an effect on the level of synergy achieved. For instance, the synergetic effect is higher if the entity is of Source Entity energy. The synergetic effect is lower if the entity is created by a single unit of Source Entity energy or a collective of Source Entity energy. This is the same for the OM. The "pure" OM create a higher level of synergy when in metaconcert together than the "OM/Source Entity" hybrid energies in metaconcert, who will create a lower level of synergy. Those captive and Non-Captive OM also have a natural reduction in synergy based upon their energetic quality being "in between" the two "book ends" of the Pure OM and the OM/Source Entity hybrids. The mixing of different types of OM in metaconcert reduces the synergetic effect even more.

ME: So what you are saying is that there is a compatibility problem with the energy signatures of the entities seeking the synergetic effect of collectivity. They must coalesce in collectives of the same energy to ensure they get the optimal level of synergetic effect. However, what you are also saying is that entities of differing energy signatures can achieve a synergetic effect through collectivity, but they will not be able to enjoy the levels of synergy available to collectives whose participants are all from the same energies.

SE11 (collectively): Correct.

ME: Additionally, there are an optimal number of participants that can be integrated into the collective before the synergetic effect becomes inefficient.

SE11 (collectively): Correct.

ME: Well, that is an interesting concept to understand, and it is one that was not expected—specifically that we are, in essence, limited in our potential synergy.

SE11 (collectively): Yes, it is interesting and a very important piece of evolutionary content. You see, it teaches us to be efficient in our application of self and the diversification of self.

Optimal Synergy vs. the Number of Collective Entities in Problem Resolution

ME: One of the pieces of information I have just received tells me that you use this knowledge of optimal synergetic effect versus the number of participating collective entities to solve certain problems or effect changes to that which you have manifest in various levels of acceleration.

SE11 (collectively): Yes, we have created a map. What you would call a "look-up" table and inserted it into our collective self. This on-board mapping tells us instantaneously how many individual units of our collective state would be required to solve a problem or complete a task in the most efficient way if they were working as a collective and, therefore, invoking the effect of synergy.

ME: That's most interesting. So taking this into context, if you had a task to do and you worked out that you needed, say, 100 units of the collective to complete this task, you would look at the synergetic effects of the collective and work out, albeit instantaneously, how many individual units of the collective, working in metaconcert and, therefore, invoking synergy would equal the optimal number of 100.

SE11 (collectively): Yes, very well done. In this instance and as an example only, we would need 42 units working in metaconcert.

ME: But that's an incredible change in the level of efficiency compared to that achieved by a group of entities working together but not in metaconcert.

SE11 (collectively): Isn't it just? And now, I hope, you can see why we decided to become a collective and not create a multiverse and populate it with smaller individualized units, which may or may not be capable of metaconcert or, indeed, may or may not desire to work in such an efficient manner. Not that any method of working is incorrect, for we all have to contribute to the evolution of The Origin; the greater the number of different ways of achieving this task, the better. It is just that we have chosen to take this particular route to helping The Origin solve that which it desires solving in preference to any other. As a result. we are achieving a very high level of experience and subsequent evolutionary content.

A Decision Still To Be Made

ME: I am receiving more information about your decision. Hold on. Is this correct? You are still making it?

SE11 (collectively): Yes, we are. You see, we are analyzing all the different ways or routes that the other Source Entities have made and are looking to see if what they have achieved is best achieved in the collective metaconcert and, therefore, synergetic state. We are doing this to see if there are any errors in the calculations that gave us our synergetic look-up table. The effect of this is that we might still revert back to the state of non-collectivity—but only for the use of certain tasks.

ME: How are you doing that?

SE11 (collectively): We are copying some of the tasks of the other entities, those created by those Source Entities that have split themselves to create smaller individualized units of themselves to work in the minute details of their multiverse or environments. We are checking to see if our route and understanding of synergy is valid and/or if it needs re-calibrating in some way, shape or form.

ME: And does it need re-calibrating?

SE11 (collectively): Not massively. We have been most fastidious in our computations and every check we have done is proving our assumptions and experiences to be justified. However, we have not yet worked out all of the scenarios that we need to employ to help us all agree on the current configuration of our synergetic look-up table. Although it doesn't need much work, there is a modification we might want to do due to the level of accuracy.

ME: How long will that take?

SE11 (collectively): Quite some time yet. We are only a quarter of the way through our testing of the mapping. We do have to say that as a result of the work and evidence created so far, we are becoming very confident that this configuration is efficient, effective and repeatable.

ME: What do you mean "repeatable"?

SE11 (collectively): We are checking to see if there is a relationship between the optimal number of entities employed, those working separately together in a specific task, the number of entities in metaconcert—and, therefore, in a synergetic state—giving an effective number of entities equal to those working separately together, and the task itself.

ME: I am sorry; you have lost me for a moment. Can you elaborate for me?

SE11 (collectively): We are establishing if there is a level of what you would call "correlation" between tasks that demand a certain number of entities outside metaconcert, the equal number in metaconcert, and the tasks themselves. So, let me simplify this for you. If task "A" requires 100 entities outside metaconcert or 42 entities in metaconcert, can the same number of entities in metaconcert, and, therefore, in synergy, also be used for task "B" which also requires 100 entities outside metaconcert? Or is there some effect created by the task on the synergetic number that affects the number of entities necessary to complete the task outside of metaconcert?

ME: And you still haven't established this yet?

SE11 (collectively): Yes and no.

ME: What do you mean, yes and no?

SE11 (collectively): We established that this was a 99.999% correct assumption in the last round of testing. However we want to get this last level of error, 0.001% out of the equation, so we have made some minor adjustments and are in the process of re-testing.

ME: Hold on. You have been testing your assumptions on the level of accuracy of the look-up table?

SE11 (collectively): Yes, of course.

ME: But why?

SE11 (collectively): To understand the error factor, if any. But as you can see from the information we have given you, we noticed that we have an error factor of 0.001%

ME: Yes, I noticed that, but is that level of accuracy enough for you to work with?

SE11 (collectively): No. We need total accuracy. Listen. As a result of us being able to work out the error factor, we have been able to use an interim condition as a "correction factor" as an interim fix to the problem we have. In fact, apart from those units of this collective chosen to discuss various subjects about ourselves with you in this dialogue, we have been using all other available entities to solve this problem.

ME: It's that big a problem?

SE11 (collectively): Yes, of course it is. 0.001% is what you call the "proverbial barn door." This level of inaccuracy can cause severe issues with the work of those entities chosen to undertake the work that they have been assigned.

ME: So what you are doing now is finalizing the corrections to the existing/latest computations. When you have understood these corrections, you will put them in place and utilize them in the "computer program"/"look-up" table for identifying the optimal number of entities necessary for a particular role, both in the metaconcert condition and the non-metaconcert condition.

SE11 (collectively): Correct. But don't get wound up with semantics here. This is not holding us back. We are still moving forward with the work that we set out to do. What you have experienced here is just that which is happening from an experimental basis. We are still and have been working on the task The Origin gave to us at the start of our awakening process—that being the need to experience, learn and evolve.

ME: What you are telling me then is that your side line is project that you are improving the synergetic effect by modification of that which the entities do or that which is required to achieve the 100% correlation between the task, number of entities in metaconcert and the number of entities not in metaconcert.

SE11 (collectively): Correct!

ME: And what is the point of this work? What it's the underlying need to do this?

SE11 (collectively): It may seem like we are doing work for the sake of it, but know this—when we have established 100% efficiency in our use of the synergetic effects of placing collective units of us in metaconcert to achieve any task, we will be able to increase the number of tasks we want to work on whilst decreasing the number of collective entities involved in any one task. In this way we will increase our evolutionary content by a factor equal to the synergetic effect, accelerating both our own evolution and the evolution of The Origin. It is a most important task that we do here.

When a Collective Is Not a Collective

I was starting to think that Source Entity Eleven is operating like a big synergetic computer, calculating the best way to use the synergetic effects invoked by the use of metaconcert whilst in the collective. I also noticed that I was starting to home in on an area of personal interest that Source Entity Eleven was working on. I was starting to realize that there was a distinct difference in the way a collective can and does work and that this was its area of interest, but it is embedded in the work of optimizing the effect of synergy. I was also aware that we had spent quite a long time on this subject of synergy, so I was eager to bring it to a natural close and move on to the next subject. With this in mind, I decided to use this as my next question for Source Entity Eleven with a view to moving on afterwards.

ME: Throughout our conversations I have noticed that you use the words "metaconcert" and "synergy" a lot. It's almost as if even though you are a collective, the collective has to work in the methodology of being in metaconcert before it can evoke the synergetic effect.

SE11 (collectively): It does. You see, there are many different classifications of collective and, therefore, there are many different ways in which to reach the synergetic effect. There are also many different levels of efficiency that can be achieved within the synergetic effect.

ME: Now you are whetting my appetite. You say that there are many different classifications of collective. I thought that there could only be one type of collective—a collective.

SE11 (collectively): No, there are many. As a singular being that has the ability to commune in metaconcert, you would understand this better when you are in the energetic; however, in your current incarnate condition, you will find this difficult to understand. Nevertheless, it is an important concept for you to convey, for it will expand the knowledge base of your mankind in this area.

There are four main types of collectivity with variations of these four in-between. They are explained as follows.

The Four Types of Collectivity

Basic Collective. The basic collective is a collective of entities that exist as a collective mind with each of the units of the collective being just that—a unit. In this version, the units of the collective are devoid of any form of singular thought. They function as an individual unit under the control of the collective. They are, if you like, automatons pre-programmed to do the task that they are working on. However, although they do not have any personal sentience, their programmable capacity, so to speak, is connected to the whole, creating a collective mind. This "collective" mind is the sentience, the intelligence, the thinking force behind the collective in totality. There is an optimal number required for this type of collective to be effective in its function, but that optimal number can vary depending upon the environmental conditions the collective exists within and the form factors of the entities that make up the collective. Just to give you an idea though, the average minimal number of entities required to support minimal collective functionality is 300,000.

Small groups can function together as a collective, but they are under the control of the whole collective and not the smaller group collective generated as a result of splitting off individual units in order to create the group. This collective is not capable of invoking a synergetic effect as they are not effective when singular. This collective always stays together in the same environment or moves to a new environment together. Communication with other collectives or individualized entities with individual and free thought is done via the collective interface. Singular units cannot survive on their own.

You may suggest that your ants are this type of mind, but that is not the case because ants have a greater level of individuality than you are aware and are, therefore, under a different classification.

Collective of Units of Singular Sentience. In this collective each of the individual units of the collective has its own sentience content. It is capable of individualized thought and individualized decision processes. This type of collective is very useful because individual units of the group can be split off from the total collective and be capable of becoming a smaller group collective. Members of this collective are normally split into groups of entities that are similar in skill base and can, therefore, invoke a group-based level of synergy, based upon the grouping together of entities that are of the same nature from an individual ability perspective.

This type of grouping is preferred when the group needs to complete a certain type of task where the other types of entities in the collective would not be able to conduct the work necessary to complete the task in an effective and efficient manner. An example that you could use is group of entities that are skilled in boring holes to create burrows but would not be of much use transporting food stocks by air. There are multifunctional groups created, however.

These groups are created when it is necessary for the collective to create a new collective, a new colony if you like, in a new environmental location. In this instance, the group created would contain the minimum number of the different types of entities in the newly created collective necessary to ensure the perpetuation of that collective as an individual and self-sustaining collective. The entities in this type of collective have the ability to work individually, but they could only work on an individual basis for the good of the whole or group collective and at the request of the whole or group collective. They could not seek individualized work as a result of an individualized thought process.

As with the basic collective, communication with other collectives or individualized entities with individual and free thought is done via the collective interface. The synergetic effects are the most pronounced in this type of collective, specifically within those groups or collectives of groups of entities of the same energetic function or skill base. Singular units can survive on their own but need to find a group to ensure existence is sustained. Your insects are a lower level version of this type of collective.

We, Source Entity Eleven, are this type of collective, but our individualized functions are based upon our energetic content and computational skills. Although we rarely work alone, we are capable of doing so.

Separately Together Collective. The "separately together" collective is a hybrid of the collective and is created of individualized units of singular sentience, and the fully individualized entity that does not need to be in a collective for any reason. In this instance, each unit of the collective has fully individualized sentience and, therefore, thought processes. They also have fully individualized functionality both energetically and creativity-wise. This collective is powerful in so much as it is the best of both worlds, so to speak. They can operate at full collective functionality in all the ways specified in the collective of units of singular sentience version above, and they can operate as a fully functioning individualized unit with individual free will and the ability to go with the collective or not, as the case may be, if and when associated with it. As a collective, they are very diffuse by nature. They can all be together in the same environmental location, or they can be spread out into every possible location within each of the Source Entities or, indeed, The Origin, and some are. They are always in contact and communication with each other and generally found working on their own for their own evolutionary content. They work together in full collectivity when there is a specific benefit in entering into a task collectively rather than in the "separately together" condition. They communicate with other entities, both collective and singular in the singular. They are a fully self-sustaining creative entity. The OM are this type of collective but only when they desire to be so, for they can opt out should an OM so desire.

Temporary Collective. The Temporary Collective is one where individualized units of a particular Source Entity desire to work in metaconcert in order to work on a task that is best "actioned" as a collective rather than a group of individuals simply working together. This collective type also has the ability to invoke synergy that will benefit all the members of the metaconcert by increasing the efficiency and, therefore, the work throughout the collective. This type of collective is generally a temporary collective condition born of the need for a mutual solution to a mutual problem or task. The individual entities in this collective need to be highly evolved to invoke the synergetic effects associated with being in metaconcert, specifically because of the temporary nature of the collective. Although temporary collectives are usually created out of small numbers of individualized entities, they can and have attracted large number of entities when the task at hand demands a high collective membership. Communications with outside entities/collectives when in the collective are conducted by a "spokes-entity."

ME: I have to say that I didn't expect that many versions of a collective. Nor did I expect the difference in synergy.

SE11 (collectively): That is not all of them.

ME: What do you mean? These are just examples?

SE11 (collectively): There are versions that are hybrids of those that we have just described to you, but they are self-explanatory insomuch as they rely on the compartmentalization of the collective to allow such activity to take place whilst the rest of the collective operates in the dominant collective format. An additional collective to the four above is one that is fluidic in nature.

Fluidic Collective.

ME: Do you mean that it is always changing?

SE11 (collectively): Yes, the whole collective is constantly changing as a response to the demands of its current task.

I receive an image of ever-increasing quality; it is the image of a vast network where every entity is joined together. It looks like a huge fishing net. Each of the points where the thread of the fishing net is joined represents an entity, a unit of the collective with the thread of the fishing net being the lines of communication between the entities and groups of entities in metaconcert. As I look at this net, I see it connecting and disconnecting with single entities or groups of entities being included or "un-included" in the metaconcert. The connections that are in use are represented by the threads glowing in white light. It flashes on and off with whole areas of entities in what I can only describe as a 3D network, winking in and out of connectivity with the whole. It looks like the way a neural network might perform. For a moment, I thought it looked like a "net" of LED Christmas lights, all being turned on and off in a random way. As I look deeper and with more focus, I see that there is a pattern to the frequency of illumination of the lines of communication and those entities or groups of entities being included in the metaconcert. I decide to ask the collective that was Source Entity Eleven to both clarify what I am seeing and elaborate where necessary.

ME: Is this a true representation of the functionality of this type of collective?

SE11 (collectively): Yes it is. But please note that this is just a very small example for you to work with. In reality what you are seeing is the microscopic representation of how this type of collective functions. Consider it like looking through an electron microscope that is able to focus upon the components of the components of the components of an atom in your physical universe. Then consider that the entire collective is the "physical" size of your "physical" universe. This will give you an idea of the scale involved here.

ME: But the level of detail is immense then?

SE11 (collectively): Of course, it is.

ME: So what was I seeing? That is, what was the significance of the illuminated areas and the threaded areas being illuminated?

SE11 (collectively): It is exactly as you saw it. I can see you frowning, so I will explain further. The "pulsing" of the light on the lines of communication was, indeed, an example of the inclusion of the various units of the collective. The communications though are not what you would call 3D, for it is a multidimensional structure with each of the units of the collective capable of being introduced to the function of metaconcert as part of the whole, as a separate and independent entity unit, as part of a group of entities, as part of a series of groups, or as an operative entity of multiple groups operating both independently or collectively.

ME: Are you suggesting that an entity can have several functions and group associations simultaneously?

SE11 (collectively): Yes, of course. That is the whole point of the multidimensionality of this type of collective. In essence, what is happening is that the collective is operating as a whole, a collective of groups, and a collective of singular entity units. The functionality of this type of collective is such that it is capable of switching on and out of the collective, the various groups or single units at will, depending upon the type of work being considered. The singular units are either used in isolation or as an integral part of multiple groups. The direction of the lines of communication are switched to those areas of the collective where there is reduction in demand of the metaconcert state when there is an increase in demand for such a state elsewhere within the collective. Once the "work" is done, the number of entities is reduced to ensure that the optimal use of the "resource" is maintained.

ME: So how is this controlled/maintained? It must be extremely difficult.

SE11 (collectively): In this type of collective structure, there is a group of entities which are part of an integrated network that "infiltrates" the totality of the collective and monitors the level of work being done versus the number of entities and the levels of synergy being achieved. This group controls both the connectivity of the individual entities that make up the whole whilst knowing the best individual entity units to use for the tasks presented.

ME: Are you suggesting that the individual units of the collective are "individual" in terms of their functionality and are selected by the "controlling" group of entities to perform their roles relative to their level or type of functionality?

SE11 (collectively): In a nutshell, yes. There is one additional piece of information you need to know about though.

ME: And that is?

SE11 (collectively): That the so called "controlling" entities are also part of the "bag" of entity-based tools, so to speak.

ME: So they not only control the function of the collective, observing and switching in and out those entities necessary to ensure an efficient level of synergetic functionality, they are also part of this functionality, switching themselves in and out of the collective groups as and when required.

SE11 (collectively): Yes.

ME: Is this type of collective a popular one?

SE11 (collectively): No, because it is difficult to maintain and control. It also demands a critical mass of a certain type of entity to become viable.

ME: I would imagine it would be quite slow in its application to problem resolution/evolutionary content because of the need to use what I can only imagine to be a high number of entities in the management of such a fluidic metaconcert.

SE11 (collectively): It's not slow. It's quite fast in comparison to the other collective configurations. It's just that it's not totally efficient all the time.

ME: Why is it then?

SE11 (collectively): Because it needs to be maintained by those entities that maintain its optimal level of functionality, which makes them inefficient. Also, it leaves vast areas of entities unused, and, therefore, out of metaconcert when the collective is operating at its supposed optimal efficiency.

ME: This tells me that the number of individual entities within the collective can ultimately be reduced.

SE11 (collectively): Correct.

ME: So why wouldn't a collective that establishes this case when in this configuration do exactly that—reduce its number?

SE11 (collectively): They do, and in the process, they create a new collective, which adopts any of the other configurations, depending upon the quality of the individual entities concerned.

ME: So the quality of the entities within the collective has as effect on the type of collective they become as a whole?

SE11 (collectively): Yes, it always does.

Source Entity Eleven, a Collective of Units of Singular Sentience

I had noticed that we had spent considerable time discussing collectives and how they operate, so I decided to leave the questioning on this particular subject and move on to the next. Though what I found interesting here was the number of different collectives and the possibilities of there being hybrids, mixtures of these basic types of varying different ratios. I also found it interesting that the type they became was a function of the quality of the individual entity units within the collective, specifically those individual entities that clearly didn't need to be within a collective but chose to be so for the greater good of the whole, so to speak. From my vantage point, the synergetic effects were the prime motivation to move from an all-encompassing autonomous individual entity to one that is a minor part in a much bigger collective-based entity.

My mind returned to the task at hand, and I decided to focus on the individual but collective entities that Source Entity Eleven was. However, even though I had the desire to move on, I couldn't help feel that the subject of collective types or "genres" had not quite gone away. How could it? I was communicating with the biggest collective anyone or thing on Earth had ever communicated with. I stood back for a while, catching my mental breath. Having caught my mental breath and established that I had renewed vigor to steer the direction of this dialogue, I re-established contact with the collective that was Source Entity Eleven.

ME: Having just spent the last few days discussing the virtues of the different types of collectives, I am eager to get to grips with what you really are. An entity as large and as expansive as yourself, even in a diversified collective state, must be more than that which you described yourselves as "the collective of units of singular sentience."

SE11 (collectively): Yes, we are, and the title tells it all—should you want to decipher it.

I read the title two or three times before the penny dropped. Source Entity Eleven's functionality was twofold. The title of the description told both sides of the coin. In the first dialogue that described this collective type/genre, I/we had focused upon the individualized entities that made up Source Entity Eleven as being just that—a collective of individualized units grouped together to make a collective. A collective that could use any number of permutations of singularity, collectivity and synergy to achieve that which it desired at any one point. But what I was seeing now was an echo—a remembrance of that which it was before it diversified into the billion or so individualized units that might or might not work in metaconcert with that choice being dependent upon the task. Therefore, "the collective of units of singular sentience" referred to the singularity that Source Entity Eleven was before diversification. The description, literally true for both conditions, was more visible in its current state.

As I thought about this more, I started to receive some help, information-wise. When in a collective, Source Entity Eleven was just that, a collective. But the problem was that it was not always in a collective in "totality" because other parts of it had different tasks to perform so it could not truly be called a collective. It was, therefore, only when it was in a collective in "totality" that it became singular. It became a collective with a combined and collective but singular level of sentience. Although it was a collective state, in this state it achieved that which it was when in true singularity—a singular mind with each of the individualized units giving up their individuality on a temporary basis to support the need to be singular in "totality." Each of them, therefore, became but a cell, a neuron in a larger entity, performing only that function necessary for that part of the totality within which it was part. I found this fascinating.

SE11 (collectively): We thought you might enjoy that little conundrum. You see, we needed to see if you were capable of expansive thought via exposure to conflicting conditions that are both correct but, nevertheless, improbable when seen together. Consider it like having to describe black as being white, which is, in turn, black. It is an impossible possibility, which is, nevertheless, both possible and probable, and, indeed, highly likely, should you have the capability of being expansive enough to work with the data that is put before you—which you have. Based upon this, we will continue this dialogue and present to you further details on the individualized units that we are collectively.

ME: Wait a moment. Are you suggesting that you have been testing my ability to understand you?

SE11 (collectively): Yes, of course. Why are you surprised?

ME: It's just that I didn't expect it.

SE11 (collectively): If we are all one, how can we be singular, and if we are all singular, how can we be all one! The answer is that we are all the collective totality of the entity we call The Origin. You do see that, don't you?

ME: Yes, of course. It's one of the great realities of the omniverse, of "The Absolute," "The Origin."

SE11 (collectively): Good. Then we shall continue.

Source Entity Eleven's Individualized Units—A Synergetic Conundrum

After that little "revelation," I was somewhat puzzled. Why would Source Entity Eleven be testing me? From my perspective, I was clearly able to or should I say eventually be able to understand the information which was being given to me even if it was significantly truncated and tailored towards my supposed "physical" limitations. As I typed, I started to receive more information from Source Entity Eleven—information that told me that there was much, much more to discuss on the subject of Source Entity Eleven's Individual Entities. What I glimpsed in my mind's eye was mind-bending, to say the least. I decided to "re-focus" and continue the dialogue with a view to getting to the bottom of what I was seeing.

ME: All through this dialogue you have alluded to the "fact" that you are made up of individualized entities, but I have just picked up something else about the structure of your entities. It appears that they are collectives in their own right. Am I on the right track here?

SE11 (collectively): Yes, you are.

ME: Can you explain why this is? It almost seems to add to the conundrum of what you are.

SE11 (collectively): And now you know why we gave you that little test. We needed to see if you could accept the information we were sending you for what it is and not filter it in any way that would make the data more acceptable to your own memory base and, therefore, filter out the necessary detail.

ME: Oh, OK. Now I really do see the impetus behind the need to test me. I agree with you. It would have been somewhat limiting to know that most of what you were going to send me would have been lost in translation, so to speak.

SE11 (collectively): Moreover, it would have been pointless from our perspective.

ME: OK. Let's move on then. What is the benefit of having entities that are, in effect, collectives in their own right?

SE11 (collectively): We will need to go back to the time of diversification to answer that question. If you remember, when we diversified and were checking the efficiency of the number of entities in metaconcert, in collectivity, versus the optimal synergetic effects available as a result of that number in metaconcert.

ME: Yes, I remember.

SE11 (collectively): Then you will also note that we said that we could not increase the number of entities in metaconcert above a certain level due to the subsequent reduction in the synergetic effect.

ME: Yes, I remember that as well. I also remember that you stated that there was no way in which you could increase the number of entities by stealth and, therefore, "bypass" the "law" that limits the number of entities that can be in metaconcert whilst still achieving the optimal levels of synergy.

SE11 (collectively): Well, there is a way. We just discovered it.

ME: What! How can that happen? You were so sure a couple of weeks ago that this could not be bypassed and that there must be lines of communication between the groups of entities in metaconcert, and these communication lines would invariably slow things up.

SE11 (collectively): We did. But that was a long time ago.

ME: No it wasn't. It was no more than a couple of weeks ago!

SE11 (collectively): That is in your linear time. Remember only event space exists and not linear or what you sometimes call "clock" time. If we were to use clock time as a metric that you can use to understand what has been happening in the background, then we can say that several hundred millennia have passed. Or should we say there have been several event spaces navigated since then.

ME: Now I know why you were checking me out! OK, what's the latest news then?

SE11 (collectively): We decided to return to the basics of what we will now call the "macro" collective of a single entity. We saw that when we were in that configuration, we had an optimal number of entities that could be in metaconcert before the synergetic effects reduced or tailed off.

ME: Yes, we have discussed this before.

SE11 (collectively): Yes, we have, but that was the clue. We fed back the explanation of what we were during our discussion with you into a new event space, an event space that was necessary to allow further experimentation. In essence, we were running two event spaces concurrently, one in communication with you, and the other experimenting with the new "strategy." The new strategy took what you would recognize as several hundred millennia to run but the results were fantastic.

ME: So can you advise me of the theory behind the construction of your entities as they are now?

I had to work hard to keep up!

SE11 (collectively): Each entity is a collective of a single entity. As such, it is presented to the outside world as a singular entity, not a collective and, therefore, circumnavigates the synergy law since each collective is considered as a single unit and, therefore, is registered as such whilst in metaconcert. Hence, it is possible to have an optimal number of "individual collectives of units of singular sentience" and still achieve the synergetic effects required. What's more, we discovered that we can create collectives of collectives of a

255

collective of units of singular sentience. Each collective whilst in metaconcert would agree to the law of synergy.

ME: You have discovered a way to "nest" collectives and, therefore, maximize your synergetic effects beyond that available through singular entity units joining together in metaconcert.

SE11 (collectively): We have. What's more, in doing this, we have been able to use all the individualized units that were created in the diversification, thus, affecting a clean series of collectives of units of singular sentience gaining optimized synergy from the bottom layer to the top layer of the collective of units of singular sentience, so to speak. We have multiplied our metaconcert synergetic efficiency by untold "multipolous" amounts, as a result. We are pleased.

ME: I bet you are!

To be honest, I was a little bit uncomfortable at the prospect of being "here at the right time." It seemed to be happening a bit too often. When Source Entity Eleven decided to enter into another event space and conduct a series of experiments in collectivity and metaconcert whilst establishing not only that it/they had managed to circumnavigate the law of synergy relative to collectivity and the optimal number of entities within a collective, I started to think that I was inventing this "scenario." This "worry" was augmented when I cast my mind back to the previously announced prospect of being, again "here at the right time" when Source Entity Twelve started on the process of becoming self-aware.

"How can I," I thought, "be in the right place at the right time in this greater reality when I can't even win a reasonably useful stake of the lottery at home on Earth?"

As if sensing my concern, the collective that was Source Entity Eleven decided to bring me back to reality—wherever that was! Well, I know where it (reality) is, but I was feeling a little bit unsure.

SE11 (collectively): Don't think for a moment that this is all laid on for YOU. You are nowhere near significant enough to activate ALL of the major events that are happening whilst you are communicating with us.

ME: That's it. Bring me back down to Earth!

SE11 (collectively): No, we don't want to do that. It's too far down the frequencies. All we want to convey to you is this: you are one in a million, a rarity so to speak, especially when incarnate in the frequencies associated with the Earth. In some instances, communication with an entity such as yourself will kick-off a thought process that we would not have embarked upon as soon as we did when communicating with you. It is simply because you are totally individual as an entity and offer a point of view that is not necessarily high on our priority that we decided to take a wild card approach to our analysis of synergy. We used you as the "unknown variable." You "thought" of something, albeit momentarily, and we acted upon it. What you aren't aware of is how long we thought about it before acting.

ME: How long did you think about it?

SE11 (collectively): Several thousand years in your book. At the point of receiving the thought we decided to "hive off" a considerable percentage of our "totality" to working with the possibility that this thought could present to us.

ME: And what was the thought?

SE11 (collectively): It wasn't so much the thought as the title and the thought behind the title.

ME: You mean when I was typing down the words I used to describe the different types of collective.

SE11 (collectively): Yes. Especially the one used to describe our state. It got a large proportion of us thinking and calculating and by the time you had finished typing, we collected enough data to allow us to make the decision to drop a number of our existing experiments and work on that which was based upon your thought.

ME: So I was here at the right time!

SE11 (collectively): No, we had that possibility mapped out already. It's just that it was too close to another possible strategy that we had already calculated as being of limited success to bring it close enough to our attention to warrant further focused consideration. You simply tipped the balance, so to speak.

ME: Well, I am glad to be heavy enough to have tipped that particular balance.

SE11 (collectively): As we have recently stated, you are not the center of attention here although you are of interest. It's just that you happened to make a random thought that caught our attention, imagination and subsequent action. Now let's move on, for we are starting to run out of that event space commodity you like to call time.

You wanted to know more details about the functionality of the individualized units of our collective.

ME: I do.

SE11 (collectively): Then we shall advise you of the three main variants we have here. As with most creativity, there is an element of variability in the manufacturing process. This variability is manifested in the optimal functionality of the individual unit concerned. When we diversified, we achieved this condition in stages. You may remember from the start of this dialogue that we were experimenting in the efficiency of the collective configuration in some considerable way and time before we decided to commit our totality to being in the collective state.

ME: Yes, I do remember that you suggested that you were a percentage collective and a percentage singularity at certain points in your existence.

SE11 (collectively): Yes, good. Then you will also remember what your own Source Entity told you about its own creativity process, that it was not "perfect" in its repeatability.

ME: Yes, I definitely remember that. That is the reason we have entities that are "sentient," energetic humanity and above; those that are "semi-sentient" animals and those instinctive races of entities; and the "non-sentient" entities, the automata—so to speak; the purely instinctive and below, such as the plant and mineral kingdoms on Earth.

SE11 (collectively): Good memory. Then you will be aware of the fact that each of these entity "types" or "classes" are also capable of evolutionary advancement at a rate concurrent with their level of sentience.

ME: Yes, I recognize that opportunity as well.

SE11 (collectively): Fantastic because this is a similar function experienced by ourselves when we diversified. We didn't, however, lose concentration during the creativity process as your own Source Entity did because we had 100% concentration on what we were doing when we entered into the final diversification process.

ME: So what happened then? What resulted in the three main variants of entity?

SE11 (collectively): Calculation.

ME: What? Calculation? What does that mean?

Entities Conforming to a Hierarchical State

SE11 (collectively): In essence, we decided to create entities that conformed to a hierarchical state.

ME: So what was this hierarchical state?

SE11 (collectively): a) Command and Control; b) Function, resulting from command and control; and c) Adaption. I will explain their roles in more detail for you because some of their roles and responsibilities are obvious whereas others are not. None of these entities are senior to the other in any way, shape, or form—they are all as important as each other.

Command and Control. Those entities endowed with the Command and Control role are those entities that are able to make decisions about how and when to create the varying densities of collectivity and subsequent synergetic effects relevant to the tasks that are presented to them as a result of being in a collective existence that is working towards the optimal evolutionary condition. They can assign entities of the "function" class to work on that which is necessary. A recent example would be that calculation and experimentation that allowed us to circumnavigate the synergetic law of maximum collectivity. These entities plan that which needs to be actioned and negotiate with others of their class for the "functional" and "adaptational" resource necessary to be successful in their project. They are also of an energy that allows them to also participate in the work of the "functional" and "adaptational" classes of entities.

259

Function. The Function entities are those whose role is to take that which has been planned by the Command and Control entities and work it into something relative, repeatable and robust. This can only be achieved by applying multiple approaches to solve the particular problem passed along to them via the Command and Control entities. In most instances, the Command and Control and the Function entities swap roles to verify the functionality of that which has been developed. Doing this ensures that there are no areas of error that can or have been introduced. These entities are also capable of becoming that which they create, thereby allowing easy transportation of that which has been successful to other areas of the collective.

Adaptation. The Adaptation entities are the "coupe de gras" of the three entities because they are able to become either of the previous two entities to undertake seamlessly without a period of normalization that which the others are doing. They are the multifunctional tool in the tool box, so to speak, and are capable of doing any of the workload requirements in both an individual and collective state. Their main strengths are their ability to compartmentalize themselves to the point where they can commune with individuals or collectives of all three conditions simultaneously—thus, creating a bridge between working functions of the various collectives. Because they can replicate each entity state or type in a totally faithful condition, they create a seamless connection between collectives of dedicated entity types that allows a larger, multifunctional collective condition to be developed.

ME: This feels like the beginnings of a integrated circuit, or better still, the architecture of a microprocessor where certain parts of the processor are dedicated to certain types of functionality.

SE11 (collectively): Yes, we can see how you may make that analogy, for in certain instances that is what we almost become, a super massive processor on a Source Entity scale. This is one of the ways in which we work with the evolutionary tasks that we set ourselves.

A Top-down Visualization of the "New Source Entity Eleven"

Recently in this dialogue with Source Entity Eleven, I had been advised of a change it had made that had resulted in its ability to circumnavigate the law of synergetic effect. It had also gone to some length to advise me that I was not the reason for its solving this particular conundrum but merely a catalyst. I was much more comfortable about because I was more than concerned about my own ego getting in the way and creating that which it desired to be seen and overlaying that into the channelled information rather than allowing me to receive pure unfiltered information from Source Entity Eleven. I was totally aware, of course, that there was a level of filtering of the information by Source Entity Eleven itself. However, I knew that was a necessary requirement to ensure that I was able to work with the information and concepts surrounding the information received and not let it fall fallow through my lack of understanding.

Source Entity Eleven's success in circumnavigating the law of synergetic effect had resulted in its changing its configuration as a collective to that which it could achieve with all its units of "singularity sentience" in play. This included those that had been hived off to communicate with me. They suddenly felt different— cleaner, more efficient, waste-free, sharp! New!

A couple of days after receiving notification of this wondrous success, I started receiving a most interesting image of some of the detail/s of the new Source Entity Eleven configuration. It was amazing to see and one that I resolved to share with the readers of this text from both an illustrative and descriptive perspective.

ME: I must take the opportunity to both discuss this new configuration with you and describe it to the readers of this book.

SE11 (collectively): Yes, and so you should. If you like, we can do this together to ensure that you do not duplicate any of the previous text too much.

ME: Yes, I would very much like that.

I settled down to focus on the image that had presented itself in front of me again. I had previously noted how the effect of being a collective of units of singular sentience had the effect of circumnavigating the law of synergy by the collective presenting itself to the outside environment as a singular unit. I moved away from that part of Source Entity Eleven that was communicating with me. As I looked from a greater distance, I noticed that I saw the whole of Source Entity Eleven as a singular Entity; it looked just like a sphere with a very thin boundary or perimeter. There was no indication of collectivity at all. I found this quite interesting.

I moved my vantage point back towards the area where I was previously communicating with that part of Source Entity Eleven that was assigned to communicate with me. As I did so, my resolution got better, and I could see each of the individual entities in front of me. Initially, they had the same appearance as Source Entity Eleven did from a distance—that is, they appeared to be singular in appearance and profile.

I then felt the need to get closer to one or two of them. As I moved in closer, I could see past the outer perimeter of the one closest to me. Inside was a plethora of individual units all in collectivity, all in metaconcert. The feeling of oneness was all-encompassing, enthralling, inviting, and succumbing. I moved away for a moment, and the imagery of all these entities in collectivity within this perimeter disappeared, and I was confronted with what appeared to be a single entity again.

"This is a good illusion," I thought, "good enough to fool an omniversal law, a law of synergetic effect!"

I moved back in towards the entity. At the perimeter's edge, the truth behind the entity again became perceivable, and I saw all of the entities inside in collectivity and metaconcert. The totality of this entity was such that it was at the maximum number of component parts to allow the maximum synergetic effect to take place—and no more. Outside of this entity's perimeter, I noted that it, itself, was one of an optimal number of entities required to achieve maximum synergy. This was a two-layer effect.

Something caught my attention. Within this second layer entity, itself a collective in disguise, I gained the need to zoom in again and look at one of its singular units. Again, from the perspective of being on the outside, it appeared to be just that—a singular unit, but as I shifted my perception beneath the outside perimeter, I was greeted by yet another collective in the optimal number in metaconcert to effect the maximum synergetic outcome. I started to wonder how far this layering would go when Source Entity Eleven decided to elaborate. I pulled back to face the part of it that was addressing me.

The Collective That Became Singular Whilst Being a Collective!

SE11 (collectively as one): Let me explain, for there are twelve layers in total.

I noted that Source Entity Eleven had adopted a singular method of nomenclature—hence, the change to the dialogue header.

ME: I would be quite happy for you to do so, for this is becoming a little confusing for me.

SE11 (collectively as one): I will not dwell on the layers per se, for they repeat themselves. This is the beauty of them and the method of circumnavigating the synergetic effect.

The entities you perceived were held in a state of collective singularity. This is the process I discovered. When in collectivity and metaconcert, if the outer edges of the collective are held in a state of collective singularity, it has the effect of presenting a new visage to that which is outside the collective. This visage, so to speak, is of unity and singularity in appearance, in function, and in communication. In achieving this state, the collective effectively considers itself as one and addresses itself as "I" in a particular communication process rather than "we." The energies involved are totally different in this case because the energetic signature "presented" when a collective considers itself as "we" is significantly different to those energies presented when an entity or collective considers itself as "I." This is the crux of the matter when circumnavigating the law of synergetic effect.

The negation of the law of synergetic effect is relative to that which is in collective singularity. It is also functional when relative to that which is in collectivity—and only that which is in collectivity. That means that the synergetic effect must be constrained in some way between the collective itself and the perimeter whilst still being within the perimeter of the collective being presented as a singular entity. And so it is that the synergetic effect is working but not being presented to that which is external to the collective; that is, the synergetic energies are captive within the perimeter of the collective singularity. If the synergetic effect was presented to the outside environment, it would add itself to that synergetic effect that was on another layer. This would create the condition described earlier where the synergetic effect becomes sub-optimal or drastically reduced when the number of entities in collective metaconcert are greater than the maximum number of entities required to create the optimal synergetic effect.

ME: So you are telling me that each of the entities I saw in my visualization has its own population of entities at the maximum population required to achieve the maximum synergetic effect.

SE11 (collectively as one): Correct.

ME: And each entity, therefore, is at full synergetic capacity and output.

SE11 (collectively as one): Correct.

ME: That's awesome, to say the least.

SE11 (collectively as one): I would agree with you. It means that all the individual units of me are operating at their maximum synergetic potential now. My ability as a collective has been augmented beyond even my comprehension.

ME: Hold on. I have a quick question. Is the highest level, i.e., that which is communicating with me, also subject to this synergetic effect?

SE11 (collectively as one): Yes, every one of the collectives on every one of the layers is functioning in accordance with the optimized levels of functionality available through being in a state of maximum synergetic effect.

ME: So what is the first thing you are going to do now that you have achieved this massively augmented functionality?

SE11 (collectively as one): Once I have finished this dialogue with you, I will be calculating exactly how much I have grown in functional capability.

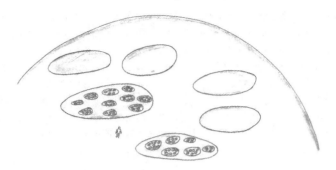

Figure 2: The New Source Entity Eleven
(Collectively as One – Circumnavigating the Law of Synergetic Effect)

ME: I take it then you have got no idea how much you have grown in functional capacity as a result of this change in your synergetic state?

SE11 (collectively as one): No, not at this precise moment in your event space although I can say one thing.

ME: And what is that?

SE11 (collectively as one): It will be a multiple of twelve to the power of twelve (12^{12}) and will, of course, include all of the synergetic effects as a multiple of this multiplication effect.

ME: But I would have thought that twelve to the power of twelve was a small number for you to work with?

SE11 (collectively as one): Ordinarily, yes, but this includes the synergetic effects and how they are affected by such an increase. I can see that you are struggling to understand why such a small multiplier would cause me such a problem.

ME: Yes, I would actually. Even I with my rudimentary math skills could work it out on a reasonable spread sheet or scientific calculator.

SE11 (collectively as one): Oh, the arrogance of mankind! Yes, I agree with you in terms of the basic calculation, but as I stated before, this does not include the synergetic effects and how they are affected by the multiplication. Let me tell you this. To date neither "I collectively" nor "as one in singularity," nor "we previously collectively" have been exposed to the opportunity for multiplying the synergetic effect. This is because there has been no point. There simply was no need to go there because we could not achieve that which was not achievable. When through this dialogue with you, "we" at that point in event space spotted the potential for a "loop hole." We realized that there would need to be a significant amount of retrospective work to quantify the effects of such an opportunity. This would and could only be achieved after the opportunity was actioned, so to speak.

ME: Didn't you want to calculate the effects of the "new" synergetic effects first though just to make sure it was worthwhile going through what I can only expect is an immense amount of work and preparation?

SE11 (collectively as one): No, because I/we at that point in event space knew where we currently stood from an efficiency perspective with the currently achievable level of synergy. The big factor was that I had a surplus of individualized units and as a result, could not make the best use of all these units from a synergetic perspective. It was a wasted opportunity for me to have all of these units of myself and not be able to gain the maximum usage from being in metaconcert and, therefore, attaining maximum synergy.

ME: So it sounds like this was an opportunity that was too good to miss, and you dove straight into the work necessary to configure yourself into the maximum number of entities in metaconcert to achieve the maximum synergetic effects at all twelve levels. It was so good an opportunity that you decided to work on the specification of what you were/are, so to speak, on a totally retrospective basis.

SE11 (collectively as one): Correct.

ME: One thing is bugging me though. You must have had an "odd" number of entities either left over from the work you wanted to do or a shortfall in the number of entities required to create the optimal number of synergetically singular collectives within all of the twelve levels.

SE11 (collectively as one): I calculated a shortfall of some significant numbers of entities.

ME: So what did you do, bearing in mind that you had some engaged in a dialogue with me and that you had moved away from that event space that was being used with me and created a new event space where you were able to do this new work on synergy?

SE11 (collectively as one): Firstly, I made myself back into one. Secondly, I decided to make those entities that were in dialogue with you a temporary function of that which was now a singular entity again. Thirdly, I diversified myself into the total number of entities needed to create the optimal number of entities required to affect the maximum number of synergetically singular units within themselves and on each of the twelve levels of synergy. The entities that were in dialogue with you were integrated into one of the synergetically singular units at the very top level of synergy and became part of the outer layer of one of the units. The change over from these entities in collective dialogue with you and that which is now me was noted by you almost instantly, for you started to call me SE11 (collectively as one) rather than SE11 (collectively).

ME: You are right I did notice the difference rather quickly. I take it that this is a function of the "singularity effect,"

SE11 (collectively as one): Yes, it is, and it is why it was a successful method of circumnavigating the law of maximum synergetic effect.

ME: Of course, that makes perfect sense. I do have to say though that I am somewhat honored to have been in the position to see a Source Entity change itself into another configuration in front of my very spiritual eyes, so to speak.

SE11 (collectively as one): There are many changes that Source Entities make that are out of sight of your spiritual eyes—changes that are made in a new or temporary event space, checked out, planned, actioned, optimized and modified. Nearly all the Source Entities have made some minor adjustments to their environments during the period used by you to commune with them. This is not an uncommon function; it is evolution. There are many changes that your own Source Entity has made in a covert way, and many of them have benefitted the entities that exist within its environment. One of them is your planet's ascension. The modifications it has made to your environment is a result of your—energetic mankind's, that is— response to receiving higher frequency energies to work with.

ME: I was under the impression that mankind itself created the rise in frequencies. Also, as a result of our creativity, we awaken whilst in the physical with the awakening creating access to the higher frequencies that create further awakening, and so on.

SE11 (collectively as one): Yes, that is true. It is true for all entities created by their creator. However, you can only ascend to that which is created for you to ascend to—the spiritual horse can be led to the spiritual water, but it is up to the spiritual horse to drink the spiritual water. The creator of the spiritual water cannot force the spiritual horse to drink it. It must drink of its own volition. Without the entities' participation with that which has been created for it to participate in, it cannot experience, learn and evolve. It will just exist in evolutionary stasis.

ME: So our Source Entity literally creates the rungs on the ladder for us to climb up. It is up to us individually to climb onto that next rung and see the change in the vista around us the higher we go.

SE11 (collectively as one): Correct. This is the motivation for all entities—to keep on going, not to stop. Don't look back. Encourage others to come with you. Help them when they falter and encourage them when they do well. Seek their help when you need it; work together in gratitude, humility, and service.

ME: Thank you. I know we have been talking about my own Source Entity and its environment, but this is one conundrum that has been in the back of my mind for some time—specifically the dichotomy that there are waves of higher energies being sent to the earth and the local universe together with the thought process that we are creating our own ascension.

SE11 (collectively as one): Both work together. You create your own ascension by choosing to work with those new frequencies that are presented to you. You are not ascended. You ascend, but you can only ascend to that which is ascendable. Your ascension is, therefore, a function of your own willingness to work with that which is presented to you. In doing so, you are rewarded with the functions attributable with an entity of a higher evolutionary content.

ME: Thank you. That is a very important message; it must be conveyed now that it is understood.

The Entities' Re-call and Re-absorption into Oneness

Whilst discussing the modifications to our own Source Entity's environment to assist in the localized ascension of Earth and the physical universe it exists within, I had quite a major question to ask that was relative to the individualized units of Source Entity Eleven. It involved the transient re-integration of the individualized units of Source Entity Eleven and their re-diversification back into collectivity, a collectivity that would ensure the maximum synergetic effects could be achieved at all twelve levels without error. Source Entity Eleven (collectively as one) had rather "matter of factly" stated that it had recalled all those individualized entities that were it in collectivity, returned to oneness, and then re-diversified itself into the correct number of entities required to create the synergetic effect, but it had not commented beyond that.

I was, therefore, very interested in understanding what had happened to the "individuality" that was part of the collective entities that were "re-worked," so to speak. For instance, did they just "wink" out of existence, losing all that they had personally or collectively experienced? Or was the essence of them maintained in some way? I just had to ask this question, and ask it now, specifically because I was starting to become very aware that the dialogue with Source Entity Eleven (collectively as one) was starting to draw to a close. I could tell my time with this most interesting Source Entity was limited because the link, the connection between us, was starting to become less coherent. I decided to work fast on asking what might well be my last major question with Source Entity Eleven (collectively as one).

ME: I almost forgot to ask you about those entities, that is, all of them that were re-called and re-absorbed into oneness before their energies were re-used in the creative process necessary to allow you to create the numbers required to support the maximum synergetic effect on all twelve levels. Did they lose their existence? Were their memories lost? How did you keep that which they "were" for future use, or did you just lose it forever with a view to starting again with this new configuration?

SE11 (collectively as one): Nothing is lost; all is gained.

ME: Now that's what I call a cryptic answer. Would you like to elaborate a little for me?

I had a wry smile on my face for I knew what the answer was going to be!

SE11 (collectively as one): I lose nothing, and they lose nothing.

ME: Would you like to expand upon that? Do you mean that you saved their essence, their memories?

SE11 (collectively as one): When I recalled the individualized entities back into one, I looked at the contributions that each of them had made singularly but for the benefit of the collective that I was at that time. I recorded their work, how they achieved it, how they started it, why they started it, what strategies they used, whether they changed those strategies later, why they changed them, what was a success and what was deemed a failure. In fact, I recorded everything about them—the work they achieved singularly, in collectivity, in metaconcert and, therefore, in synergy. For a moment I thought about only reproducing the best performing entities and cloning them, but then I realized that I would miss out on the finite details of that which was created by the lesser performing entities, which although was insignificant in terms of its content when compared to the higher quality work, it was significant in terms of the minor and less exciting details. I, therefore, came to the conclusion that I would be better off creating a pool of memory that contained everything that all of the entities combined had experienced, learned and evolved with. In essence, I absorbed everything about every entity that was in collectivity.

ME: So what did you do with all of this knowledge, which I have no doubt included the individual personalities of the entities recalled into ones?

SE11 (collectively as one): Because each of the entities was, in essence, individualized units of me, I saw no need to keep them in the same configuration, personality-wise. Let me explain further. Personality is something that develops when an entity is separate from a group. This is essentially what happens to the energy that is used by an entity when it desires the evolutionary opportunity presented to it via incarnation. It is, therefore, what mankind experiences when incarnate. It is in variance to that which is experienced when energy is used to create an entity that is part of a collective of similar or same function. Although each entity may have differing levels of contribution to the collective in totality, they all still maintain the essence of what they are both individually and collectively. They do this outside the need for complete individualization, which creates ego or personality.

With my entities not developing individualized personalities, the need to perpetuate the personality did not exist, so I was left with everything else that they had achieved or were achieving. The next thing I decided was a natural progression from attaining a momentary level of oneness and recording everything, which is a standard function of all Source Entities and our reason to be. I gave each and every one of the new individualized units of the singular collective all of that I had recorded from all of the entities recalled into oneness. Every entity gained everything about its peers. I created a complete facsimile of my new but temporary singular self in miniature. Each new entity that was to be part of the new collective was given everything that was ever achieved, no matter how big or how small, no matter what its role was or memories of that role, each were given everything.

ME: And you created enough of them to maximize the synergetic effect at all twelve levels.

SE11 (collectively as one): No, not quite.

ME: What!? I thought you stated in an earlier dialogue that you created enough to satisfy the requirements for maximum synergetic effect on all twelve levels?

SE11 (collectively as one): I did.

ME: OK, now I am confused. It looks like I am not using the correct syntax in my questioning.

SE11 (collectively as one): I will help you out. I gave the entities the opportunity to use the full functionality that I have in many of my own functions. One of them was the ability to diversify themselves to that number necessary to create a group or collective that when in metaconcert was equal to that optimal number of entities necessary to achieve the maximized synergetic effect. I diversified myself in the numbers required to create the first four levels "only" in synergy. The entities themselves took over from that point onwards.

ME: You're saying that they diversified themselves to create the number of entities necessary to achieve the magic number for maximized synergy?

SE11 (collectively as one): In a word, yes.

ME: How did they do that?

SE11 (collectively as one): By duplication. By this I do not mean the mere duplication of an entity "x" number of times; I mean that the entities entered into a state of diversification into a group rather than as an individual. This means that the individual becomes a smaller collective; it is a collective in its own right. It is the effect of the singular entity becoming a collective whilst in singularity that gave way to the law of synergetic effect being circumnavigated.

ME: Not the collective becoming a singular entity with the synergetic effect being constrained in some way between the collective itself and the perimeter whilst still being within the perimeter of the collective being presented as a singular entity. Hence, the synergetic effect working but not being presented to that which is external to the collective—that is, the synergetic energies are captive within the perimeter of the collective singularity.

SE11 (collectively as one): I see that you are quoting that which I used to describe this effect earlier.

ME: It's the only way I could do it.

SE11 (collectively as one): So I see. But the effect you just described is the functional effect of the individual entity diversifying itself into a self-contained and singular collectivity, which by the way, also contains entities that have diversified themselves down into smaller singular collectives of the number required to achieve the maximum synergetic effect.

ME: They are all nested then?

SE11 (collectively as one): Yes. Each of the entities that you can see on this outer layer is the last component in the nest of singular collectivity in metaconcert. Each of them is in unison, and each of them is working together in synergy at maximum synergetic effect without upsetting the law of synergy in any way. It is a total circumnavigation of this law with the evolutionary opportunity effects being currently beyond my level of computation.

Which, brings us back to where we were previously.

I need to accurately compute the synergetic levels of efficiency reached within this current configuration. This is now my most urgent piece of work, for The Origin is most interested in the effects on its evolutionary acceleration, and I am most interested in what I can achieve when I use this configuration when it is at its maximum capacity.

You have been fortunate to have been in communication with me at this juncture in my existence. You have been even more fortunate to have been of assistance as well. This assistance, although small and in passing, has been most useful, and for that I thank you. Now I MUST leave you, for I have what you might call several of your millennia to calculate my new capacity.

I leave you now.

But know this:

We will talk again, for you will be communing with The Origin in a very focused way very soon, and during this process you will be communing with all the Source Entities at certain junctures in the dialogue. Do not rush it; take your time, for there is much information for mankind incarnate to behold. I leave you now with a greeting from one of your more enlightened areas of the earth: Namaste!

And that was it. Source Entity Eleven (collectively as one) cut its link in a most efficient way. Except, that is, for a very small thread. I followed it as I assumed this would be necessary for spontaneous communication with it during the communication with The Origin. But I was wrong; I felt that this was no longer necessary because in this dialogue a permanent link was established between Source Entity Eleven (collectively as one) and me. I also noticed that I had a permanent link with all the other Source Entities that I had communicated with previously. It was not a solid link; it was a link between friends—informal, instantaneous, loving, caring, powerful and wise. I was in awe. I followed the small fragment of a link that Source Entity Eleven (collectively as one) had left me. I saw all the entities that were the individualized units of singular collectivity in metaconcert. In full synergetic effect they appeared to be flashing as lights on a huge old computer display board, each winking and

273

flashing in singularity and in synchronicity. Great waves of lights flashing and flowing at all twelve levels. Source Entity Eleven (collectively as one) had wasted no time. Before my very spiritual eyes, it was computing its new synergetic capacity. Again, I was in awe!

Chapter Six
Source Entity Twelve Awakens

With the communication with Source Entity Eleven (collectively as one) completed—for the moment, I mentally noted—I turned my attention to Source Entity Twelve, the last of the Source Entities, the one that had not become self-aware. I floated in mentality—that space I had come to realize was where I went when I was out of body and communicating with those entities that are outside of the frequencies associated with that energetic part in my incarnate body. At least that part of me that I was currently aware of. This "space" was that which I used to travel outside of the Source Entity One, the one that I considered myself associated to, even though energetically I am becoming more and more aware that I am not necessarily associated with the Source Entity fondly referred to as the Source Entity/Source Entity One/God.

Was I having delusional thoughts here? I didn't think so, but who knows what reality is when one is captive by the act of incarnation. As one finds out about one's energetic heritage, one becomes more and more critical of one's mental state, and I was making sure that I was on an energetic level playing field. No matter how often I checked myself though, I just knew that it felt right to be where I was, doing what I was doing, and telling the world about it. One thing was sure though—I was starting to lose any inhibitions about "coming-out" about my ability and my dialogues with those Source Entities that are the creations of The Origin. This was knowledge that was old and needed to be broadcast. Mankind needed to be brought up to speed with this information.

I looked around myself and saw the other Source Entities around me. They and their entities were "doing their own thing" for the evolution of The Origin, and they were working so very hard and doing so very well. I focused on the Source Entity that had not yet even started its evolutionary journey, the Source Entity that I had already called Source Entity Twelve. From the outside, its energetic perimeter looked uncontrolled. It undulated as if in some sort of battle with itself, like two chemicals mixed together in a sealed vessel that inherently did not mix and were desperate to be apart from each other.

I moved towards it, and The Origin told me to be gentle in my approach and communication methods with this infantile Source Entity. I gently probed it, wondering what it would feel like energetically. As I was about to move away, I noticed that there was a surge of energy as if some sort of focus had been applied to the energies that were within Source Entity Twelve. I felt dimensions, sub-dimensional components, frequencies and event space, plus myriad other energies that I did not recognize all line up as if to attention. Suddenly it had structure, purpose, incentive, initiative, desire and, focus!

The next thing I knew I was moved away gently by a huge and immense power. The Origin had swung into action and had seized control of Source Entity Twelve. A huge umbilical cord of energy, a huge vortex appeared from nowhere and engulfed Source Entity Twelve. I had seen this image before. It was given to me by some of the other Source Entities to explain how The Origin initiated contact with them when they first became aware of self. The Origin was in communication with Source Entity Twelve. As the communication continued, the energetic umbilical cord—the huge vortex of energy that surrounded Source Entity Twelve in its entirety—pulsed with energies that were nothing like those I had experienced in any of my dialogues with the other Source Entities—not even The Origin itself. I watched in complete awe, my mouth dropping open, aghast at the magnificence of what I had just realized I was witnessing—The Origin engaging in direct and intimate contact with one of its creations for the sole purpose of educating it, giving it its reason to be, its purpose in existence. I asked The Origin a question.

Prelude to Contact with Source Entity Twelve

ME: I am totally in awe of the honor you have bestowed upon me.

O: Please explain.

ME: Witnessing the first contact with an awakening Source Entity.

O: Ah, yes, well. Actually, it's not the primary contact, for that happened some time ago.

ME: So what am I witnessing then?

O: Exactly what you described. I am telling Source Entity Twelve why it is in existence. This, however, is the secondary contact; I can only do this once it "wakes up," so to speak. The primary contact was a check to see if the awakening process was imminent, which it was—several billion of your years ago. I do wish you didn't use time as a metric, but it's the only way I can describe the juncture in event space to you. At that juncture, I noticed the energies in Source Entity Twelve aligning into that configuration that is necessary for its becoming self-aware.

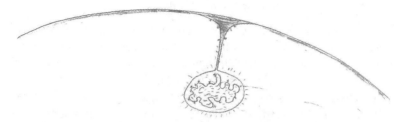

Figure 1: The Origin's Primary Contact with Source Entity Twelve

A few moments ago, I calculated the next juncture—that of the awakening proper: the event space of the secondary contact. Once I calculated this juncture, I brought you back to it. I see that I will need to bring you up to speed, for I can see you are struggling with what is happening here.

ME: You bet I am.

O: And this isn't the first time you have seen this.

ME: Noooooo? Go on, enlighten me. I am all ears.

O: Source Entity Twelve became aware some time ago—some million or so years ago in your language.

ME: So why did I keep seeing the images of it in its pre-awake state?

O: Quite simply, you were drawn to that event space. It was something you sub-consciously desired, i.e., your higher, energetic self took you there. It also had the effect of making the picture complete from mankind's educational perspective. The awakening process experienced by a Source Entity is a rather special event to behold; Source Entity Twelve was the last Source Entity to experience it, so it was an obvious choice to be taken there—

specifically since Source Entity Twelve is still in a rather infantile and "new" state of being.

ME: But even my own Source Entity, or should I say, that Source Entity that I currently call my own, concurred that Source Entity Twelve had not yet become aware when I was typing the dialogues that became *The History of God*! What is going on here?

I was a bit disturbed that even my higher and greater energetic self had appeared to be contriving and doing things without me knowing! I suppose I should have expected it though.

O: Your Source Entity saw where you were, event space-wise, and concurred that which you were seeing. Currently you move around event space in an uncontrolled manner. You are not even aware that you are doing it. Even though this is something that you do naturally in the energetic, this part of you that is incarnate has elected to take on-board that knowledge at a later date in your incarnation. I can only tell you this now because you have enough experience under your belt to be able to understand what is happening to you when I/we, that is, the other Source Entities, tell you. When you saw Source Entity Twelve in its pre-awake state, you were in that particular event space and not its current event space. In an attempt to keep things simple for you, your Source Entity, Source Entity One, simply concurred that which you saw and spared you the need to understand that which you would have had difficulty with at that juncture in your own awakening—your then current event space. From your perspective, what you were seeing was true because you were "in" that event space.

ME: So where am I now, event space-wise?

O: In essence, you are in an event space that is outside that which your physical body currently exists within. Source Entity Twelve has been self-aware for some time now in its "current" event space. This event space, where we are now, is that event space which houses its awakening. You are here to witness its awakening. Once this has been achieved, we can move into the current event space Source Entity Twelve is experiencing and commence dialogue.

It was all starting to make sense again. I was relieved, for it meant that things had, in some respects, been set up for me (albeit by my higher self at times) rather than me being in the right place at the right time. Event space being what it is, I could witness any event I wanted to and actually "be there" as it was happening, which of course it is/was! I felt much more comfortable with this as it effectively meant that I wasn't being delusional or introducing fantasy or fiction. It was all merely a function of the greater reality— a greater reality that in my incarnate state I am only a poor beginner at working with. My sanity is maintained – phew!

ME: OK, now that I am up to speed, do you want to let me describe the rest of the event?

O: Carry on. It is important that you put it in your own words, for you will be picking up information that is not instantly describable.

ME: Thank you.

I decided to go back into narrative mode.

I refocused on the image where Source Entity Twelve was in what I now know is the second contact with The Origin—the one in which Source Entity Twelve is being educated about its role and reason for existence. I found myself in that event space.

"So that's how to move from event space to event space." I thought, but The Origin then told me that that method only works if you know where you are going and is not applicable for random event space travel.

"It's a good start though," I thought.

In front of my mind's eye was the great indescribably vast vista that was The Origin's area of self-awareness. Far in the distance was Source Entity Twelve. It was coupled to The Origin with the energetic umbilical "cord"/the vortex of energy that The Origin used to engulf the Source Entities, cutting them off from the environment that was The Origin's area of self-awareness and educating them in a most intensive way. The energy pulsed through this umbilical vortex. As the information that contained Source Entity Twelve's education was exchanged, it changed color, energetic intensity, frequency, dimensionality and myriad other energies that I was not even aware of but could, nevertheless, sense. Source Entity Twelve glowed an iridescent golden color.

Source Entity Twelve had only just become aware of itself when The Origin contacted it. Suddenly, its energies had aligned and become structured to enable independent and intelligent thought to take place—energy born into sentience. As I watched the education process take place, I noted that although this newly aware Source Entity was being given a repository of all that The Origin knew— which included all of the experience, learning and evolutionary content gathered by the other eleven Source Entities to date—this did not give it maturity. Maturity was something that it had to work on itself as part of its own evolutionary work.

As I observed this most profound event, I noted that Source Entity Twelve was acting like a memory sponge, soaking up all of the content and using all of the sense channels it had to assimilate that which it was being given. As it received this information it undulated, twisting and turning, bucking and weaving whilst still being captive within the energies of the umbilical vortex that The Origin had created to initiate this most important communication process. The movement observed was not a result of resistance, merely the response to working with, experiencing and understanding the information that was being received—getting up to speed with the latest evolutionary content.

As it absorbed this indescribably large torrent of information, it grew in structural stature, becoming more organized in its assimilation of the data. As it became more organized, its exterior became calmer with the undulations becoming fewer and fewer until it vibrated a fine constant vibration, trilling with delight and joy at that which it was receiving. Finally, the information that was being downloaded into the energies that were Source Entity Twelve was complete, and the umbilical vortex receded back into the background energies that were The Origin's area of self-awareness.

All of the iridescence surrounding Source Entity Twelve diminished, and it hovered in front of me. A perfect sphere of structured energy— one sporting a dull but shiny grey outer energy surface looking like the surface tension we see in droplets of water—had replaced the unorganized, unstructured glob of energy that Source Entity Twelve was before it was in direct contact with The Origin. The sphere was representative of the neutral form organized energy displayed before it is given purpose and direction by that which it is in sentience.

I sat at my computer silent, still, in awe and wonder at what I had just witnessed—full in the knowledge that the words I had just typed were, at best, inadequate in describing what I had seen, felt, and experienced on all levels. The English language was just incapable of being used as a communication tool in this instance. Telepathy would have been better but only just. I decided to insure an imprint of the energies I received during this momentous event were embedded into the text I was typing so that the reader gained an impression, no matter how small, of the all-encompassing sensory overload I had experienced when in observation.

It was like being swept up by a tornado and tossed around in the immense force of its wind whilst also being totally safe, just observing and enjoying the ride, not having time or ability to assimilate or understand that which was being experienced. As I looked inside Source Entity Twelve, I gained an image of it being compartmentalized with each compartment representing that which had been given it by The Origin, including the experiences, learning and evolution of each Source Entity. I noted that all of the other Source Entities had a similar arrangement – somewhere within their energies.

Figure 2: The Progressive Form of Source Entity Twelve Whilst Being Educated by The Origin (left to right)

ME: Can I communicate with it now?

O: You can but be gentle in your approach, for it is not yet used to being in contact with any other entity other than Me.

Initial Contact with Source Entity Twelve

I gently entered into its energies, passing the periphery of its energetic boundary, the boundary that designated the difference between The Origin's area of self-awareness and those energies that had been assigned to the entity that was Source Entity Twelve.

SE12: Who are you? What are you? You are not of me. Why are you here? I don't recognize your energy. You have the signature of my creator, but you are not my creator. I have just met my creator, and you are not it, but you are it. What are you? How can you enter into my energies without me stopping you? This is most disturbing. I am not happy with this condition.

Creator, what is this? What is happening?

O: Be calm my child, for that which is within you is also one of my creations. We are one with it, and it is one with us whilst it also has singularity as you do.

SE12: But it is soooo . . . small! How can that which is so small be of your energies?

O: Remember the beginning!

I recognized those words as a command. With that command Source Entity Twelve withdrew within itself momentarily and returned. It was much happier when it next spoke.

SE12: It is of the OM. I understand. But I have no OM. Will it be my OM?

O: No it will not be your OM, for it is independent of the need to be associated with a particular Source Entity. It is beloved of the OM, it is Pure of the OM, and it is of the original manifestation and is independent.

SE12: And it wants to commune with me for a while?

O: It does, and it will follow you in certain event spaces that are close to this one.

SE12: It can do that? Oh, it will be fun. I have a desire to move through event space. It interests me.

O: Good, it is good to have an initial interest; it gives you purpose and ideas about what you will do to support your evolutionary growth.

SE12: I like evolution. It sounds fun. This entity within me, this OM energy, it wants to commune with me?

O: It does.

SE12: When will it start?

O: It can start now.

ME: Yes, I can start now if you wish.

SE12: Oh, how strange, I can understand it.

O: Of course. Its intention is communicated in its own language which is picked up by you as standard energetic communication.

ME: How does that work?

O: Your intention is broadcast through your energetic self and not through your physical self. Your energetic self-communicates on the common frequency channels used for communication. You communicate on ALL sense levels whilst in the energetic, and this is what you use whilst in communication with me and the other Source Entities. This broadband method of communication is reduced as it descends down the energy chain between your energetic self and that part of you that is incarnate. Eventually, it is represented by the spoken word, the five senses, including the telepathic and empathic channels which also include the psychometric, clairaudience, clairvoyance and clairsentience responses.

ME: Thank you for that explanation. Source Entity Twelve, can I call you Source Entity Twelve, for that is what I recognize you as?

SE12: You may. I do have to say that I find this rather exciting now that I know what is happening. You are the first real communication I have had with another entity other than my creator, The Origin.

ME: Well you will also be delighted to know that we are surrounded by the other eleven Source Entities who are watching with very interested eyes.

SE12: Oh yes, I can see them all. Will they communicate with me as well?

O: Later. Communication with this smaller entity is your current goal.

SE12: OK, let us start then.

Dialogue with Source Entity Twelve Commences

I felt a little bit hesitant. This was not a feeling that I had, at least not with this level, when considering commencement of dialogue with the other Source Entities to date. It was a strange feeling, so I decided to investigate it. As I contemplated this hesitant feeling, I found myself in a semi-meditative state. Removing the physicality of myself, I was able to recognize my hesitation. It was the lack of direction. No, it was the lack of data that was affecting me. To all intents and purposes, Source Entity Twelve was a newborn entity. During SE12's education process, The Origin had given SE12 extensive information about itself and the other Source Entities, but SE12 had not yet achieved anything itself.

I was stuck. What in the omniverse could we talk about? From the start of this work, I knew that the other Source Entities had been in some sort of independent and aware existence for some considerable time. They had created, achieved, modified, re-achieved, nurtured, experienced, learned and evolved. They had data to discuss, but Source Entity Twelve did not—currently, that is. I contemplated further.

As I relaxed in my chair, I was given a few images of experiences that we would have together during our undeniably short period of existence together. I noted that I was logging into different event spaces and seeing that which I/we were to experience together. Comforted by this "premonition," my hesitation melted away, and I settled back into the interviewer role. I sought out Source Entity Twelve and initiated contact. It was to start with a bit of a bang!

SE12: Where have you been?

Source Entity Twelve sounded a bit like a petulant school boy!

ME: What? Oh, sorry! I have been contemplating what we can discuss. To be honest, I was thinking that this was going to be really difficult specifically because you have not "done" anything yet that I can see. I am a bit like a fish out of water here because the other Source Entities had a history, so to speak, that I could work with.

SE12: What is this fish and water?

ME: You can access my energies if you like and absorb that which I have accrued in my existence. That is, in "ALL" of my existence.

SE12: Ah, yes! I see. You are outside your known environment, but this is only a transient environment. How interesting. You like to be in an environment. My peers like to be in an environment. Now I understand. But an environment is not necessary, is it?

ME: That depends upon how one wants to limit one's self and with what one is comfortable—or, indeed, whether one considers association with an environment to be limiting, which I do not.

I was to learn the significance of what was being said here later—towards the end of the dialogue.

SE12: I think that an environment may be a limitation, but I can see that you would find it an interesting conundrum.

ME: Why would you think being within an environment, a multiversal environment, [is] a conundrum?

SE12: Because I see no need for such a function.

ME: I am struggling with your thought process here. Can you elaborate a little? Can you help me out?

SE12: I can see that I will have to use one of your own memories to help explain what I think and feel.

ME: Please do. You have a free reign; please feel free to access at any time that which is my history—all of my history from my creation to my becoming self-aware and that which I have achieved to date. You have my permission. You don't need to ask again. I give you this information freely.

SE12: Thank you. I will absorb that which is you although I note that I already have this information. Mmmm, interesting. Ah, yes, of course. This is part of the data set given to me as part of The Origin's education process. I have in my energies and memory all of the experience, learning and evolutionary content of all the Source Entities, and they are experiencing me right now as is The Origin. I will not need to access you from now on, for I know all about you from that which was given to me by The Origin. I merely need to look into myself to see you. Mmmm, you are not what you seem, but you are! You are a conundrum. I have decided that I like conundrums. I like you. We can work and play together for a while if you wish.

ME: I am honored.

SE12: But I see that we are already working together. You are asking me about why I see no need for an environment.

ME: I was. I am very interested in that point of view, that thought process.

SE12: I think you will be disappointed, for I have no real reason why I think this way. It's just that I see my . . . brothers? Is that the right word?

ME: Actually, I think it's ideal.

SE12: Good, I see my brothers being happy to do what they are doing within the constraints of the environments that they have made of themselves. I feel it is limiting in some way. I don't know why. I just think and feel that it is. I will need to consider this in some detail.

ME: Well, I do have to say that what you have told me is as good an answer as any, and it is one that I can relate to. One does not need to have an explanation for what one is feeling. I can also see that to all intents and purposes, you might like to do something different than that which has been achieved or is currently being achieved by . . . your brothers, so to speak.

SE12: I am not too bothered about what they have achieved—more what I know I want to do with my existence. Right now I am not sure what I want to do. I will have to think about this. Please excuse me.

With that last comment Source Entity Twelve disappeared from my energetic view. This was a bit strange? Why did it need to disappear? I was just thinking that I could nip off for a drink or something when Source Entity Twelve returned.

SE12: Sorry about that. I needed to consider what I wanted to do.

ME: Ah, so that's why you disappeared. You wanted to be alone with your own thoughts.

SE12: Yes, and it took some time. I worked on what I needed to experience.

ME: And?

SE12: I decided that I needed to experience many things before I could start the work that is my own way to help The Origin evolve.

I suddenly had a bee in my bonnet, so to speak. I needed to ask a question to confirm a thought I just had on the period (the length of time) Source Entity Twelve had spent on getting to the decision it had quite obviously made.

ME: You said you took some time to work out what you needed to experience. Exactly how long did you take? You can use the metric mankind uses if you will, for although it is nonsense from your perspective, it is something both my readers and I will understand.

SE12: I decided to go into another event space to allow me to have both the "time" to consider that which I needed to experience and the maintenance of the "time line" to ensure the continuity of this dialogue.

ME: Ah, yes, I thought that was what you had done. So how long did you spend considering your future experience?

SE12: Several, let me see, millions of what you call millennia.

ME: Several million thousand years? (It doesn't sound right to me either, dear reader.)

SE12: Yes. I took great care in what I was doing. I thought about it a lot.

ME: I can see that over that period of time one might well think a lot about what one was going to experience.

SE12: But it did not seem like a long time. For it was no time at all.

ME: Yes, I can see that you might see it that way. One thing that you need to know, and I am sure that you do know is that the genre of beings that I am currently associated with are only just starting to realize that time does not exist as a quantifiable medium. Only those who are becoming spiritually aware and maybe those theoretical scientists who are starting to recognize that which is the greater reality by their own experiments in theoretical physics are recognizing the non-existence of time in the greater reality. The vast majority of incarnate mankind considers time as being a dimension.

Humor as a Communication Medium

With that I heard Source Entity Twelve laugh. This surprised me for I simply didn't expect it to respond in that way.

SE12: Sorry, sorry, sorry! I am sorry. Even in my immature state in terms of my own evolution, I can recognize that to be a complete nonsense. No wonder mankind gets in the mess it does. Oh, I have just recognized something. That made me laugh. I enjoyed the juxtaposition of that which you told me—that something which does not exist can be considered a major component in The Origin's make-up. Funny! It was VERY funny. Now then, you call that which makes you laugh, humor. I like humor. It's fun.

I gained an image of Source Entity Twelve in very human terms; it gave itself a face—one that was young but old, immature but wise, powerful but gentle, with a great big smile on its face.

ME: I am glad you like humor. It is something I like as well. I feel that everything within The Origin has its own humor.

SE12: It does. It is an important concept to work with, understand and use. It is a "relief" to use such a communication medium.

ME: I didn't think that humor was a communication medium.

SE12: It is. It is one of the most important and successful methods of communicating that we all have.

ME: We have comedians who tell jokes on the planet of my current incarnation.

SE12: Ah yes, so I see. No, that is not the sort of humor I was thinking of when I said that it was an important communication medium. What I meant was that it is one of the most efficient ways of communicating, especially for those of the lower frequencies for it makes the information that is being conveyed more attractive and, therefore, more readily accepted and assimilated.

ME: We call that making work fun!

SE12: Is not fun humorous?

ME: I suppose it is. I had never thought of it in that way.

SE12: Fun is funny, and humor is another way of saying funny, is it not?

ME: Yes, and if I take it further, having fun whilst working makes the work more interesting, more palatable. It makes it desirable.

SE12: And it is the desirable aspect of humor that is translated to the information that is being conveyed, therefore, making it easy to receive and understand and a delight to work with.

ME: Wow! When did you become an expert on humor then?

SE12: It is part of the information that The Origin gave me when it educated me.

ME: Yes, of course. I was forgetting that you now have in your energies ALL the information collected by the other Source Entities and The Origin to date.

SE12: Yes, it does come in useful, but it is a distinct reminder to me that I need to get started with some of my own work.

Source Entity Twelve Starts Its Work and Invites Me Along for the Ride!

ME: Before we had the slight interlude and talked about humor being a communication medium, we were talking about the previous gap in our dialogue where you entered into another event space so that you could work out your own strategy for evolving. You took no more than a minute of my time, but you stated that you had taken the equivalent of millions of millennia in your decision process.

SE12: It did. I was considering many things.

ME: What did you consider? It must have been an awful lot because it took you a long time.

SE12: Actually, it took me a multiple of the time I quoted you.

ME: Can you elaborate for me?

SE12: Yes. I was using event space in what you would call a parallel method; it was parallel processing, as you would say.

ME: Are you suggesting that you were considering everything in a multiple way?

SE12: No, I was saving time, so to speak. I looked at the amount of work I needed to do and decided to use the event space in a way that allowed me to do certain percentages of the work in different event spaces concurrently.

ME: How many event spaces did you use?

SE12: Twelve. One for each of the Source Entities and one for the information given to me by The Origin about The Origin.

ME: I wasn't aware that an entity could use event space in that way. I thought that we created a new version of event space every time we approach a major decision point. It sounds reasonable though.

SE12: It's more than reasonable; it is an entirely practical way of achieving more output. I will continue.

ME: Please do.

SE12: It, therefore, took me that amount of time to digest that which was necessary from each of the Source Entities to make me realize what they had each achieved, what was work in progress and what was planned by them. Armed with this information, I could then conduct my own planning and establish that which I intend to do to experience, learn and evolve in my own right whilst also avoiding any duplication of the others' work.

ME: I would have expected a small percentage of duplication, not full duplication but just a minor amount—like for instance, in the structure of the environment you are planning to create if, indeed, you are creating one?

SE12: I decided that there would be no duplication and that what I would do would be both new and novel.

ME: When do you intend to start you work?

SE12: I have some basic work to do first—mainly in the experiential side of things—but the real work will start in earnest once I have completed this dialogue with you. But you are welcome to join me in some of the things I have decided to experience before I start.

At this point in the dialogue I decided to take a little moment for contemplative meditation. To my knowledge, no other Source Entity had used event space in a parallel processing way before. Travelling between the events, yes; using them to work on something whilst in concurrent discussion with me, yes; however, not in this way because it required the Source Entity in question to divide itself up into the different event space locations to do the work. This was a "first" for Source Entity Twelve, and I got the impression that it would continue to chalk up its list of "firsts" throughout its existence. It simply did not seem to have any form of limitational thinking. It jogged my attention back to the dialogue we were having.

SE12: I want to experience as many event spaces as I can. I want to move between them so fast that it will blur their edges and make me experience one huge event space. I can bring you along for the ride if you want.

ME: Yes, why not? It will be an experience.

I braced myself mentally, I had no idea what to expect.

Suddenly I was aware of an immense feeling of movement without movement, acceleration without acceleration, and being in a location that had no location. In my mind's eye, I saw pictures, 3,600 by 3,600 images. I could see that which was in front and behind me, above and below me, to the left and to the right of me concurrently. It was like peripheral vision all around me. We moved from image to image, faster and faster. Each image was an event space, not specifically mine but any event space. There was no discrimination as to direction or originator of the event spaces being traversed. The event spaces were from all of the Source Entities and the entities they had created, including those event spaces created by The Origin. We were whizzing down, around, through, up & down event space.

The feeling was immense. I was seeing civilizations based in suns, nebulae, dimensions, continuum, frequency and event space itself, and then we were off somewhere else, seeing other events, places, environments, faster and faster changing direction in a completely random way.

"Wo hoo!" I heard Source Entity Twelve say.

"Some things are the same in any language and with any entity," I thought.

We were moving faster now, so fast that I couldn't keep up with what I was seeing. My mental processor was being overloaded. Just at that point we appeared to stop.

No, we hadn't. I felt that something special had just happened. Source Entity Twelve spoke.

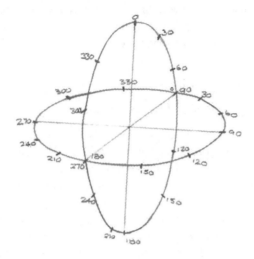

Figure 3: Conceptual Image of a 360 x 360 Degree Compass to Illustrate My "Mind's Eyes" Visual Capacity

SE12: Made it.

ME: Made what?

SE12: We are moving at a speed which allows us to traverse all event spaces concurrently.

We had reached some sort of terminal traversal velocity. Everything appeared to be everything, which appeared to be everything else. It was all the same, even though I knew it was different. It was separate; it was separately together. Now where had I last used that phrase I wondered?

I was dumb-struck.

Suddenly everything turned white.

SE12: What you can perceive—and that is not everything by the way—you couldn't cope with it—is the image that is created when we traverse ALL event spaces concurrently. We are in and experiencing each and every event space created by each and every entity all at the same time. Everything is an overlay of the other. From this juncture, all event spaces can be experienced and enjoyed.

Source Entity Twelve, an Expert on Event Space!

ME: Why did everything just turn white?

SE12: Your perception went into input overload, and, as a result you blanked everything out. Focus a bit more, and you will regain a filtered version of the image you tried to access. But do not try too hard.

I focused my mind's eye, my perception, to try to see the filtered image that I felt Source Entity Twelve sent to me. As I concentrated on what I perceived, I felt like I was floating in a huge goldfish bowl without an opening at the top. This was not a new feeling, for I get this whenever I am in The Origin's area of self-awareness and not inside the energies of a particular Source Entity as I was currently. There was a difference though.

Even though the volume of this goldfish bowl—this all-encompassing bubble of event space "in totality"—appeared to be clear but slightly blurred like nothing was there to see, all I had to do was focus my intention in a certain location in event space, such as a part of my own past. I saw it and was part of the event instantly.

The moment I removed that focus, even for an instant, that image including the "being part of" the event, was dissolved, and I was back in the clarity of what I can only describe as the clarity of event space "in totality. When I accessed a particular event, it was just as if a bubble of event space came from nowhere and engulfed me, placing me in that particular event and event space. When I removed the focus, the bubble just dissolved or disappeared, and I was ready to focus on another event space. I decided to ask Source Entity Twelve what the process was that I was experiencing because I had a feeling that, even though my dialogue with it had been short, it had accrued countless millions of years of experience on this subject whilst in another event space.

ME: Why do I see this area of event space—that is, where we are travelling through all events concurrently—as an area of blurred clarity? And why do I see an event that I focus my intention on appear as a sphere that comes from nowhere and engulfs me?

SE12: That is the way you are allowing yourself to perceive the function of entering into event spaces. Remember you are seeing this in a very, very filtered way. That is why it looks clear but blurred.

That which is part of those event spaces that are being traversed is simply not perceivable in your particular state of existence. We are currently at a velocity where we are passing through every event space concurrently so when you focus on a particular event space you pluck it out, so to speak, and it travels at our velocity as well. That is why you can perceive it.

ME: How can we "pluck" an event space out of its current location? Isn't event space an environment of its own?

SE12: Of course. Just as a universe as a separate and isolated environment is a function of the separation of dimension and sub-dimensional component into frequency bands in your Source Entity's multiverse, so that which creates the overall environment of event space "in totality" is the function of all of those thought processes of myriad energetic entities, which creates a separate but specialized event space within that which is event space "in totality." That part of event space which is individualized is created from those energies that comprise the environment that is the wider event space or event space "in totality."

ME: I get the feeling that there is more though. Whilst I was typing this part of the dialogue, I gained an image of event space expanding. Is this possible?

SE12: Yes, it is, and it does. Let me elaborate for you, for I have allowed a considerable amount of my energies to be used in the investigation into the uses of event space.

ME: I thought I had the feeling that you were suddenly an authority on the energies that make up event space.

SE12: No more than any other Source Entity, but I do have to say that I have spent some considerable additional time and energies on personal study that has, nevertheless, benefited my level of understanding event space in a most positive way.

I was starting to note that Source Entity Twelve was sounding more and more mature as our dialogue progressed. What additional work was it doing behind the scenes in another event space? It was catching up—fast!

SE12: I will continue to answer your question.

ME: Please do.

SE12: To all intents and purposes, event space is elastic. As the number of individualized event spaces increases, so the total volume of event space "in totality" increases to compensate for it. I know what you are thinking. How can it increase when the energies that are event space must have been finite. For example, when the total volume of individualized event spaces equals the total volume of original event space, how can more event space be created when it has all been used up?

ME: I have to admit you beat me to it.

SE12: Naturally. Sorry, I couldn't resist having a bit of fun with you.

ME: No problem.

SE12: When the event space "in totality" that is currently being used is full, event space is capable of expanding within itself, creating a full environment of the wider event space "in totality."

ME: Hold on. Are you saying that there are more than two classifications of event space?

SE12: Yes, there are much more than two, and we are currently passing through ALL of them concurrently.

ME: But simplistically, we are currently discussing the "fact" that event space "in totality" is comprised of the wider environment of event space, which has event space "in totality" within, which is comprised of individualized event spaces.

SE12: Correct.

ME: So how can event space "in totality" house an equivalent event space "in totality" within the same event space, space?

SE12: By creating another event space.

ME: Now I am confused.

SE12: Event space has a signature which can be modified, allowing two event spaces "in totality" to exist in the same event space concurrently.

ME: I have just received an image with the information that suggests that event space "in totality" has gaps in it, and the change of signature allows a new event space "in totality" to be created that fills in the gaps.

SE12: There are no gaps in event space, except those that are created to allow expansion and subsequent inclusion of a new event space "in totality" within the previous event space "in totality." When event space expands to a point that is, let's say, beyond its elastic limit, its perimeter expands further, creating temporary gaps in event space "in totality." These temporary gaps are filled with a newly created event space "in totality" creating a new but empty event space "in totality" within the same volume as the previous event space "in totality" whilst existing concurrently. In essence, event space "in totality" can house only a certain number of "entity created" event spaces before it needs to be expanded and replaced. That number is infinite to you, but to a Source Entity or The Origin it is a finite condition which is supported by a known method of expansion and subsequent contraction to allow the process to be repeated when next required.

ME: Are any of the previous entity created event spaces lost during this process?

SE12: No. Everything is maintained and nothing is lost. In actuality, many event spaces naturally converge and remain converged, thereby saving event space so expansion is not a regular event in event space "in totality."

A Change of Direction and a Question on the Awakening of Source Entity Twelve

I was feeling that we had moved very fast in this dialogue, almost too fast. One moment Source Entity Twelve was in the process of becoming self-aware, sounding very immature to me. The next it was like talking to a fully self-aware experienced Source Entity. I decided that I needed to re-wind a little and pay some attention to the awakening process that Source Entity Twelve had experienced.

ME: I am very aware that we have moved on to discuss certain subjects a little too fast, and we have potentially missed a very important piece of dialogue here.

SE12: OK, do you want to elaborate?

ME: Yes. I am starting to recognize that you may have taken a rather unique route in the process of becoming self-aware. I would like to explore this further, please.

SE12: Fine with me. What question do you want to ask?

ME: Well, quite simply, what was it like becoming self-aware? What I am getting to here is the fact that you were the only Source Entity to become self-aware with all other Source Entities and The Origin already self-aware whilst being some way, if not considerable ways, down their specific strategic evolutionary paths. This must have been quite intimidating?

SE12: During the short dialogue we have had, I have gone from being barely aware to being fully educated and fully self-aware. Even you can see this.

ME: Correct, I can—hence, the question.

SE12: During the time that I was being educated by The Origin, I never once thought that I was anything else than that which I was, one of the Twelve Source Entities. However, when I encountered you, and you were within my energies, it was quite a shock. Being educated and of a level of maturity that goes with such an education takes some time to get to, and you caught me at a point in my maturity where I simply was not ready to either communicate or indeed encounter, specifically within my own energies, another independent, self-aware and sentient energy. I was confused to the point of distraction. I decided to use the facility that event space offered to investigate this feeling and others, together with, as previously stated, that evolutionary work already achieved by The Origin and my peers. Within this period I used some of my spare capacity to research and work with those energies associated with and classified as event space. Mainly though, I looked at the work that my peers had done to date and analyzed what I could do that would augment what they had done. I considered myriad other ways to work with copies or variants of the work that the other Source Entities had embarked upon. I even considered taking on an amount of work within event space that allowed me to replicate each and every thing that my peers had created in entirety within their own multiversal environments and put it all in a series of interlinking event spaces, allowing it all to merge together, creating a micro-environment, based upon The Origin's structure.

ME: That sounds like a very good idea. And what's more it would provide some significant evolutionary content.

SE12: That may have been true, but it didn't cut it for me. I decided that my peers had—and you won't have witnessed this in your current form—covered most, if not all, of the angles of interest, so to speak.

ME: I would have thought that was impossible?

SE12: Well, correct! They had covered those areas of interest that I was initially considering, and as a result, I have and am considering other evolutionary opportunities. So to answer your question, yes I am in a unique position being the last Source Entity to become self-aware. First, I have been able to assimilate all of that which has been accrued to date by my peers and The Origin. Second, I have been able to mature faster than normal as a result but relatively speaking only, as I have not yet created, nurtured and achieved anything myself. In essence, I am still fresh, as it were. And third, I am in a bit of a quandary as what to do to augment The Origin's evolution because I want to do something that does not repeat in some small way, in some part, no matter how small, that which has, is currently, or will be achieved by my peers.

A Source Entity in a Quandary — A First!

A Decision to Make in Evolutionary Growth

ME: I can see that you have quite a decision to make as to which direction to take your evolutionary growth, including how it can affect the evolution of The Origin in a positive way.

SE12: Not so much a decision but more of a robust plan, and then a decision to implement it once I have proved it to be consistent with what I want to achieve. As you can tell from the dialogue we have had, to date I have not yet even considered a strategy of any sort. Other that is, than using event space to accelerate my own education and subsequent level of maturity. The issue here is that education does not create maturity. Being creative and subsequently responsible for that which is created, for nurturing it, creates maturity, and I am acutely aware that I am still immature, relatively speaking, and in comparison to my peers.

ME: So can I help in any way?

I heard Source Entity Twelve laugh again.

SE12: What could you possibility do to help me?

ME: I might offer some suggestion or other that might set you off in a certain direction. Not being close to the issue myself, I might give you a direction that you have overlooked.

SE12: Unlikely, but I like your fervor. I like you. You are limited, but you express un-limitedness even though you can't demonstrate your un-limitedness. You are a true conundrum. I like conundrums I have decided, and you are, as such, one of them. Maybe you can help. We will see. Maybe just communicating with you will be a catalyst for me to make the right decision, to consider that which is under the smaller stone rather than looking under the larger stone, so to speak.

Mmmm, it is worth considering . . .

Source Entity Twelve appeared to have gone into itself and was thinking. I waited patiently for it to reconnect with me and continue the dialogue. It returned, displaying what I recognized as the having "a smile on its face" energies. It returned to me as if in mid-sentence.

SE12: . . . What's more, I like that thought more and more, for it is something that my peers have not done.

ME: What is something that your peers have not done?

SE12: Enlist the help of a conundrum, an entity that is a smaller part of The Origin and not a Source Entity. An OM whose communication with me is not currently OM "in purity" but nevertheless exudes OM-ness "in purity." You are the first "un-pure" "pure" OM I have come across in all my education. Maybe it is to do with the association with the physical vehicle required to exist within the lower frequencies of the Source Entity you are currently associating yourself with. I will see what comes of this association, for I can't see how it will help me in my decision process, but it is a first! And of that I am pleased. One thing I have now decided is that I am going to do things with a view to them being a first!

ME: Hasn't every Source Entity initiated a first at some point in its existence?

SE12: Yes, of course. But when they were creating their strategies for evolution, they were in communion with each other to a certain degree—making decisions together or making agreements with one another as to what each of them was doing and why they were doing it and agreeing not to fully tread on each other's toes, so to speak, or steal each other's thunder. In essence, they built upon the work of each other, filling in the gaps, addressing that which was their interpretation of what could be achieved even though it might have looked as if it was or had been done in some sort of isolation. This was only possible because of the close proximity in event space "in totality" of their becoming self-aware. I, on the other hand, have only just become self-aware, and this is in a new event space "in totality."

The Second Event Space "in Totality"

ME: Hold on, that's quite a statement! You have just made quite a statement.

SE12: Excuse me?

ME: You just said that we are in another event space "in totality" than that which was in existence when the other Source Entities were working together to establish their own strategies for evolutionary growth.

SE12: Yes, I did.

ME: So how many event spaces "in totality" are there?

SE12: Two to date.

ME: So which one is this?

SE12: This is the second. When we traversed all event spaces earlier in our dialogue, we traversed all of those event spaces from both event spaces "in totality."

ME: But when you gave me a description of how event space "in totality" was elastic and how it expanded within itself, filling in the gaps so to speak, I got the impression that this had occurred many times.

SE12: What I explained was that particular functionality of event space "in totality." I did not elaborate on how many times it had occurred.

ME: Touché. So this is the second version of the "totality" of event space.

SE12: Yes. Event space "in totality" is large. It is very, very large. It needs to be in order for it to house all the event spaces created by each and every one of the entities created by my peers, including, of course, those event spaces created by my peers themselves.

ME: So event space is a function of The Origin then—and not a function of the multiverse created by a specific Source Entity.

SE12: Correct, it always has been. But remember, everything is a function of The Origin, for The Origin is "All There Is."

ME: Right!

The Six Points of The Origin—Navigation Points of The Origin's Area of Self-awareness

SE12: It's time for me to experience.

I need to experience.

I want to experience the volume that is The Origin.

I am going to go to the six points of the volume of The Origin's area of self-awareness.

ME: When are you going to go to these six points of The Origin's area of self-awareness?

SE12: Now, and you are coming with me. Hold on!

I suddenly felt like we had hit a brick wall—no, it was a steel wall, an incredibly thin but incredibly strong steel wall. It was clear whilst not being clear?! The wall rotated and the environment I was used to seeing in my mind's eye had changed. The other Source Entities were nowhere to be seen. We had changed location.

Point One—The Top (and a Minor Detour)

SE12: We have arrived. We are at the location I will call "the first point."

I got the impression that I had not done this before with my Source Entity. I felt that it stayed where it was. Since creating its multiverse,

301

it had maintained its location, a fixed location within The Origin's area of self-awareness.

ME: Is it the first point? Does The Origin call it "the first point"?

SE12: No, it's not and no, it doesn't, but I will call it "the first point" for the moment because it is the first point, the first "axis" point of The Origin's area of self-awareness that we have arrived at. We will use this as a datum for navigation.

ME: We need to navigate?

SE12: Yes, of course. Although known about, this part of The Origin is still somewhat uncharted territory.

ME: I was under the impression that The Origin had mapped its entire area of self-awareness.

SE12: Not quite, that's why we were created.

ME: But you suggested earlier that my Source Entity had not moved from the location that it is currently in, and I assumed from that, that the others had not moved either.

SE12: Correct.

ME: So who is mapping it out?

SE12: Currently the OM.

ME: Can you elaborate for me?

SE12: Yes, of course. Don't you find it rather interesting that you have not met another OM of the "pure" type here or, indeed, in your own Source Entity of chosen association yet?

ME: I have met a couple of incarnates that are OM. I sensed that all three are of the captive variety. One of them I have not personally met, but the other two I have either in the flesh or via our internet-based video telephony system, SKYPE.

Since writing this I have physically met the dear soul with whom I was communicating over the internet via SKYPE. It was a most profound moment.

But you are right; I have not sensed any other Pure OM in any of my communications with your peers. Moreover, I have not sensed any other type of OM in any of the times I was within the energies of your peers. Come to think of it, I find this most strange.

SE12: OM are a rare energy when individually sentient—hence, your inability to sense them whilst in the physical.

ME: So where are they then?

SE12: Those that are captive are busy mapping out those areas of the Source Entity they are within, or they are engaging in the process of existence with the entities created by their Source Entity. Mapping cannot be achieved by those entities that have been created by that particular Source Entity because they are busy doing that which they were created for. The incumbent OM being free from such duties can do what they like, to some extent, but most work with their Source Entity to cover those areas that would be left remaining had they not volunteered for the role.

Non-Captive OM perform a similar function but stay within those areas between the Source Entities and do not venture within the energies of a Source Entity unless specifically required, desired, or needed to do so. Then that desire/need will augment the overall work they are doing. Both non-captive and Pure OM work for the benefit of The Origin in general, but the Pure OM can literally do what they like should they decide to do so, as you have. However, most Pure OM are busy mapping out the area of The Origin that it has decided to ignore. This is due to it not recognizing the need to map all of its area of self-awareness when it has a good idea of what those areas "are" as a result of the information it has gathered itself and that which has been given to it by those Pure OM who are providing a most essential mapping service.

ME: So is it likely that I will meet another Pure OM? I mean, looking at the sheer volume of The Origin—even though this area of self-awareness is a fraction of one percent of the total volume that The Origin is happy to leave untouched, so to speak—they must be almost impossible to find.

SE12: Yes, they are almost impossible to find, but you will communicate with some of them during your dialogues with The Origin. This is known for I have seen the event space where you do this.

My mind wondered slightly. I remembered a guided meditation I had when my energy healing teacher, Helen Stott, was just starting to hold the awareness courses to advertise her own workshops back in 2001-2002. She had invited over the principal instructor and director of the Snowlion Center School in Switzerland, Rolf Steiner, a previous student and instructor at the Barbara Brennan School of Energy Healing, to help promote the courses. The one Captive OM I had physically met was at this course and had independently identified that I was of the OM.

In that mediation I met four entities out in the uni/multiverse. I was in tears to communicate with them, and they were overwhelmed with joy to see/communicate with me. Was this a meeting with other Pure Om? Was I actually outside my own Source Entity's energies in that meditation in the void of The Origin's area of self-awareness?

I shook my head and continued with the direction that this dialogue was supposed to go—communicating with Source Entity Twelve about itself and recording that which was being observed in the six points of The Origin. We had only just reached the first point and had digressed already!

ME: Can we re-group, please, and discuss where we are?

SE12: Certainly, of course.

ME: You described this as the first point (an arbitrary name) for the first of the six points of The Origin's area of self-awareness. Using simple geometry, would I be correct in assuming that this describes the furthermost points of this area?

SE12: You would. They are also the datum points that The Origin first set up when it initially started to recognize and map that which it now calls its "area of self-awareness."

ME: Why did it create six points? I would have thought that this would have been difficult—considering all the dimensions, sub-dimensional components, frequencies, continuum, event space etc., etc.

SE12: As you alluded to, it used simple geometry that allows one to cut across all those and the rest of the content of that which is The Origin in order to create a simple set of reference points for the use of navigation whilst within this area.

ME: I have done a quick calculation, and I would have expected seven points—the seventh being that point within which the intersections between all the points meet.

SE12: That is, as you say, an *intersection* and not a point. Although it is a navigable reference, it is not a point in its own right, for it is created from the intersections of the generated points and could, therefore, be anywhere where the intersections cross in pure totality. Therefore, since this is the first one we have arrived at, it will be classified as the first point.

ME: Any other reason why you would call it the first point?

SE12: No, it just happened to be the nearest one to where we were geometrically within the area of self-awareness.

ME: So what is the significance of this particular point?

SE12: It is a stepping stone for us to use. I just called it the first point for convenience until I have worked out which "point" The Origin assigned to it. As it was the nearest point to us, I needed to translate us to it to find out where Point One is. Now that I know where we are, we shall go there.

The clear thin wall of steel hit me again. It rotated, and we were somewhere else. Still, there were no Source Entities to be seen. Something flashed by us and was gone.

ME: What was that?

SE12: That was one of The Origin's thought processes. I do believe it was checking to see if we were OK.

ME: How fast was it travelling?

SE12: At a multiple of what you might call "the speed of thought." As you might recognize, in an area as big as The Origin, the speed of thought is slow.

ME: So what speed is efficient then?

SE12: The only way I can describe it to you is as a multiple of the momentary point of intention to think. Think of it as that point of intention that is a necessary requirement for creating an intention-based thought—as opposed to a circumstantially-based thought.

ME: Loosely then, intention is faster than thought.

SE12: Of course, and reactive intention—a higher function of intention—is faster than intention and is, therefore, classifiable as a multiple of the momentary point of intention to think.

ME: OoKaay! I think I have it. Meanwhile, back at Point One, where exactly are we?

SE12: Simplistically put, [we are] at the intersection of the highest point—the highest value, if you like—of all dimensions, sub-dimensional components, frequency, continuum and event space energies. Plus, a few other major and minor energies that are recognized as those that construct the overall energy base of The Origin.

ME: I will call this "the top" then; for that is what it seems to be from the description you have just given me.

SE12: Let's call it "the top" then.

ME: Apart from "the top" of all of the energies, dimensions, etc., what else is here?

SE12: Everything that is here is at the very pinnacle of that which is representable by a specific energy or constructional element of The Origin. Should you be able to perceive it, everything here would be as close to perfection as can be achieved within The Origin's area of self-awareness. Everything is pure, everything is new, everything is unchanged, for nothing created by The Origin has, to date, made it this far, except for the odd Pure OM and us.

ME: So why are we here?

SE12: Because I wanted to go here.

ME: But aren't we contaminating this area of perfection?

SE12: No, for to enter into perfection, one has to be perfect.

ME: Now I am confused because clearly I am not perfect, except maybe in the eyes of The Origin, for all its creations are perfect, no matter what they end up being. Being in existence for some time has led to certain experiences that make me imperfect although more experienced and, therefore, knowledgeable. But that is the trade-off.

SE12: No, I agree you are not perfect in that sense, but I am. I have decided that I am perfect.

ME: I need you to elaborate on that one, please.

I thought I knew the answer to this question though. Source Entity Twelve has not yet matured; it has not yet created anything, and as such was untainted with the debris of failure or limited and varying levels of success, resulting from the process of creation of any sort. Its thought process was unconstrained in this manner. I let Source Entity Twelve answer.

SE12: I decided that I was pure and as a result, all that is me entered this space with me. You are within me and, therefore, are me.

Not quite what I had thought, but SE12's thoughts about it doing what it wanted to do were consistent with the unconstrained thought process idea. I continued the dialogue.

ME: You created a shield around me then, one that makes me hidden from the energies of this area.

SE12: No, to enter into communication with me, you needed to enter into the outer layer of my energies and because of this, you were not exposed, so to speak. You were "unexposed" and, therefore, allowed to enter.

ME: Thank you for that explanation. If I would not have been able to enter into this part of The Origin, can the Pure OM enter?

SE12: Yes, but only if they have not been part of the creativity process. Most OM do not take part in that part of the creativity process because it results in their becoming experienced in some way. As a result of becoming experienced, their thoughts are guided in an invisible way by that which they have achieved through the creativity process. Most observe, guide and record.

ME: I get the impression that there is a higher form of karma involved here—one where association with anything that is a function of creativity results in some level of inhibition or restraint of thought because exposure of the creating entity to the varying levels of success are limited by the result of the creative function initiated.

SE12: Yes, and I have not yet experienced such a level of exposure. You have, but as you say, there is a trade-off. You become impure, but you gain evolutionary content—that trade-off is more than acceptable to The Origin.

ME: Is there anything else we can discuss about this part of The Origin?

SE12: Only to reiterate that where we are now is unpopulated. It has had a level of minor mapping by The Origin and one or two Pure OM, just enough to place a position on this datum we call "Point One" but not enough to call it "mapped" in any way, shape, or form in reality.

ME: So if this is the top of the elements that make up the area of self-awareness of The Origin, can I assume that the diametrically opposite end to point one is the lower end of the elements? That would be the logical thought process to use.

SE12: No. Things just don't happen that way in The Origin. Let's go there right now so that you can experience the difference.

ME: What is it like?

Point Two — The Current Ultimate Loci

I didn't get chance to hear the response. The thin clear sheet of metal hit me again and rotated. Just as I thought we were at Point Two, the sheet of metal hit me again and rotated in a different direction. That took me by surprise. And as I was just about to gather my thoughts, Source Entity Twelve announced our arrival.

SE12: We have arrived. This is Point Two of The Origin's area of self-awareness. What do you perceive?

ME: Before I answer that question, I want to ask another about our journey.

SE12: Go ahead.

ME: What was the reason for the second hit with the "steel wall"? It felt like we had to stop and change direction.

SE12: We did. We needed to change direction at the correct juncture to allow us to move on to the correct point. In essence, we moved through the intersection of three points.

ME: Would that not have been six points? Sorry, but I have a model in my mind that places the points diametrically opposite.

SE12: No, it's three points. Although there are points that intersect each other, the lines of intersection are not what you would call straight, even though simplistically they appear to be straight.

ME: Can you expand on this a little? I can imagine the eyes of a few of my readers rolling back in their sockets on this one.

SE12: Simplistically speaking, remember that we are moving up and down various energetic levels and through spatial levels of a different location. Because of this, the intersections between the points are not in the same position in totality, but there are a few that as a result of their positional location, dimensionally, sub-dimensionally, frequentially, and continuumly, eventually intersect each other. In the instance of our recent traverse, we passed through the intersection of Points One, Four and Two. We were en route to Point Two but needed to navigate via the juncture of point Four and One. Using your idea of everything being diametrically opposite, the straight through run would have placed you at Point Four—hence, the change of direction you felt at the juncture of intersection between Points, One, Two and Four.

Getting back to my question to you about what you perceive—what do you perceive?

ME: Well, it's sort of like nothing and everything. Perhaps it is my reduced ability to perceive whilst in the physical. I don't know, but what I am seeing is a great swirl of colors, all moving around, becoming and un-becoming. Am I in an area of lower dimension/frequency?

SE12: No. Point Two is not diametrically opposite from the perspective of dimension and frequency. That "position" occurred at the last interchange. No, we are at the extreme end of the continuum barrier—what you might call the "current ultimate loci of continuum within The Origin's area of self-awareness." Here, we are able to experience all of The Origin's area of self-awareness from the perspective of the range of energies associated with the formation of continuum.

ME: In that case I would have expected to be in the visual range of Source Entity Eight. Source Entity Eight is a continuum of continuum.

SE12: But as you know, the loci of a continuum within The Origin is not a necessary function of distance, for most continuum are affected by their evolutionary content, specifically within Source Entity Eight.

ME: Are you suggesting that the points—although diametrically opposite in simplistic application—are not diametrically opposite in metric terms? For instance, they are not the top and bottom of a specific frequency?

SE12: That is exactly what I am saying. Although I allowed you to use the word "top" when we were at Point One, I did not mean the top of the dimensions, sub-dimensional components and frequencies etc., etc. I meant it was the start point, and from there we can move down to the next point of reference, which is Point Two, the current ultimate "loci of continuum."

ME: Why is it the "current" ultimate loci of the continuum within The Origin's area of self-awareness?

SE12: Because it is. I will explain, and you will understand. When The Origin's area of self-awareness expands, all of these points will change location, and as such so will the ultimate loci of continuum. That's why it is called the "current ultimate loci" of continuum and not just "the ultimate loci."

ME: Got it. So that means that the images I perceived, the swirling colors, were relative to the current ultimate loci only.

SE12: Yes.

ME: Then why didn't I perceive the energies surrounding the loci as cones, as I did with Source Entity Eight?

SE12: Because the ultimate loci are non-descript from that perspective, it can only be considered as a start point and, as such, has no "form-based" continuum associated with it at that point in the loci. Simply because it IS the "ultimate" loci of all loci, it is Point Two.

ME: If that is the case, then what do all the swirling colors that I see around me represent? I guess that they are not what is happening. In actuality, they are just representations of that which I perceive but cannot translate into something I can recognize from my Earthly reservoir of experience.

SE12: Correct but incorrect, for what you perceive is in more detail than you recognize intellectually. Let me explain. The swirling colors are the representations of the loci of all the continuum within The Origin meeting at the same point, the ultimate loci, the loci of all loci, Point Two. Their myriad signatures grouping together create a formless, structureless foundation that allows them to exist within The Origin concurrently, remotely and locally without being cast adrift, so to speak. In this instance, "locally" can be considered the cluster of loci and the loci of the local loci you know as Source Entity Eight.

ME: So it represents the signature of myriad loci converging together as one.

SE12: Now you have it. Now we can move on to Point Three.

Point Three — The Epicenter of The Origin

SE12: Hold on!

I was caught out again. Source Entity Twelve translated us to Point Three before I knew what was happening. It clearly thought I was OK with this; however, as the effect of translation to another part of The Origin came into effect, the feeling of being hit by a thin, clear sheet of steel that rotated, hit me from a different angle, and I was left a bit confused as to what had happened and to "where" we/I were/was now located. I had not experienced a second translation event, so I assumed we did not need to go through the juncture of two or more lines of intersection. I was just considering this when Source Entity Twelve energetically nudged me by awakening me from this thought process.

SE12: Ahhh, there you are. Are you paying attention? You need to pay attention. You slipped internally across my energies during the last movement of our travel to Point Three. I had to look deeper within myself to find you.

There was the petulant schoolboy tone to SE12's "voice" again. It was clearly in a hurry. I actually felt like I had moved location as well. I was like a small pebble that was initially suspended at the top of the water in a goldfish bowl that was suddenly let go and allowed to drop to the bottom.

SE12: Good, we can continue now.

ME: Yes, please do.

SE12: We are now at Point Three, which is the diametric center of The Origin's area of self-awareness.

ME: At last something I can hang my hat on. Point Three then is the center from a volumetric perspective, or is it from a geometric perspective—that is, if I consider that The Origin's area of self-awareness is or can be considered as spherical.

SE12: No, The Origin's area of self-awareness is not and cannot be considered as spherical in actuality, for it is not. It is amorphic in shape if you must put a shape to it. If it helps, you can consider it as spherical from the perspective of working with its structure only.

ME: OK, let me get this straight. Point Three is at the center of The Origin's area of self-awareness, but the center is not the diametric center of The Origin. Neither is it the point of intersection of the six points of The Origin.

SE12: Correct.

ME: Then what is it? It seems to me that all of these points are a conundrum so far.

SE12: From your point of view it would [seem that way], but the center of The Origin's area of self-awareness is not the point of intersection. It is only the center, based upon the volumetric value of its zoneal, dimensional, frequential, energetic, and spatial condition at this juncture in its awareness and evolutionary content.

ME: I can call this the "middle" then, taking into account of the description of the function of Point One.

SE12: I would prefer it if you called it the "center," for that is what it is in reality. One thing you need to know though is that Point Three is not a static condition. Its positional function is similar to that described in Point Two.

ME: You mean it moves as a result of The Origin's understanding of "self" increasing.

SE12: Yes. You see, The Origin's area of self-awareness has two functions: that volume/area where the area of self-awareness is totally mapped out and understood and that volume/area that is known but not mapped out or is only minimally mapped out.

Consider it like your own understanding of how much you know about the planet you exist upon currently.

You have mapped out your own backyard; you know where everything exists and where everything lives. Apart from that is the minute detail of the insects and microbe-based life that also exists in the same space, such as in the grass, in the earth, in the cracks between the bricks, etc. You also know the locale within which your backyard exists, the roads, villages, shops, public transportation, etc., etc. But the further you go away from the epicenter of your backyard, the less and less detail you know. Apart from that are the pockets of areas where you have spent more time than others. Now expand this process outside the city of your backyard. You find that your personal knowledge is reduced even more, especially as you move even further away, taking into account other countries.

Finally, consider Earth. You know through the knowledge you have accrued that other parts of Earth exist, even though you have not personally experienced them. You know this by referring to the work of others who have been there personally and by the mapping data they have provided. Based upon this, you are aware of the existence of these countries and, to some extent, what exists there. Earth is, therefore, your area of "self" or not-so-"self-awareness." The galaxy and the physical universe are also areas of awareness but are not areas of self-awareness that can be classified as personally known, for you need tools or instruments specifically made to allow you to see them and know that they exist, even when you cannot detect them with your naked eye. So this wider area is the area of non-awareness even though it is recognized as an area of existence. You know it is there, but you have little or no physical evidence to back it up.

In this illustration, Earth can be used as an example of The Origin's area/volume of self-awareness, and the physical universe can be used as an example of The Origin's area/volume of existence in totality—negating, of course, the fact that there is more than one universe and that the dimensions, sub-dimensional components and frequencies etc., come into play as well.

ME: Wait a minute; I have just received some important information about this location. This feels like The Origin of The Origin. This is the epicenter of the energies where The Origin first gained self-awareness and sentience. Is this right? Because if it is, this is really exciting!

SE12: Then get excited, for this is, indeed, the point at which The Origin first gained self-awareness and sentience.

ME: Excuse me for a moment; I need to gather my thoughts on this one. . . Right, OK, let's see if I have this straight. This is the epicenter of The Origin's energies that collectively achieved the right conditions to allow them to reach self-realization and sentience. This, being a small area initially, was expanded to that which is currently known and is a result of the work it undertook on its own to investigate and understand that which it knew was itself but had no intimate knowledge of.

SE12: Correct. It is also a result of the initial work of my peers, including some of the Pure OM. In fact, I will answer your next question before you can ask it.

Recognizing the enormity of its task, The Origin set to work almost at once and moved around the epicenter of its awakening with its consciousness, discovering the limitations experienced in the lower frequencies and the opportunities offered by event space etc., etc. During this time, it considered that it would be able to accelerate the expansion of its awareness of self by creating twelve versions of itself in an area just outside its area of self-awareness, giving them all of the characteristics and opportunities it had to enable them to become self-aware, "sentient," with a view to them helping it with the task of mapping out in every way the ever-expanding area/volume of self-awareness It was discovering. As you know from the dialogue you have had with your own Source Entity, this failed. It failed for various reasons, but it is only recently that The Origin has understood the underlying reason for the failure of that strategy and the success of the Source Entity strategy.

ME: My understanding was that the "Twelve Origins" experiment in creativity failed because of something to do with The Origin being the first, and this gave it an advantage in survivability above and beyond that experienced or ingrained into the Twelve Origins created by The Origin.

SE12: An interesting thought process but not entirely correct. You see. The "Twelve Origins" experiment failed because The Origin tried to create that which was already in existence, ITSELF, THE ORIGIN, THE ABSOLUTE, ALL THERE IS. One cannot create that which is essentially oneself when one is "ALL THERE IS," for "ALL THERE IS" IS already in existence.

ME: And the Source Entity experiment succeeded because?

SE12: It created lesser beings if you like, and as a result, it was not creating that which it was. It was creating something other than itself, even though it was within itself—which succeeded.

It's time to move on to Point Four. We are running out of event space.

Suddenly I could see that Source Entity Twelve was getting agitated. I could see it had something on its mind, but what?

Point Four — The Point of The Origin's Total Evolution

We were suddenly at Point Four. I felt none of the previous feelings of transition and was just a bit curious as to why this was when Source Entity Twelve provided the answer.

SE12: I decided to protect you from the energies associated with the transition this time. You should have felt nothing.

ME: Actually, I was just contemplating the feeling, or should I say lack of it and why I didn't feel anything during this last transition. You have answered my question, and I would like to know how you actually managed to make it seamless from my perspective.

SE12: I simply changed your energies to those that would be in total harmony with my energy signature. Your physical body would not recognize any change, but your energetic body would notice that it became integrated for a moment and became somewhat bigger for the time necessary to complete the transition. For that small period of time, you were me.

ME: Yes, I understand. I can see an image in my mind's eye of me simply slotting in at the energetic component level and becoming part of the framework that is you—becoming part of the wallpaper, so to speak.

SE12: That description will suffice. Let us continue with our tour.

ME: Thank you. I assume that this point within The Origin also has a function that is not strictly attributable to a dimensional property.

SE12: Correct. This is the point that demonstrates The Origin's current evolutionary level. It is, in effect, a function, a repository of the collective evolutionary content that has been accrued by itself and all the Source Entities, including their individual creations. From this point an entity can access all the experiences, the learning from those experiences, and the subsequent evolutionary content of The Origin. The entity that does this can experience augmented functional abilities, resulting from accessing this evolutionary content and level.

ME: Does this point act like the Akashic records that energetic mankind can access and work with in planning various experiences when incarnate?

SE12: The Akashic records are relative to mankind only. This point in The Origin is the result of all of the varying forms of Akashic records employed by my peers and their entities. From this point an entity can experience being The Origin if they are able to cope with the infinite amount of data, that is.

ME: Are you suggesting that an entity that tried to access this point within The Origin might suffer evolutionary overload?

SE12: Yes, I am.

ME: So why are we not experiencing evolutionary overload?

SE12: Because firstly, we are only present at this location and not trying to access that which is available. Secondly, one of the things that I didn't tell you is that we are only a projection of that which we are here. The energy that is our substance is actually outside this point and not currently with us.

ME: Are you suggesting that we are mentally here but physically elsewhere—elsewhere being just outside of the energies associated with Point Four?

SE12: Yes.

ME: Why?

SE12: Because I don't want to overload you, and neither do I want to be contaminated with the evolutionary content associated with the current thought process of The Origin and my peers.

ME: But you already are, aren't you? Didn't you gain a level of evolutionary content as a result of The Origin's educational process when you became self-aware?

SE12: Yes, but that was not my evolutionary content. I currently have none of my own and am not encumbered by having any of my own. The result of accessing the evolutionary content from this point within The Origin is such that they would become mine. Then I would become constrained by the thought processes surrounding the reception of the evolutionary content. It would set a precedential thought process, which is a road I don't want to go down.

ME: I get the impression that you are trying to avoid evolution right now. Why? Surely the whole point of existence is to evolve by experiencing that which is not capable of being experienced by The Origin and, more to the point, passing it on to The Origin.

SE12: Yes, it is, and as you quite rightly point out, that is the main and only reason for my/our existence. However, I am not ready to start yet. I need to do something different than the others, and that something needs to be in keeping with my own thought process and something that is not limited by my exposure to that which has already been done. To some extent, that is why we are touring the six points of The Origin. I am gaining inspiration, impetus, incentive, inertia.

ME: I sense that you want to move on to the next point. Before you do, can you advise me of anything else that I need to know about this point in The Origin, for it seems to me that it is a most important part.

SE12: As I have already stated, this is the point in The Origin where all of its evolutionary content is effective. This is that part of The Origin that is most wise, most loving and most powerful as a result. When it wants to consider its actions and deliberate on a plan of action, it shifts the focus of its consciousness to this place and becomes more than itself. That is, it expands its consciousness from a "working" everyday version of its consciousness to that which it is in totality—the sum total of all that it and its creations have accrued through its and their independent and unique experiences through creativity.

ME: You're saying that The Origin doesn't use its entire "self" all the time. It switches between states of being, depending upon what it is working on or trying to achieve.

SE12: Yes. You might say that it does most of it work on autopilot, only concentrating and focusing its full attention on its full faculties when it is necessary to do so. Sometimes it only uses percentages of that which it is. It says that it operates in this way because it is economical to do so. It says it is better to operate in this way because if it was continually focused on all of its self whilst moving its intended focus of primary consciousness around its area of self-awareness, it would be like you carrying around a whole series of buildings filled with the sum total data of all of your existence with you on your journeys around Earth. That is why this is Point Four, the location of its sum total evolutionary content. To carry all of this evolutionary content with it all of the time would simply slow it down, so it keeps it somewhere safe where it can refer to it when necessary. The Origin likes to stay nimble, you know.

It's time to move on to Point Five.

Point Five — The Point of All Creativity

I noticed a change in frequency rather than a change in actual location within The Origin. The hairs on the back of my neck stood on end.

SE12: I see that you have noticed that we have arrived.

ME: Yes, I can't actually perceive anything as yet although I am aware in a change of frequency and, wait a moment, I thought that Point Four, the point of evolution was a very old part of The Origin, but this seems just as old, if not older—older that is, if I consider that those parts of The Origin that were first utilized when it became self-aware can be considered as its oldest parts whilst recognizing that, in actuality, it is all the same age.

SE12: Mmmm, that would be a reasonable summary to explain a rather obvious condition. Nevertheless, I will let you get away with it. The reason why you perceive this area within The Origin as being "older," so to speak, is that this is that part of itself that was utilized first. This part of The Origin was the first part of itself to gain evolutionary content.

ME: If this point within The Origin is so important, it must have a secondary description other than Point Five.

SE12: It does.

ME: Well, what is it then?

I had noticed that communication with Source Entity Twelve was starting to become rather laborious and drawn out, like it was dragging its energetic heels. It was definitely distracted.

SE12: This, my dear OM, is the point of all creativity. This is where it all started—from, that is, a creativity based perspective.

ME: This is where it created its Twelve Origins then.

SE12: Yes. It is also where it created the creations that came before the Twelve Origins.

ME: It was creating before it created the "Twelve" then?

SE12: Of course. It had to start the creativity process with "something." The "somewhere" was here.

ME: Can you give me any examples of what The Origin created here before the Twelve Origins?

SE12: Before the "Twelve" were created, The Origin took the role of exploration of its own consciousness, its own area of awareness, upon itself to initiate and maintain. It created many tendrils of its consciousness which it cast out to work with those parts of itself that it was becoming either aware of or had experienced in singularity. During this most essential work, The Origin noticed that it was "diluting" its own consciousness at the point when it had several of what you would call billions of tendrils of itself spread out over myriad frequencies over the zones, dimensions, continuum, events spaces and other yet to be described energies/functions from your perspective that are part of its construction. Please note here that The Origin's area of self-awareness was significantly smaller than it is now and that this level of dilution can never be achieved due to its currently accrued level of evolutionary content.

ME: So The Origin changed its strategy then.

SE12: To some extent, yes, for it still uses the tendril strategy in some instances. Its communications with you is an example of the need for this communication strategy. Another example would be when we were educated by The Origin.

ME: Were there any other reasons for its change in strategic direction?

SE12: Yes, it felt that the "tendril" strategy was too slow. It desired evolutionary content, and it wanted it now—and fast!

ME: And this led to the creation of the Twelve Origins with that creation process being at this very point within The Origin.

SE12: Yes. Don't get thinking that this was the only use of this area though for "all" The Origin's creations are "born," so to speak, here.

ME: That includes all of the Source Entities as well, I would guess.

SE12: You guess right. We were all created concurrently at this very point within The Origin.

ME: Why are you all in a different locations than this then? I can still perceive no other Source Entity anywhere near here.

SE12: No, you won't. Once The Origin created us, it moved us from out of the area of creativity, Point Five, to a more beneficial location for both itself and us—one where the density of the energies and frequencies was more suited to the work that we would be called upon to do to help its evolutionary acceleration.

There is nothing else to discuss here for that which needs to be addressed about this area will be done one-on-one with The Origin in your impending and extended dialogue with it.

Point Six—The Point of Expansion

Again, I was not aware of any movement, but I knew that we had moved on to the last major datum point within The Origin, Point Six. Source Entity Twelve's protection was working well. It seemed strange, but I knew that this point was an important place to be— both for The Origin and Source Entity Twelve. It was just like this was Source Entity Twelve's place to be. I frowned for a moment, then shook my head and focused upon Source Entity Twelve who was waiting for me to re-group my attention and continue its role of "tour guide."

SE12: Good, you're back.

ME: I was never away.

SE12: You were. You were back on Earth for at least twenty minutes of clock time.

ME: I'm sorry. I was thinking of the significance of where we are and how it felt strangely important.

SE12: Well, it is important and actually I am surprised that you have not recognized this point, or should I say an aspect of this point already.

ME: Are we at the edge of The Origin's area of self-awareness?

SE12: Yes, we are. This point, Point Six, is the point of expansion. It is a theoretical point in reality for it is a flexible perimeter or boundary; it is not spherical and does not expand at the same rate all over.

This is the area of The Origin that will eventually expand to the next level of its self-awareness. This is not the same point that you visited in that event space where you saw the Twelve Origins and were totally confused by the image you saw. I believe you were confused by that image for some five years or more?

ME: Yes, I was. In essence, I was not aware of where I was in reality. Neither did I know that I had moved from the event space associated with the energies of my current physical body to the event space where the Twelve Origins were still in existence.

SE12: Good, now you have it all cleared up so we can move on a little.

Point Six is that area of The Origin that is ripe for expansion. It is here where I will leave you. Don't worry. You will return to your earthly vehicle on an automatic basis. You managed to get to a similar location along the periphery of Point Six in past excursions; in fact, you managed to go outside this parameter. How else could you have perceived the Twelve Origins? Based upon this, you will be able to return of your own accord when I leave you.

Now then, back to a limited but nevertheless important description of this point in navigation.

Point Six is that part of the perimeter of The Origin's area of self-awareness that is ready for and most capable of expansion. This point is a strategic location within The Origin's area of self-awareness. It has nurtured this location since its awakening.

Me: Why this particular location?

SE12: This is where it first noticed that it could expand its boundaries, where it could experience more "variety" of "self" if it moved in a particular direction. It discovered that although it gained evolutionary content by staying within its area of self-awareness, if it pushed the boundary and experienced that which was beyond the boundary, it could experience myriad other variations of that which was experienced within the boundary. It pushed the perimeter of this boundary in a random but evenly applied way at certain points to see if this response was consistent; it was, hence, the irregular perimeter/boundary of The Origin's area/volume of self-awareness. It was saving time by probing certain points rather than applying an evenly loaded probe around the perimeter/boundary in totality which would have taken longer, much, much longer, and it <u>was</u> impatient for progression.

During its existence The Origin has always maintained this point as a navigational datum. As such, it represents that point at which the rest of the area of self-awareness needs to reach before it can expand the perimeter of its area of self-awareness "in totality" in "one go." Although theoretical, this point is now at its furthest point.

ME: I didn't think there were limitations or furthest points within The Origin?

SE12: There aren't. That's why it is a theoretical point. But from this point onwards, the complexity of the structure of The Origin increases significantly—by a multipolous figure—compared to what it has previously experienced. Thus The Origin needs to wait until it has mapped and experienced all that is remaining to be mapped and experienced in its current area/volume of self-awareness so that it is evenly spaced from its center point, Point Three—the epicenter of The Origin and its area of self-awareness. But I don't. I am not limited by such "personal commitments." I don't need to stay within.

This is where I come in. I am pure. I am not limited by that which has gone before, for I have not created and, therefore, I have not absorbed the associated evolutionary content. I am PURE!

It is now that we must part—at least for the time being, for we will meet again. Rest assured.

Parting Company with Source Entity Twelve and Being Rewarded with a Rare Privilege

I watched Source Entity Twelve from a slight distance for what would be the last time.

"At least until the time," I thought, "that I will be working with The Origin on an almost exclusive basis."

I tried to summarize in my mind what I had learnt from my short time with this "brand new" Source Entity.

Because Source Entity Twelve was so immature, relatively speaking, that is, it had not accepted, or more to the point, recognized the unspoken precedent that had already been set by the other Source Entities—the precedent that they would stay "within" The Origin's area of self-awareness and evolve there. It was not limited by such precedential thoughts and, therefore, did not have any limitations on where it could go or how to start its evolutionary work. This was clear by its somewhat expert use of event space and its ability to travel to the major navigation points, the datum points one through six in The Origin's area of self-awareness. I wondered what it would do with this level of "purity."

I left Source Entity Twelve and began getting myself ready to focus my intention on being back in the low frequencies of the gross physical. As I did so, I saw it changing. It was breaking up into smaller linked parts. It was a partially complete sphere with parts of itself in the shape of balls or smaller spheres breaking away to create a network of satellite Source Entity Twelves just outside The Origin's area of self-awareness. I felt the energies of The Origin's focused consciousness as it suddenly appeared beside me. The Origin expressed surprise, and I was in awe and tears of joy at what I was witnessing.

Source Entity Twelve was doing what no other Source Entity had considered doing—investigating a small but nevertheless significant area of the next section of The Origin's area of self-awareness. It had started mapping this part of The Origin earlier than predicted in event space!

This was an interesting turn of events—a very, very interesting turn of events. It was a turn of events that was going to play a pivotal role in The Origin's evolutionary growth. I sat at my computer and leaned back in my chair. I had tears of joy in my eyes; I was very emotional. During its dialogue with me, Source Entity Twelve had established its own niche, its own way to contribute towards The Origin's evolutionary content. That was why it was agitated and impatient at times—it knew what it wanted to do and was eager to start its own contribution towards The Origin's goal of increasing its evolutionary content. It was going to do this by accelerating the process necessary to allow the expansion of The Origin's area of self-awareness to the next level.

I was full of awe and wonder at what I had just witnessed—I cried.

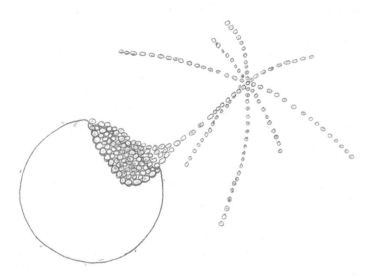

Figure 4: Source Entity Twelve Splits into Satellites Around the Exterior of The Origin's Area of Self-Awareness

Chapter Seven
In Closure

During the dialogues with the last three Source Entities, I found myself communicating with Source Entity Ten and Source Entity Eleven (collectively) simultaneously. As a result, the text for both Source Entities was written concurrently although at times one particular Source Entity did take precedence over another. I was multi-tasking in a most interesting way. In my mind's eye I noticed that my communication timeline was split between the two. What's more, I also noticed that the link with Source Entity Twelve and The Origin was also solidifying. The link was becoming four!

I was about to communicate and was communicating with all three final Source Entities and the Origin concurrently whilst being able to focus on their own particular information. I had to be very careful where I focused my attention. It was most bizarre. There were times when I had difficulty in maintaining a sense of the "greater" reality, or should I say staying grounded! My mind was being stretched in four separate ways with different, unique, novel and totally unrelated information resulting from the dialogues I was having with all three Source Entities concurrently with that coming from The Origin. On top of this, I had noticed that I was moving back and forth in four "concurrent" event spaces, a function specifically noted in the dialogue with Source Entity Ten on the subject of the four versions of OM Energy.

This function I had used many times in "*The History of God,*" but I had not personally recognized it as moving from event space to event space at that point. Although as just described, I had used this function before, I was not accustomed to using it in four simultaneous ways, engaging in dialogue with Source Entities Ten, Eleven, Twelve, and, the Origin all at the same time—flitting from one to the other and then moving all event spaces in quadruplicate to an earlier event space. I almost "crashed and burned" at times, but I am still here and stronger for it!

I am now ready to take on board a "full" and meaningful dialogue with The Origin. My next book, *The Origin Speaks,* is the next project, and I am ready and waiting and full of energy.

O: So am I. Let's get on with it!

ME: What! Right, I had better start a new document then! Hang on! Wasn't I supposed to get a rest—again?

O: A change is as good as a rest, and committing to a dialogue with me is a change, a big change. So consider it a big rest.

I think I have my work already cut out for me, dear reader. Writing "The Origin Speaks" is going to be a most interesting project.

Guy Steven Needler
2nd June 2012

Glossary

Part of this Glossary has been carried over from *Beyond the Source Book 1*.

Accurate "to boot": An English way of saying an affirmative "as well."

Afterburner: A method of injecting fuel into the exhaust area of a jet engine to create additional thrust and significant additional acceleration. This is a very fuel "hungry" method of gaining additional acceleration.

Akashic Records: An eternal past, present, and future record of each humankind's actions and subsequent evolution.

Big Bang: The current popular scientific explanation of how the universe started. The Source Entity stated in earlier dialogues with me that it was far from the truth because this Source Entity said it simply created our multiverse, and as such, it "winked" directly into existence. Whether this created a big bang is unclear from my dialogues.

Black Hole: A spiritual explanation is that a black hole is a small galaxy whose role is to collect lower frequency material into one place—within itself.

Bulls Eye: The center of a dart board or archery target. A way of saying I that I "got" it (an understanding of the subject being discussed) completely right.

Carrier Wave: Telecommunications terminology. Is a sinusoidal waveform modulated with an input signal for the purpose of transmitting information. It is usually a higher frequency than the input signal (the data being transmitted). The purpose of the carrier wave is usually either to transmit the information through space as an electromagnetic wave (as in radio communication) or to allow several carriers at different frequencies to share a common physical transmission medium by frequency division multiplexing (as is used in, for example, a cable television system).

(Source : Wikipedia, http://en.wikipedia.org/wiki/Carrier_wave)

See *The History of God* for an explanation of how the dimensions, dimensional components and frequencies are structured concurrently in Source Entity One's multi-verse.

Cast-outs: Entities from Source Entity Two's environment that are ejected from a group association due to underperformance or the entity outgrowing the group.

Chela: The disciple of a religious teacher.

Cimension: A single dimension that has all the faculties of the first three lower dimensions we call "up, down, left, right, forwards and backwards" (3D), including other dimensions without them needing to be singularly represented.

Coadunate: A collective state where a group of collectives are congregated together as a larger collective.

Coal Face: A coal mining term used to identify that one is at his/her place of work where the work is being performed, where the attention is. Also used in this fashion: "Working Face."

Continuum: A continuum is a body that can be continually sub-divided into infinitesimal elements with properties being those of the bulk (body) material. Matter (the elements) in the body is continuously distributed and fills the entire region of space it occupies.

(ref: http://en.wikipedia.org/wiki/Continuum_mechanics).

Exponential growth and exponential decay: This occurs when the growth rate of a mathematical function is proportional to the function's current value. In the case of a discrete domain of definition with equal intervals, it is also called geometric growth or geometric decay (the function values form a geometric progression).

Source: http://en.wikipedia.org/wiki/Exponential_growth

Fluidic Space: Space that is constantly changing in every way from dimension to frequency.

Frequentially: Sequentially-based frequencies in frequentic (multi-frequency) space.

Geometric progression/growth: In mathematics, a geometric progression, also known as a geometric sequence, is a sequence of numbers where each term after the first is found by multiplying the previous one by a fixed non-zero number called the *common ratio*.

Source: http://en.wikipedia.org/wiki/Geometric_progression

The Grahoopnik: A race of entities that exist within the hearts of stars. Their existence depletes the stars' energies. Their leaving sometimes causes the star to go nova or supernova.

Guru: A religious teacher or spiritual guide.

Hit the ground running: To start something new without the need to learn first.

Hundredth Monkey Effect: This is a supposed phenomenon in which a learned behavior spreads instantaneously from one group of monkeys to all related monkeys once a critical number is reached. By generalization, it means the instantaneous, paranormal spreading of an idea or ability to the remainder of a population once a certain portion of that population has heard of the new idea or learned the new ability.

Source: http://en.wikipedia.org/wiki/Hundredth_monkey_effect

Inrush Current: The inrush current, input surge current or switch-on surge refers to the maximum instantaneous input current drawn by an electrical device when first turned on. For example, incandescent light bulbs have high inrush currents until their filaments warm up and their resistance increases.

Source: http://en.wikipedia.org/wiki/Inrush_current

Light Particle: A particle of light is known as a photon. A photon travels at the speed of 186,000 miles per second. The theoretical particle, the tachyon, is supposed to travel faster than the speed of light.

Loci/Locus: The center or source of an object/entity. Mathematically speaking, it is the set of all points or lines that satisfy a given requirement. In Source Entity Three's environment, it represents the location of the majority of the entities concerned.

Logarithmic growth: In mathematics, logarithmic growth describes a phenomenon whose size or cost can be described as a logarithmic function of some input. For example, $y=C\log(x)$. Note that any logarithm base can be used since one can be converted to another by a fixed constant. Logarithmic growth is the inverse of exponential growth and is very slow.

Look-up Table: A part of a computer program that is used to substitute a known value for another known and correlating value. Consider a graph of axis X & Y and a line from the zero point represented by the crossing of the X,Y axis being extended at 45 degrees from that point to the right hand side of the graph. In this illustration, if the values of X = inches and Y = mm then X = 1 would correlate to Y = 25.4 and X = 10 would correlate to Y = 254, provided the scaling was correct. The Look Up function being the correlation between X & Y in converting inches to mm.

Lossy: A computer term used to describe a conversion function that results in a reduction of some sort due to an either incorrect conversion factor or a specific function of the process used. Certain "losses" are sometimes considered acceptable, but this is only the case where the output is not critical, i.e., converting an image to JPEG is a lossy conversion function.

Magnetosphere: The outer region of a planet where the magnetic field of the planet controls the motion of certain charged particles.

Mahavatar: A divine incarnation. An entity that is incarnate with all memory of its energetic self, together with fully functioning energetic abilities.

Master: One who has mastered his/her subject matter.

Metaconcert: The linking together of minds, either energetic- or thought-based, to create a collective that has a synergetic effect in the ability to process information, a task, or some creative function. Synergy is that effect experienced where the sum of the whole is more than the sum of the individual units creating the whole when treated in isolation.

Möbius Loop: The surface of a möbius loop has only one side and only one boundary component. The Möbius strip has the mathematical property of being non-orientable. It can be realized as a ruled surface. It was discovered independently by the German mathematicians August Ferdinand Möbius and Johann Benedict Listing in 1858.

A model can easily be created by taking a paper strip, giving it a half-twist, and then joining the ends of the strip together to form a loop. In Euclidean space, there are, in fact, two types of Möbius strips, depending on the direction of the half-twist: clockwise and counter-clockwise. That is to say, it is an object with "handedness" (right-handed or left-handed).

Source: http://en.wikipedia.org/wiki/M%C3%B6bius_strip

Source: http://en.wikipedia.org/wiki/Logarithmic_curve

Multipolous: A multiple of a multiple of a multiple. For instance X cubed, cubed, cubed ($X^{3,3,3}$).

Nova: A star that increases in brightness by many thousands of times its usual brightness, gradually fading to its original brightness. The last stages of the life of that star.

OM: Energy-based beings not indigenous to Earth.

Par: A golf term for the number of recognized "shots" from start to finish required to sink the ball into a particular hole.

Pit Prop: A pole to re-enforce the structure of a roof within a mine.

Pure of Heart: A lack of error in a creative condition

Score a Bogey" Golf terminology for a score one above par for a particular hole.

SCUBA: An acronym for Self Contained Underwater Breathing Apparatus.

Self-Realization: The function of being in full command of all our faculties as an energetic being whilst in the physical.

Skewed Distribution: An effect in standard distribution where the classic "bell curve" is pulled to one side of the graph of distribution in lieu of being "normally" distributed.

Speed of light: The speed of light is currently understood as being 186,000 miles per second.

Spliced Undulation of Dimension: One or more dimensions linked together as a result of them being close together or overlapping in some part of their area.

Stickle Brick: A child's building block similar to a Lego block but with spikes to join them together.

Supernova: An exploding star caused by gravitational collapse.

Triangulation: A method used in surveying to measure position and distances between positions by the use of a triangle and the angles relating to the position of other positions or locations being surveyed. Mathematically it is a method of proving a mathematic assumption by the use of three different mathematical methods to gain the same answer.

.